BOOKS BY JEROME L. SINGER

The Inner World of Daydreaming

The Child's World of Make-Believe:
Experimental Studies of Imaginative Play

Imagery and Daydream Methods in Psychotherapy
and Behavior Modification

The Control of Aggression and Violence:
Cognitive Psychological Factors

Daydreaming: An Introduction to
the Experimental Study of Inner Experience

The Inner World

Jerome L. Singer

# of Daydreaming

HARPER COLOPHON BOOKS
Harper & Row, Publishers
New York, Hagerstown, San Francisco, London

THE INNER WORLD OF DAYDREAMING. Copyright © 1975 by Jerome L. Singer. All rights reserved. Printed in the United States of America. No part of this book may be used or reproduced in any manner whatsoever without written permission except in the case of brief quotations embodied in critical articles and reviews. For information address Harper & Row, Publishers, Inc., 10 East 53rd Street, New York, N.Y. 10022. Published simultaneously in Canada by Fitzhenry & Whiteside Limited, Toronto.

Designed by Dorothy Schmiderer

First HARPER COLOPHON edition published 1976.

STANDARD BOOK NUMBER: 06-090519-0

76 77 78 79 10 9 8 7 6 5 4 3 2 1

For Dorothy

Contents

Acknowledgments

A book like this, representing as it does a quarter century of research, would not be possible without the cooperation of literally dozens of colleagues and student collaborators. In my other technical books and publications I have tried to acknowledge each of these individuals, and I will not present a long list now. I must, however, acknowledge the inspiration I have gained from Professor Silvan Tomkins, whose theoretical research has seemed to me the most original of the past two decades. I also must single out Professor John Antrobus, who served as my closest collaborator on many of the research studies described herein.

The making of this book was greatly aided by the work of David Diamond, by my sons, Jon and Bruce Singer, who assisted in bibliographic research, and by Delores Hyslop, Roni Tower, Katherine Meech and Audrey Klein, who helped with typing and other aspects of preparing the manuscript. The wise editing of Ann Harris was impressive indeed.

The book is dedicated to my wife, Dorothy, who has also collaborated on some of the research described in the following pages.

Part I

CHAPTER 1

Daydreaming:
A Basic Human Experience—
An Exciting Psychological Problem

Daydreaming, our ability to give "to airy nothing/A local habitation and a name," remains one of the most fascinating, if perplexing, phenomena in the vast range of human behavior. Associated in common language with terms such as "reverie," "brown study," "woolgathering," "castles in Spain" and "looking into the middle distance," daydreaming has long been recognized as a wispy, mysterious and yet intriguing facet of our behavior. Because of its completely private nature it is impossible to formulate a generally agreed upon definition of this act. Probably the single most common connotation is that daydreaming represents a shift of attention *away* from some primary physical or mental task we have set for ourselves, or *away* from directly looking at or listening to something in the external environment, *toward* an unfolding sequence of private responses made to some internal stimulus. The inner processes usually considered are "pictures in the mind's eye," the unrolling of a sequence of events, memories or creatively constructed images of future events which have varying degrees of probability of taking place. Also included as objects of daydreaming are our awareness of our bodily sensations, our emotions and our *monologues intérieurs,* those little inner voices we hear talking to us somewhere in our heads.

The child dawdling at his dinner who can be heard softly imitating the sounds of Indian war whoops and pioneers' gunfire or talking seriously to an imaginary playmate is engaged in an early form of daydreaming. The busy executive who finds himself contemplating a forthcoming romantic rendezvous while reading over financial statements, and the harried housewife who pictures herself as a chic guest on a Greek magnate's yacht while stirring the soup are familiar examples. The absent-minded professor who fumbles with his key at the wrong apartment door while he is inwardly contrasting two alternate readings of an ambiguous passage in a medieval manuscript is demonstrating the distracting nature of daydreaming as well as some of its problem-solving characteristics.

Actually, daydreaming is probably best understood as one manifestation of the "stream of consciousness" so beautifully described by William James in his classic work *The Principles of Psychology,* which appeared in 1890. Daydreaming or conscious fantasy seems most likely to occur under conditions relatively similar to those of night dreaming. A person who is alone in a situation in which there is very little outside stimulation, perhaps most often just prior to going to sleep, is likely to find himself engaged in an extensive reverie or interior monologue. James introduced his term "the stream of thought" to try to characterize the complexity of the process of waking awareness in which one experiences an interplay of direct perceptual responses, interpretation of such responses, and then the intrusion of associated phrases or memories, fantasies, fleeting images and half-heard sounds. An important literary trend in this century has been the effort on the part of poets and novelists to capture the complex layers of man's ongoing mental activity, conscious and unconscious, in vivid and communicable form. James Joyce's

Ulysses and *Finnegans Wake* probably represent the most effective of these attempts but many writers, such as Saul Bellow, continue to make intriguing use of the method in novels and short stories. From the standpoint of the artist, daydreaming and fantasy are processes that are just *there*. Artists seek to capture them in prose, paint or music, and more recently on the moving picture screen, because of their value in communicating with an audience. We can enjoy the flow of good stream-of-consciousness writing and identify with the way the character's experience meshes with our own, but as a rule we are not concerned about precision and consistency in material of this kind expressed in fiction.

Since daydreams are so often visual, the movies are especially effective in capturing their quality. In *Midnight Cowboy*, for example, there is a scene in which the Cowboy and the ever-hungry gamin, Ratso, find themselves at a pseudo-hippie party. Ratso stands by the lavish buffet table wolfing down sandwiches. Suddenly in a quick cut we see his long-dead shoeshine-man father standing beside him. We feel the poignancy of Ratso's fantasy—"If only my poor old man could be here to enjoy this"—without a word being spoken.

Issues in Psychological Science

For the student of human behavior working in a scientific orientation, daydreaming must be approached with much greater care in definition and technical analysis; it must be examined in a way that lends itself to experimental and empirical research approaches. To catch hold of so elusive a phenomenon as daydreaming in a scientific fashion demands a very strict discipline in the investigator. It is too tempting to use one's private experiences and to generalize from these to all humankind. For the scientific psychologist the first task is to establish a series of rea-

sonably delimited definitions of daydreaming and related phenomena, and then to set up a series of operations which can test
fairly specifically the conditions under which daydreaming occurs,
its different characteristics as a consequence of different environmental situations or the personal qualities of the individual, and
the various adaptive or maladaptive human functions it appears
to serve.

Science is indeed a stern taskmaster but it may also be the most
democratic institution man has yet devised. The goal of science is
to establish processes and formulations that are capable of being
examined by other scientists anywhere in the world. One must
provide sufficiently specific descriptions of research or experi-
mentation so that investigators in other laboratories can repeat
the results obtained from any given study. In this sense there can
be no authorities in science, for each investigator is duty-bound
to make explicit all his assumptions and to present all his results
as clearly as possible. Despite the unquestioned genius of Sigmund Freud as an innovative thinker in the psychological realm,
there is no assertion that he makes that is not subject to question
by the lowliest of graduate students, provided the student sets
about proposing a logical argument or some kind of formal
experiment or research that can test the great man's dictum.

In daydreaming all of us are in a sense authorities because of
the very private nature of our experiences in this sphere. We
must be especially cautious, therefore, that we do not attempt to
impose our own view on the whole human species. Thus, research
on daydreaming calls for making a very simple and direct start at
systematic inquiry of large numbers of people about their experiences under conditions in which we can establish some degree of
commonality across groups, and where others in other parts of
the country or in other nations can repeat and extend the nature
of our research.

Does everybody daydream? Does everybody experience the
kinds of stream of consciousness that have been so vividly pre-

sented by Virginia Woolf or William Faulkner? Despite the many uses made by psychoanalysts of individuals' daydreams as a basis for interpreting significant reaction, the clinician's data is based on the limited sample of people to whom he has had access. Much of the research work done in questioning people about their inner experiences has been carried out with very small numbers of persons, generally relatively well educated and often enough already trained for introspection by the nature of their literary interests or professional activities. A good deal of our information in this area is drawn from neurotic or psychotic patients undergoing treatment, or from unusually gifted and creative individuals whose private fantasy lives are expressed in culturally attractive forms. That Hieronymus Bosch or Coleridge or James Joyce had vivid fantasy lives can scarcely be doubted. But can we assert with any certainty that some of the prototypes of characters depicted in fiction by Joyce, Proust, Faulkner or Bellow as manifesting complex layers of inner thought actually possessed such differentiated patterns?

To study daydreaming more systematically, therefore, we need to obtain information about the extent of inner mental activity in various samples of our human species. To what extent do people generally engage in daydreaming and with what frequency? Can we speak of daydreaming as a single phenomenon, or is it possible that people differ consistently along a variety of dimensions in their patterns of fantasy activity and private experience?

Let us consider such other questions that one might look at in a more formal fashion:

1. Can we specify the conditions under which it is possible to increase or decrease someone's awareness of an ongoing stream of thought? What are the conditions that govern an individual's assignment of priorities for attending either to externally derived stimuli or to those drawn from his own memory system?

2. Can we move toward formulating any theoretical statement

about what function daydreaming may serve in the structure of personality? Much of the original effort of developing a theory about daydreaming came from Freud and the psychoanalysts, who particularly emphasized its relationships to wish fulfillment, solutions of conflicts related to bodily needs, and as a partially drive-reducing expression of energy. The conclusions that psychoanalysts have drawn about daydreaming have depended mainly on persons who were seen under circumstances oriented primarily toward treatment of their emotional problems, and who are therefore not ideally suited for establishing repeatable scientific formulations. Psychoanalysis has provided hosts of brilliant insights, described vividly many intriguing phenomena of human thought; but its very nature precludes the possibility that it can provide precise enough definitions of phenomena that can meet the highest scientific criteria.

3. We may also ask what role fantasy plays in the child's development. Can we specify some of the conditions of a child's experience that foster the development of increased responsiveness to inner stimulation? How does the child move from talking out all his fantasies toward either giving them up completely or internalizing them in the form of private daydreams? Is there a continuity between fantasy play in childhood and the daydreams of adolescents and adults, and the whimsy of the humorist or novelist?

4. We may also carry this inquiry further by exploring some of the adaptive and pathological characteristics of daydreaming in human beings. Is daydreaming inevitably a sign of neurotic tendencies or personal disturbance, as has so often been proposed—at least by American psychologists, psychiatrists and educators? Are there any advantages to systematic training of children in imaginative play and fantasy? What are the therapeutic uses that have been made and could be made further in the use of imagery and fantasy techniques? What role, in the end,

does daydreaming play in our ability to lead effective and interesting lives?

While I can scarcely pretend that these questions are capable of being answered at this stage of our scientific knowledge, it is my hope that this volume will guide the reader toward an understanding of what information we do have and, especially, how this information can be developed in a reasonably scientific fashion.

The Psychological Study of Daydreaming

Artists in painting, music, literature, the theater and the cinema have sought to depict the quality of man's ongoing stream of thought, his daydreams and the moods they evoke, and the variations in the fantastic quality of these waking reveries. These works point up the complexity of the problem that faces the psychologist seeking to study more directly a process such as daydreaming. The range of experience covered is from momentary and fleeting associations generated by external stimuli through more elaborate memories of recent or even fairly remote events from the past, and then more extended fantasies that combine material from the past in novel forms, into expectations of future possibilities or into bizarre or constructive reorganizations of past material, wishes and hopes. How can psychologists approach such a complex and yet ephemeral content?

It is not my intention here to present a review of the history of research in this problem. Some indications of previous efforts will come up as we deal with various facets of the study of daydreaming in subsequent chapters. What I do hope to indicate is the degree to which the scientific approach hinges essentially upon a certain type of careful methodology that does not restrict the artist.

In the nineteenth century, psychology, while essentially the science of mental life, attempted to limit the range of the problems it investigated to those manageable by the available technology of the period. The focus was therefore on the studies of the individual's percepts, sensations or images. Despite William James's emphasis on the stream of thought, it was clear that what he was describing, while phenomenally a seemingly accurate image, was not yet susceptible to careful study. Thus psychologists busied themselves with attempts to analyze through introspective methods, or through the use of reaction times to colors or sounds, the differences between sensations and perceptions, or to measure where possible the persistence of an image of an object once one looked away from the object itself. The more self-generated imagery with which we are primarily concerned, *the image evoked by an image,* was scarcely dealt with in academic psychology.

At the turn of the century, the major controversy in the field was based on whether all thought necessarily involved imagery in one of the five modalities—taste, touch, smell, sound or sight. The leader of the group proposing that all thought did hinge on imagery was Titchener, who dominated American academic psychology during that period. Titchener's students used a variety of introspective methods to try to capture the quality of their own thought and perception, but they were oriented primarily to reproducing in their imagery some clearly visible external object. For psychologists the controversy was resolved against Titchener by the research of the so-called Würzburg school, whose investigators were able to show that an important part of human thought involves anticipatory sets or intentions which themselves are not ordinarily reflected in direct images.

Perhaps one might say the origins of research on more extended aspects of daydreaming come really from the clinical investigations of Sigmund Freud or Carl Jung. In his exhaustive examination of almost every phase of human experience through the medium of his psychoanalytic work with patients, Freud not only realized the great importance in daily life of one's fantasies and night dreams but also built the method of the stream of thought directly into his treatment process. Freud combined his own self-analysis with the material he obtained from his patients to put together a remarkably comprehensive view of the private experience of man.

While introspection has always been a method of psychology, it had fallen into disfavor in the early part of the twentieth century for the obvious reason that it was difficult to get two people to agree about their private experiences. The effectiveness of the clinical method was that it was derived not only from the intuitions of gifted individuals such as Freud or Jung, but was supplemented importantly by material gained from extensive analyses of patients done under what for those times were reasonably controlled conditions. The clarity and brilliance of Freud's case studies led to a vast growth in the case method in psychoanalysis and related forms of psychotherapy, with the development of a very impressive body of material on the nature of human wishes, dreams, the variety of fantasies, the possible psychological meaning of slips of the tongue, the great variety of symbols shared across different cultures, and so on. Much of the focus of the psychoanalytic research was upon verifications of aspects of Freud's theory, and primarily upon the content of dreams and fantasies produced by patients. The more structural characteristics of thought (its organization, logic, relationship to basic biological needs), which were also important to Freud, were somehow neglected in the analytic literature until David Rapaport and others revived interest in them in the 1950s. Apart from the case method there was some continuation of the introspective approach, moving in a somewhat more experimental direction, by persons influenced by Freud, such as Varendonck and Silberer, who tried to explore their own daydreams or their experiences of thought in drowsy conditions. We shall have a chance to look a little more closely at these methods in the following chapter when I discuss some of the introspective approaches to studying daydreaming.

Psychologists and other behavioral scientists have tended to be somewhat impatient with the anecdotal qualities of the clinical method. It is fairly obvious, when one sees the proliferation of schools of psychoanalysis and of divergent theories, that one man's interpretation based on his own private examination may deviate dramatically from that of another. If one generalizes from private experience to all mankind one is in trouble indeed. In attempting to study daydreaming, therefore, some investigators began to move more in the direction of survey research techniques as a means of establishing a normal base line for understanding the phenomena, using large numbers of persons who respond to interviews or questionnaires. An early work on daydreaming by Greene attempted to tabulate the fantasies of British schoolchildren, and a questionnaire approach by Shaffer in the 1930s sought to determine if there were uniformities in daydreams across a large sample of college students.

Much of my own work has taken the form of trying by various technical methods to survey the frequency, content and structural characteristics of daydreaming in fairly large samples of the American population. Here the focus is upon getting at the daydreams of the average person rather than focusing—as in the clinical method—on those produced by individuals consciously seeking help for specific maladjustment. The survey method clearly has the advantage of larger numbers, but it lacks the intensity and detail of clinical investigation. The clinical method suffers, of course, from the fact that the patient is in treatment with the therapist, that the therapist's own report is what one relies on primarily, and that these reports are often strongly influenced by the theories or self-justification needs of a given therapist, however objective he may try to be.

A whole new series of developments have taken place in the

study of daydreaming and the stream of thought within the past twenty years. Some of these developments stem from the important breakthrough in the study of night dreaming, when it was found that laboratory measurements of brain-wave patterns and eye movements, in addition to some other physiological measures, could provide remarkable insight into a hitherto unknown aspect of human behavior, the sleep cycle. These methods have opened the way for studying waking behavior as well, including daydreaming and fantasy. There have also been important advances in our ability to measure imagery and ongoing thought processes in situations that call for the performance of tasks requiring intense concentration in the laboratory. Because they are laboratory procedures subject to fairly precise control, these methods have the advantage of being more objective and capable of replication in other laboratories; and thus they meet some of the highest scientific standards.

That does not mean, however, that one can dispense with the individual verbal report of the patient. This continues to be a critical part of learning about private events and daydreams. But we now have in psychology the technology for classifying such ongoing private events more precisely and in more objective ways; and we are even developing methods for simulating the stream of thought by computer in a fashion that may give us new insights. These experimental methods may lack some of the glamour of the clinical method, but they have made possible a very significant advance in our ability to state more precisely the conditions under which one becomes aware of daydreaming, the difficulties of increasing or decreasing the regular flow of the stream of thought, the functional value or utility of ongoing daydreaming and some of the differences in personal style that are evident in the patterns of fantasy activity.

An important new feature in research on imagery and fantasy stems from the fact that many of the current methods of psychotherapy rely more heavily than ever before upon the patient's capacity to produce images and fantasies in the treatment process. These methods include the behavior modification techniques, which have been much more closely linked to academic psychology and are by their circumscribed nature more capable of experimental study than psychoanalysis or the more humanistic treatment methods. The result is an interesting confluence of the experimental and the clinical methods in the study of imagery and fantasy around these new therapeutic techniques; and I will attempt in Chapter 9 to point out how our understanding both of the therapeutic process and of the nature of imagery has been enriched by these new developments.

Psychology is now entering a phase that is extremely exciting for those who have been concerned with the nature of human thought and private experience. For years following the development of behaviorism by John B. Watson around 1910, psychologists were afraid to attempt to study some of the most significant facets of human experience lest they not be able to express them in sufficiently objective terms. Today we are at a point of a breakthrough in our technology that will allow us again to tackle the study of human imagery and understand the role it plays in the overall process of learning and emotional development.

We are also at a point where we can study the connected images that go to make the stream of consciousness or the daydream and extended fantasy so much a part of our normal life. Though this book will not emphasize the technical details of method, it is my hope that the critical reader will find the exploration of the various facets of daydreaming especially rewarding as he sees unfolding before him the increased ingenuity of method available for its study in a scientific fashion.

Introspective Studies of Fantasy: The Individual as the Starting Point for Scientific Observation

The unique characteristic of daydreaming is that it occurs in solitude, in the privacy of the consciousness of a single individual. Let us therefore begin our exploration of fantasy at its source. It is my hope that by exposing my own experience in daydreaming and the stream of thought, I can encourage others to consider seriously more intensive self-examination and self-experimentation as an explicit starting point for psychological research.

Obviously there is a certain narcissism as well as fascination in sharing one's most personal experiences and thoughts—a fact that can often explain why some people persist in going to psychoanalysts for years at great personal expense and without much change in their life patterns; but I am convinced that most psychological research ought to begin by such self-examination. Though an individual's self-awareness is not a satisfactory basis for drawing conclusions or for formal testing of hypotheses in psychological science, it can sharpen the psychologist's critical awareness of the *relevance* of the material under examination. If more psychologists took the trouble to undergo the tests they

devise or to first put themselves through the experimental procedures to which they subject others, we would find the quality of
much of our research deepening in significance and excitement.

Self-examination can also serve as a basis for raising legitimate
questions that require more systematic research. The critical
thing in beginning with oneself is that the information be
scrupulously presented and that it be formulated not as a rule
for the whole human race but rather as a phenomenon that, since
it occurs in at least one individual, must be included in any
comprehensive view of human personality.

I would like to show here how one can start from the self, then
gradually move out to observation of others through interview
and questionnaire, and then eventually to tightly controlled
experimental studies. At each point in this process one must
examine the new level of information by checking back with the
experience of other individuals. I am sure that for some readers
the experiences that I am going to describe may seem foreign and
indeed uniquely mine. I can only say that most of what I do
describe has also been reported by other persons, sane and
insane; some I have read, other accounts I received personally. I
should like to invite the reader who is quick to interpret the
psychopathology in the material I shall present to take a fresh
look at his own stream of thought and daydreams before casting
the first diagnostic label!

The daydreams that I have observed fall for presentation
purposes into two general categories. On the one hand, we have
the great bulk of reverie activity—one's own ongoing stream of
consciousness, the private interior monologues and sometimes
somewhat more elaborate fantasies, all of which seem to occur
spontaneously in association with events noticed in the outside
world or in chains of sequence to early memories. Somewhat
more dramatic examples of daydreaming are the recurrent, self-
consistent and fairly elaborate fantasies that have persisted for

years since childhood. These longer, recurring fantasies will be described first because I believe that they may be easier at the outset for the reader to identify with and use to enter into the spirit of self-examination I would like to encourage. Many people have told me that my presentations of childhood and adolescent fantasies have touched off a revival of many early memories about their own experiences in this realm. It will please me if, as I recount my own fantasies, you too drift away occasionally into your own.

Recurrent Daydreams

If I had to describe the main feature of my own mental life in childhood and adolescence I would characterize it by stressing the interest I had in a series of recurring fairly elaborate fantasies. Most of these dozen or more themes involved the adventures of a heroic figure, generally a person of outstanding character and accomplishment in a specific field of endeavor. Without question the closest approximation of this pattern that one can find in literature is described in the famous short story about Walter Mitty by James Thurber. Within the brief time span of the story the relatively mild-mannered Mitty drifts into a series of elaborate images in which he has become a great aviator or surgeon who fearlessly confronts the tasks before him. It is not clear whether these characters recur regularly or whether they are newly created each time Mitty drifts into a fantasy. In my own case, while I am sure that I have had hundreds of fleeting daydreams of heroic achievements or the attainment of specific goals that resemble Mitty's, the main focus of my fantasy life has been around the lives of my recurring characters. Unlike Mitty, who gives all the characters his own name, I generally made a clear separation between myself and the characters (with one exception) and each of these individual heroes was allowed to run an independent life course through a particular phase of their adventures.

The fantasies grew out of reading, attendance at movies and radio listening, since I am of the pre-TV generation. As far as I can recollect, most of the themes began between the ages of six or seven through eleven. At first the particular characters were part of my private play. Alone in a room, or sometimes just in the corner of a room, I would carry on an elaborate game with toys or makeshift props, talking out loud and actively playing the parts of the various characters. Some of these same characters probably were included when I joined other children in what is called sociodramatic play. When the elaborate make-believe games shared by other children diminished and gave way to organized formal "games with rules" or sports, the heroic figures I had been interested in persisted in my private play or in my cartoon drawings and doodles. As schoolwork, sports and organized games took more of my time, and as I naturally became embarrassed by continued overt make-believe, I indulged in these fantasy characters more and more by drawing pictures of them in notebooks. Eventually the sequences were almost totally internalized in private visual imagery.

My drawings were much like comic strips elaborating particular sequences of adventures, except that no captions were necessary because the fantasy was played out internally. Whatever skill I had in sketching was applied to delineating the main details of a fantasy sequence. The emphasis was really much more on plot than upon artistic detail. I became fairly good at suggesting activities with a few strokes of the pencil but I used this skill primarily for my private fantasy play and I rarely demonstrated it in school art courses or in attempting to win approval from others for drawing abilities. I believe that from a technical standpoint, the fact that I did rely on drawing played a part in feeding back for me more crystallized and vivid images of the characters. Often these visual images were made even more vivid by my tying them mentally to particularly appealing personalities I saw in the movies or met occasionally in real life.

The most interesting of my daydream activities in puberty and adolescence were built around the recurring "central figure" fantasies. Many of these were associated with sports and they changed with the sporting season. I had in particular an entire baseball team which I followed throughout the many years of its imaginary career. It was named after the New York Giants (alas, long removed now to San Francisco) but the team consisted of imaginary characters whose identities I had created and whose arrival to join the Giants I developed individually. I would spend a good deal of time alone or in school classes writing out box scores of typical games, illustrating them with drawings of scenes in which various of my team heroes played out their roles. Philip Roth's recent book *The Great American Novel* undoubtedly reflects one of his own early baseball fantasies of a similar type, presented in the form of a wild parody. Occasionally my Giants traded for new players or a particular figure retired, but I can still remember the names of the superstars at the peak of the Giants' fame in my fantasy league. My lead-off batter, for example, was the auburn-haired Red Raymond, who shared many of the batting and base-stealing qualities of the original Ty Cobb but was much more gentlemanly. The team's home-run star, Jim Lane, was also a successful operatic baritone who overlapped into another one of my fantasies, to which I will refer shortly.

When I was nine years old I discovered in the library a series of boys' books that described the adventures of a group of friends living in a mythical small midwestern town, Tutter. As I read each book of this extensive series I became particularly attracted to one of the characters, Poppy Ott, who seemed especially clever and intellectually gifted. I lost interest in the books themselves after a few years, but my identification with the character of

Poppy Ott persisted. Although the Tutter books had almost nothing to do with sports, I found myself incorporating Poppy Ott into some rather elaborate fantasies about football games. In the earliest years of this fantasy I would privately go through the physical motions of a complex football game, with the imaginary ball being snapped, my running or darting in different directions and then in effect tackling myself or catching my own passes. Soon I had created my own football league and adapted the characters and locales from the Tutter books to my purposes. Beginning as a player on a local town team, Poppy Ott and some of his friends moved on to professional football. Poppy Ott emerged as the superstar, the shifty-hipped, clever broken-field runner and accurate passer. Gradually I had to restrict my elaborate physical enactments of the football games, as I had less privacy and as with age such play became less feasible socially. I started to draw the games on paper. I would visualize an entire league series, sketch highlights from each game, sometimes write out detailed play-by-play accounts of games, and maintain elaborate statistics on the achievements of my imaginary players just as the newspaper keeps records of running or passing averages.

As I grew into adolescence Poppy, who was presumably a few years older than I was, grew up too. After some well-documented setbacks in his career because of the envy of other players, he emerged as the greatest football player of all time on a Boston professional team of my own creation. Gradually less of this material was written down or drawn and more and more was simply visualized. The fantasy was closely correlated with the football season; in spring and summer it was shelved for the revival of my baseball fantasy and the heroic batting and fielding of Red Raymond, Bob White, Jim Lane and Val Arnett.

In time the entire fantasy sequence built around Poppy Ott settled into a fairly circumscribed pattern. In high school and even in adult life, confronted with situations that were monotonous or dull I would find myself resorting consciously to playing out a particular game in which Poppy Ott starred. Sometimes at classes in school I would doodle cartoons depicting events of the fantasy games. Even in a variety of military situations in World War II, I found that during periods of long waiting I could amuse myself by fantasizing football games. By now many other demands have preempted my consciousness, but the fantasy continues to be available and on occasion it can help me to while away a long train ride when I do not feel up to more "constructive" thinking. It has also recurred in situations such as sitting up all night with sick children and it has helped me to tune out rock-and-roll music when I have been a captive audience. In childhood and early adolescence I eagerly looked forward to moments of privacy or occasions when I could elaborate on Poppy Ott stories, but this is not the case now. What is true is that I have found ways of using some of these stylized fantasies to help me get through particular periods in which attention to the external environment would only lead to frustration.

My football or baseball fantasies have been especially valuable in the period of preparation for sleep. Although I have never been especially troubled by insomnia, I have noticed that the increasing range of activities in which I participate and the many complex responsibilities I have as an adult—as a psychotherapist or as a university professor, in helping to run a household or in sharing concern about my family—leave me with so many loose ends and things to be done that dwelling on these before bedtime can only be a fruitless exercise. I have therefore recently revived my baseball and football fantasies for use in helping me get to sleep. Now as I compose myself for slumber I begin the sequence of one of the famous games in which Poppy Ott starred. I start running through the sequence of plays and within a short time I awaken in the morning to realize that I left Poppy Ott and his teammates with third down and five to go on the opposition's ten-yard line. This use of the fantasy as a means of getting to sleep is now so effective (very much like a hypnotic suggestion) that once I start the sequence I rarely get more than a few plays run before I fall asleep. As I write this it is the baseball season and for almost a week now I have been starting out at night with Red Raymond batting in an all-star game early in his career. The count has now worked up to three and two but he still has not hit the ball before I fall asleep, and I wake up in the morning to realize that I haven't yet got through the lead-off batter.

Unlike some other characters in my fantasies, Poppy Ott grew up only between the ages of fourteen and thirty-two; he has been more or less stabilized as a mature and experienced football player ever since. But after all, who really is interested in the exploits of aging athletes?

Another general category of fantasy that developed and included a number of characters or themes was built around forms of heroic achievement. The earliest character with whom I identified was Tarzan of the Apes, whom I had seen in early serials on Saturday afternoons at the movies. I had devoured all Edgar Rice Burroughs' books avidly by the time I was nine. My knowledge of Tarzan's exploits was so extensive that between the ages of seven and nine I would often entertain the boys on my street in the evening by telling them stories of Tarzan's adventures. Indeed, I was nicknamed "Tarzan," a ludicrous designation for one of my then rather scrawny figure.

Perhaps as an outgrowth of my participation in elementary school debates, a new imaginary figure of a great senator began to occur in my daydreams. He started as a sort of crusading reform district attorney who fought corrupt political bosses and racketeers and eventually rose to become a dynamic and distinguished senator. In the same way that Poppy Ott was the greatest football player of all time and my baseball heroes rivaled Ty Cobb and Babe Ruth, the Senator developed in my daydreams as a towering national leader. In fantasied incident after incident he showed his stance as a great moral figure in the

American life, a foe of corruption or blind conservatism, defender of the republic, a towering individual in the service of his people.

Though the last sentence is a compendium of clichés, sounding a great deal like political campaign oratory, it nevertheless reflects truly my imaginary senator. It is painful for me to reveal my private fantasies not only because one gets some clues to the inner dynamic trends in my personality, ordinarily concealed, but also because I am forced to expose the soap operatic quality of much of my thought. This, of course, is hindsight, because from ages eleven to eighteen the Senator fantasy did not seem at all banal to me.

For some reason I never settled on a name for the Senator. In early phases the play was acted out sociodramatically, that is, in my speaking some of the parts aloud and enacting many of the scenes privately. Later I again transposed the fantasy to cartoons and eventually only to mental elaborations. In my drawings the Senator and some of his co-workers or antagonists took on very clear-cut physical appearances; even though I don't have the daydream anymore, I can still draw the face of the Senator. He is a rather distinguished, white-haired, Vandyke-bearded gentleman, resembling Henry Cabot Lodge in physiognomy but scarcely in political orientation. The Senator undoubtedly represented an updated version of my grandfather, whom I had known until his death, when I was seven, and who had been a kind of legendary family idol.

This daydream faded away almost completely in early manhood but I recall quite clearly the content of specific incidents and the physical appearance of some of the characters. Unlike the football or baseball fantasies, the Senator theme (perhaps because it required more creative effort) never developed the automatic nature that would qualify it as a time-passing private game during adult life.

My third example of a recurring fantasy has the same central heroic figure but it is different from the others in being somehow more transparent; indeed, I gave my own name to the main character. The mixture of obviously self and nonself identification in this fantasy is odd, because while it is certainly true that I have a great love for music and really do wish I could be a composer, I never actually thought of the character in the fantasy as being *me*.

The fantasy began around my crude attempts to play the piano when I was nine or ten. Although I had had no formal training, I gradually learned to play by ear. I had no particular technical skill but I became pretty good at making up original melodies and developing them in symphonic or operatic fashion. As I sat banging away, I started to substitute an inner harmony for the rather mediocre external efforts I was producing. I began imagining operas, symphonies and a variety of musical works, a full *oeuvre*. Gradually the character of "Singer the Composer" emerged in my mind, as well as a host of associated characters, entirely fictional, with appropriate Italian or other European names, who were soloists or conductors in the various operas or orchestral works produced by the composer. As I suggested above, the great home-run hitter and left fielder of the New York Giants, Jim Lane, somehow sneaked into this fantasy as a great operatic baritone, James Lane.

Little by little my musical technique improved. I also read extensively about music and about the history and form of various compositions. Soon I began keeping notebooks documenting the various works of Singer the Composer from his first major success (a five-act grand-opera setting of Longfellow's "Evangeline," a poem my English class had been studying in seventh grade) to his later mature chamber works and great symphonies. In these notebooks I wrote out detailed accounts of the action and of the musical qualities of the various operas or symphonies and at the same time I played through them at great length, undoubtedly with much variation since I could only write down the main themes or note the structural lines of the development. In my imagination Singer grew older as his works developed and by the time I left off active involvement with the fantasy somewhere in late adolescence, Singer was a very old man, still working on his Seventh Symphony, which, like Sibelius's Eighth, it appears he will never finish—unless I find myself reverting to this fantasy in my own old age.

Gradually I spent less time in make-believe play at the piano or in writing notebook descriptions of the music with pictures and critical comments, all contributed by myself. As in my other fantasies, Singer lived on in private imagery, however, and from time to time I would think about him when I sat and improvised at the piano, particularly since most of the music I improvised would be music *he* had composed. When alone, I often drifted into a musical daydream, sometimes imitating the sounds of an orchestra out loud or running through a section of one or another of Singer's works. This kind of fantasy activity has never really stopped. I still have musical daydreams, which take the form of audibly or inaudibly humming or singing excerpts from Singer's works or from some of the compositions of a number of additional composers I eventually created, who had different styles but were more or less contemporary with him. On the whole, however, the fantasy has faded to a pale shadow of the richness and excitement it had for me in early adolescence as, alas, my own gift for composition has disappeared. Like the baseball and football fantasies, the Singer music fantasy has become crystallized into a relatively narrow form for use in idle moments, as I drive or sit in a bus or occasionally when I have some time to sit down at the piano and I lose myself pounding away again the themes of a Singer opera or symphony.

For many years, except for an occasional revival of Singer's works or those of one of his contemporaries, no new musical fantasies developed. In the past seven or eight years, however, I have noticed the emergence of a new make-believe hero. Just as

Singer or Poppy Ott or Red Raymond towered above their coevals as nonpareils in their fields, a new operatic tenor has appeared, particularly when I am driving the car on an extended trip or occasionally in the shower. He has no name. He is an American who at a very early age went to Italy, where he sang obscurely in local church choirs until at a private performance before a group of wealthy Italian businessmen he was recognized as so outstanding, with such a combination of purity of tone and vocal power, that they offered to sponsor him in his career. In my imagination he has by now reached a mellow age and is clearly the greatest tenor since Caruso or Bjoerling. Naturally I have also made up a few operas in which he can take the lead, as well as having him sing roles by Verdi, Puccini or Wagner. Occasionally, on a long automobile trip alone or with my family in parts of the country where all that comes out of the radio is rock-and-roll or Nashville country music, I have preferred to sing operatic arias aloud in this young man's powerful yet mellifluous tenor, to the dismay of my family if they are with me: my wife and children seem unable to appreciate the truly beautiful quality of this great tenor's voice.

SOME IMPLICATIONS OF THESE RECURRENT FANTASIES. Let me now summarize some of the main implications of my observations based on a study of my own recurrent daydreams. It does not take much technical psychological knowledge on the part of a reader to guess that one theme that occurs again and again suggests a great deal of general achievement motivation—a striving for accomplishment, which certainly characterizes my overt behavior as well as my private fantasies. There is, however, an interesting subtle relationship between the content of these fantasies and my actual accomplishments, since obviously I have never become a senator, a composer or a sports star. A small reality is nonetheless involved in each fantasy. In school and in professional activities as an adult, I did play some role in politics, though without the distinction or great nobility of my fantasy senator. As a youngster I did play sandlot baseball or football with a moderate amount of success and as an adolescent I did learn how to write music and produced at least a few compositions.

The composer fantasy, obviously closest of all to a conscious wish on my part, points up an important principle which is supported by clinical observation. My actual musical efforts turned out to be so inferior to my fantasies of what they should be that I very quickly gave up the attempt to learn music properly. Clinical observation of patients who are blocked in writing or other creative work has often suggested that a grandiose fantasy standard may make their every initial effort seem hopelessly inferior, so that the attempt to narrow the gap between the fantasy and their own product becomes too burdensome. This is the kind of theoretical notion about the relation of aspirations in fantasy and the capacity for direct production that could be tested experimentally by further research.

Let us take a closer look at some of the emotions that accompanied these fantasies. Most of my daydreams were associated with a moderate amount of pleasure and excitement. Occasionally I developed fantasies that would be particularly associated with sexual arousal or excitement. Relatively early, however, the specifically sexual fantasies took on a rather circumscribed form, and did not overlap the more extensive recurrent fantasies I have described. While a daydream was rarely as exciting or joyous as an actual success—the exhilaration, say, of getting a long hit in a baseball game—I still experienced a great deal of good feeling in the course of my daydreams.

As a matter of fact, I was rarely aware of much negative emotion in my fantasy life. The most common negative feeling associated with daydreaming that I recall was shame. This seems to have been closely related to the normal growth process. It occurred when I imagined being discovered in overt make-believe play or talking aloud to myself. I also was aware that my fantasies were outrageously grandiose and unrealistic and I would have been embarrassed to have others know about them. I realize today that my family was probably much more than usually tolerant of overt fantasy play, so that I carried it on with a minimum of interruption or teasing during the period from age five through thirteen or so. But I soon learned that the acceptance I got at home was quite unusual compared to what was likely to happen in the outside world.

It seems very likely that internalization and, probably, the relatively early disappearance of daydreaming in many people are closely linked to the association of such processes with childishness. A particular set of circumstances in my life made it possible for me to continue my pleasurable investment in my own daydreams but I also learned that circumspection was necessary if I was to keep this experience private. By the time I had internalized my daydreams in the form of private imagery I had already developed a series of well-crystallized, recurrent *structures,* of which the drawings and the musical compositions are an example. In effect, fantasy had become for me a kind of generalized reinforcer, as B. F. Skinner might put it, so that many experiences could be translated into that realm for me with ease. This is less likely to happen to persons who have been forced to suppress their make-believe or fantasy play relatively early in childhood, and have not had the chance to elaborate or develop organized ways of keeping it going, privately, into adult life.

In addition to the obvious theme of achievement motivation in my daydreams, and the narcissism expressed in the outstanding success of my characters, I think the persisting element in my fantasies was my need for creative expression and organization. At every point I turned my wishes or anticipations into elaborate stories.

Storytelling requires reasonable originality and organization.

My tendency, even at an early age, to impose some logical structure on daydream material indicates the operation of what Freud
has called secondary process thinking. Even my night dreams
showed a similar quality of elaborate detailed story lines, which
were bizarre only in their general adventuresomeness or in the
introduction of changes in space and time. While psychoanalysts
and other theorists have tended to emphasize the wish-fulfilling
and "primitive" nature of daydreaming and fantasy, my introspection accords with the views of writers, such as Robert Holt,
who have emphasized that from earliest childhood one can see
evidence of organized logical processes side by side with the more
directly egocentric and need-related thought of the child.

In my own fantasies there always was a certain orientation of
the fantasy to reality. Despite the fears of many people that
daydreaming leads to loss of contact with reality and practical
concerns, I do not believe this was the case for me at all. I always
made a clear distinction between myself as an individual boy and
the characters in the fantasies, so that even Singer the Composer
was not myself exactly. Also, while I did attribute great powers to
my characters, these were always within the realm of reasonable
possibility for an athlete, a senator or a musician. The Superman
or Batman fantasies in the comic books of my childhood, which
are now popular on television, involve activities beyond normal
capacity (flying, invisibility, X-ray vision) that were always
somewhat repugnant to me. My heroic characters accomplished
what they did without magical resources.

At no time that I recall did I confuse my daydreams with the
reality of my experience. I never experienced hallucinations nor
did I ever attribute to myself any of the great powers of my
imagined characters except in the most fleeting moments of
fantasy. I certainly did develop some of the kinds of elaborate
private worlds (including an entire Graeco-Roman nation with a
dynasty of kings whose history I elaborated in drawings of the

busts of the various rulers) constructed by the young patient in "The Jet-Propelled Couch," a case study in Robert Lindner's *The Fifty-Minute Hour.* Unlike the character in Lindner's book, I never, even in times of severe emotional stress, considered immersing myself in these fantasies to the exclusion of the real world. On the basis of my own experience, I therefore feel that an extensive fantasy life does not preclude, and may in some cases actually strengthen, the establishment of a clear distinction between what is reality and what is fantasy. Indeed, it is possible that regular exploration of one's daydream world makes this world a familiar realm and one less likely to evoke anxiety. A possibility, worth exploring in research, is that many people who have failed to indulge in fantasy play may be the very ones who later misinterpret their own daydreams or images as hallucinations and thus may be made much more anxious by the sudden seemingly autonomous occurrence of a fantasy image.

The relation of fantasy to reality is really a profound philosophical question. Writers like the French Gaston Bachélard have urged that we recognize that our own private experiences and images, our own symbolic alterations of the natural world or our mythological elaborations of it, are as much a part of our reality as the physically measurable stimulus field that surrounds us. Our task as mature adults is not to ignore the more private set of experiences in favor of close attention to the external environment, but rather gradually to learn the conditions under which we can use both sources of stimulation for adaptive purposes.

The relation of reality to fantasy that I experienced in my daydreams also seems to be somewhat contradictory to the so-called catharsis theories. These theories have argued that fantasizing is in general the opposite of behaving. It seems to me that the relationship is far more complex. My own fantasies were often closely related to my direct achievements—although of course these were far less distinguished than those of my characters. Research carried out by Symonds and Jensen at Teachers College, Columbia University, followed up in adult life persons whose adolescent fantasies they had obtained earlier. These investigators found that many of the major fantasy themes of the young people were occurring in reality—at least in moderate degree—in their adult choice of occupation, style of life, selection of mate and degree of success.

I hope that this account of my own fantasy material has evoked in the reader a somewhat similar exercise, and somewhat similar kinds of memories of extended private fantasies. If not, it is possible that one can look alternatively to the use of identification with certain current notable figures in society as a storehouse for private fantasies. Whatever they may be in their private lives, Elizabeth Taylor and Jacqueline Kennedy Onassis have become focal points for the fantasies and elaborate private imagery of large numbers of women. Many of those who follow the ins and outs of the careers of these celebrities in the popular magazines spend at least some private time elaborating their own fantasies of identification with them. Is it conceivable that the special appeal of such glamorous living individuals lies in the fact that at early ages many people have been shamed out of elaboration of fantasy, or have lacked the kind of privacy and opportunity that I clearly enjoyed? The fact that the huge world interest in television, movie or popular-music personalities has become a mammoth industry in itself attests to the great need all of us have for a constellation of ego ideals or alter egos, whose adventures we can follow and whose fates we can share vicariously. For relatively young persons such fantasies and identifications form a critical part in the molding of their personalities and of the direction of their goals, as well as their aesthetic tastes. For the adult who can no longer seek to emulate such figures directly, they still play a role in providing an alternative source of stimulation and elaborate thought which helps one escape occasionally from the tedium of one's own life, and also helps one evaluate different patterns of living—not necessarily always in favor of the glamorous ones.

The Stream of Thought and Spontaneous Cognitive Processes

Elaborate daydreams of the type I have been describing are only a fraction of the total amount of the ongoing internal cognitive activity to which we are prone. For as long as I can remember I have also been aware of the kind of stream of thought that William James described and that has also emerged in the interior monologues of great literature. Sometimes my associations are rapid and pass quickly; but more often, if I am not actively engaged in a very demanding physical or mental task, I discern considerable complexity in their content. The stream of thought is made up of a series of ongoing associations, some of which are like little cognitive or emotional footnotes to external perceptions. As one looks out at heavy black clouds or a turbulent sea there may be a momentary feeling of excitement or awe at the vastness and power of the universe. Or one may be piqued by curiosity over a distant light that shines out across a dark void of countryside at night. More often the stream of thought takes on a character of an ongoing interpretation or inward comment on one's perceptions. The associative image is Proust's example of the madeleine crumb, which revives by its taste a sudden flood of memories unfolding like Japanese paper flowers in a bowl of water. Ratso's fantasy in *Midnight Cowboy* would be a clear instance of the associative image which though only a brief flash still has some degree of vividness, and leads one a couple of steps away from the external stimulus.

Robert Humphrey's analysis of the famous monologue of Molly Bloom in James Joyce's *Ulysses* makes clear how sensitive

Joyce was to the relationship of the stream of thought to external stimulation. At first, aroused by her husband's late return, Molly stirs restlessly and responds to many external stimuli—the clock, the wall, the paper, the lamp. Gradually she is immersed more and more in internally stimulated fantasy, until amid warm thoughts of her romantic courtship by Leopold Bloom "beneath the moorish wall" in Gibraltar, she drifts again into sleep.

The interior monologue, which is like a verbal stream of associations and comments on an ongoing set of events, is also used effectively by detective story writers or radio script writers, as, for example, a character like Sam Spade comments wryly on his experiences while he undergoes them. For me the interior monologue has the quality of a dry inner voice that seems to be annotating my external stimulus world or, sometimes, more internal experiences, such as an awareness that my toe is twitching or my stomach gurgling. In my own case interior monologue is not as frequent or as common as associative imagery. I have a feeling that this inner voice is not as fundamental psychologically, and that it is influenced strongly by the fact of reading literary materials or by identification with particular characters of fiction. Often it becomes a way of dealing with loneliness or of finding a basis for interpreting new experiences. When I am alone in a new city or traveling in a place I have never been to before, I will sometimes find myself carrying on an internal commentary to my wife or a friend, describing various aspects of the scenery or interpreting odd sights, sounds or customs. In adolescence I would occasionally conjure up a kind of imaginary companion to whom I would describe what was going on. Often he might be an ancient Roman or Greek, to whom I was pointing out the wonders and complexities of New York City. Many people in psychoanalysis or some other form of psychotherapy carry on a kind of dialogue with their analyst in the interim between sessions as a means of identifying with him, looking at things through his eyes, or perhaps training themselves to be more sensitive to the psychological nuances of social interaction.

For myself the running off of the interior verbal monologue has been more often closely connected with defensive behavior. As a shy adolescent feeling awkward and uncertain at a dance or a party, I might stand against the wall and picture myself as an inscrutable observer of the world's foibles. Masking my shyness with an air of all-seeing detachment, I would allow my interior monologue to race along with witty and penetrating insights on the appearance or character of the pretty girls with whom I was really dying to dance, or putting down the obviously empty-headed fellows who actually embraced them.

This interior monologue will still emerge at times when I find myself in a novel and self-conscious situation. On occasion I have served as a subject in some of the research on the electrophysiological concomitants of daydreaming or night dreaming. As I was wired up to the polygraph and then established alone on a couch in another room, knowing full well that my reactions were being carefully monitored not only by the EEG machine but also by my own staff or some distinguished researchers, I became aware of the vivid "loudness" of my interior monologue. The novelty and necessarily self-conscious characteristic of the situation probably contributed to this upsurge of the detached, dry voice reporting to me on all my reactions. As time passed and I relaxed more, the inner monologue subsided somewhat but it stayed in evidence almost concurrently with my awareness of my visual imagery or daydreams during the experiments.

Classification of the Dimensions of the Thought Stream

In order that the reader realize the full range of possible private experiences that can characterize the stream of thought and daydreaming, it may be useful to employ a system of classification that starts with the seemingly most external source of associations. Under most waking conditions, when our eyes are open, a vivid external stimulus can absorb all our attention, and leave us little opportunity to make any kind of conscious interpretations of what is happening. An explosion, a sudden flash of light, a vividly colored landscape, a new face—these all make so strong a demand on us that we are unlikely to be aware of inner activity. As a matter of fact, in attempting to formulate the nature of brain functions, it is this kind of experience that leads us to conclude that our *processing* capacities, though fairly extensive, are still limited.

Consider the common situation of being introduced at a party to a circle of individuals whom you have never met before. The host quickly runs around the room calling out the names of each of the new people. You smile and proceed to shake hands with each. By the time seven or eight people have been identified, smiled at and greeted, you realize that none of the names is retrievable. Clearly what has happened is that the complexity of the new face (and the human face is probably the single most significant social stimulus in our environment), the physical sizing up of the new person, and the handshake, which demands some motor activity, all combine against storing the name. Remembering a name requires some degree of repetition in our so-called short-term memory system, in order that the name eventually be assigned to the brain's long-term storage system. Only politicians, whose success depends upon instant recognition of large numbers of people, or skillful social butterflies are likely to retain names under these circumstances. My hunch is that most of these people have learned tricks of rapidly repeating the names of newcomers and replaying them as soon as possible after the greeting phase, in order to be sure they remember as many as possible.

Physical activity—whether shifting gears in an automobile, diving into a swimming pool, hitting a tennis ball, or laughing or shouting with excitement on a roller coaster—also limits the likelihood that we will be aware of our inner cognitive activity. As any good tennis player knows, to become aware of a stream of associations or images while engaged in a game is apt to lead to a disastrous loss of concentration.

Sometimes, of course, one can choose deliberately to concentrate on one's inner cognitive activities to the exclusion of external stimulation. This circumstance takes place primarily when one is in bed or relaxing in the privacy of one's home. There are relatively few other situations that safely permit extended self-awareness. Patients in psychotherapy are notoriously self-indulgent of their own cognitive processes; indeed, they are paying for the right to focus on them and this is one of the attractions of the process. Once while I was practicing in New York City, a patient of mine was free-associating on the couch when I became aware of a great deal of noise in the street just below us, loud bells and sirens. The patient talked on and on and finally, unable to resist any longer, I stood up and walked to the window to discover that the building was on fire. "I still have ten minutes to go," said the patient when I called this to his attention, and continued his free associations.

While it is true that many of our bodily sensations are not located in the "outside world," pains, cramps, the rumblings of our stomach, an awareness of the need to urinate or defecate, or twitches that signify sexual arousal, all function in much the same way as a more readily observable external stimulus. As we grow up we train ourselves to ignore some of the "noise" of the "running machinery" of our organs. We are in many ways made up of a whole host of gurglings, rushings in the ear, odd tastes in the mouth and flashes of spots before our eyes.

Many people, in fact, are sometimes surprised or frightened by the occurrence of certain commonplace sensory or perceptual phenomena, such as afterimages, manifested, for example, in the persistence of the image of a light bulb for a few minutes after we have looked away from it. We can also become aware of the kaleidoscopic firework display that takes place frequently when we shut our eyes, seemingly right there on the interior of our eyelids. These phenomena, known technically as *phosphenes* or *entoptic* activities, are parts of the normal firings of the nerve endings, but many people have ignored them or not taken the trouble to enjoy them. When they do become aware of them they may be frightened or troubled. The same is true for experiences we have during the transition to sleep, which are known as *hypnagogic hallucinations*. These may be characterized by a great rushing in the ears which sounds as if there are huge crowds in the street or, sometimes, by the seemingly repetitive sound of one's own name being called. A corresponding phenomenon upon waking in the morning is called a *hypnopompic* experience and may be characterized by a sense of paralysis or again of repetitive sounds in the ears in the period before one is "fully awake."

Psychologists are discovering that the ways in which we learn to label certain phenomena, or the causes to which we attribute their occurrence, determine the quality of our subsequent reactions. Some of the seemingly self-absorbed behavior described in chronic schizophrenic patients, which has often been interpreted as "an immersion in a private world of daydreams," turns out upon direct inquiry of the patients to be an extreme preoccupation with their bodily sensations, with perception of stomach processes or muscular twitches and with the play of lights in blurring vision.

Are there ever any truly "blank periods" when we are awake? It certainly seems to be the case that under conditions of fatigue or great drowsiness or extreme concentration upon some physical act we may become aware that we cannot account for an interval of time and have no memory of what happened for seconds or sometimes minutes. I have had moments when very tired when in retrospect I realize that I have been gazing in an unfocused fashion at lights which took no definite form, were assigned no meaning, apparently produced no association and evoked no interior comment or curiosity. These periods do seem most like genuine breaks in the stream of consciousness. They are probably in microcosm very much like the experience of severely anxious persons, so-called chronic or "burnt out" mental patients, or patients suffering from severe brain damage.

Some people may say that their day-to-day experience is much more full of blank spots than I seem to be suggesting. Introspection tells me that that may seem to be the case when a person is not actively attending to the fact that the stream of thought is running along, and has not developed a *labeling* system for the stream of thought. In a sense, if we are to remember things or at least assign them to a long-term storage system with a tag that makes it possible for us to retrieve the material in the future, we have to adopt an attitude that is somewhat more deliberate about the labeling process. A good many people, whether for defensive purposes or simply because it has never occurred to them, do not ticket their free associations as they occur for later recall. Nor do they replay these associations and "rehearse" them during idle moments. Without replay there is a strong likelihood one will not recollect how much daydreaming or interior monologue has actually characterized one's experience.

The next phase of the stream of thought involves the interpretation of sounds or sights that engage a more active sequence of connections. We hear a sound in the next room which we quickly interpret as running feet of a small child. A sudden silvery flash against the blue sky may not be seen clearly but is quickly represented in imagery as a jet airliner. Recently our home was subject to a series of regular attacks by a brightly colored large cardinal. For days we were at a loss to interpret the repeated bangings against our windows, since they occurred early in the morning before anyone was awake and prepared to look outside. Eventually we saw the large red bird charging again and again at our windows. Until we saw this happen, we had no basis for interpreting the strange repetitive banging sounds that occurred all around the house. Was someone throwing stones? When we finally saw the red bird dashing against the windows it led us to think that he had perhaps gone mad, a nice example of anthropomorphism. Then, independently, several of us in the family came up with the fantasy that he may have represented some transmigrated lost soul—perhaps a long-dead relative—trying to communicate with us or to get back into the house. We spun further fantasies, which we communicated to each other in a playful but puzzled manner as we tried to understand the odd behavior of the bird over the next several weeks. Finally the Audubon Society clarified the matter. They reported that during the mating and breeding seasons it was common for male cardinals and robins to note their reflections in picture windows and attack what seemed to them to be a rival encroaching on their territory. This simple explanation had eluded us in favor of much more speculative and wilder fantasies.

This example of our naturalistic naïveté suggests how in many cases people are led into what often may be seriously self-defeating patterns of behavior or thought when confronted with situations for which they have no anticipation or preprogramed set of expectations. This situation was nonthreatening, of course, and our fantasy explanations were carried out playfully and without any serious beliefs in their truth. But consider the situation of a person in a strange community who experiences behavior from neighbors that does not coincide with any of his own cultural experiences, and who in turn shows them behavior that is grossly at odds with established social patterns. Speculation can develop very quickly on both sides as to the meaning of this behavior and it may be tied in with suspicions of evil intent or wrongdoing. Internal as well as external stimulation can set up a train of associations which, by the feedback of memories or joining of the memories into new fantasies, leads a person into such a profound immersion in daydreaming that it in turn creates a new psychological situation.

An important new theory of emotion has been proposed by Silvan Tomkins, one of the most original thinkers in psychology. He suggests that we have evolved as a species with a fairly limited but rather differentiated set of emotions, which are triggered from birth by patterns of new stimulation that the organism seeks to assimilate. For example, a sudden loud noise will inevitably evoke a startled reaction from the individual or, if the material is not quite so sudden but still difficult to assimilate, one may respond with terror. But if the new stimulation comes in at a much more moderate or less abrupt rate, we will respond more positively, with interest or curiosity. Much therefore depends on the timing and relative complexity of the material with which one is faced.

All too often we do not have already developed labels for many of our emotional reactions in particular situations, and without them we may be led to threatening or frightening interpretations of our own feelings. A new approach in psychotherapy has involved helping people identify their own emotions or the relation of these emotions to the attempt to interpret events in their social environment. Here is a simple example of such a use of attribution in helping a person come to terms with a very frightening reaction. A young woman consulted me after a nightmarish few days in which she thought she was going crazy. The sequence of events was triggered by a seemingly trivial incident. She was reading a book on Indian meditation exercises in bed early one morning just after awakening. The preliminary material was followed by a discussion of the different mantras, the repetitive phrases that each individual is encouraged to develop as part of entering a meditative state. The young woman tried to say one of the mantras and suddenly felt herself transformed, as if she could hear the phrase echoing round and round in her head to the point where she felt a wonderful clarity and good feeling and lost all interest in anything but the reverberating sound. The whistle of her teakettle suddenly called to her attention the fact that she had lost a period of time which she could not reconstruct.

This strange experience, and her inability to explain the intense reaction she had had, confused and distressed her and for several days afterward she was preoccupied at work, mispronouncing names and stumbling over words. Finally she heard of an unfortunate occurrence which had no personal relationship to her and found herself moved to tears.

As we explored the situation, it became clear that the experience of lying in bed and saying the mantra had revived an early memory of a particular pattern of fantasy in which she had indulged when she was three or four years of age. When she was put into her room for a midday nap in those days, she would often find that she could not get to sleep and developed a fantasy of herself being up on the ceiling and looking down at her own body. She found this very relaxing and it often put her to sleep. While this woman had never personally been hypnotized or experienced hypnosis, what in effect she had learned, as she quickly realized, was a form of self-hypnosis, an intense concentration on a specific image to the exclusion of external distracting stimuli. The power of vivid imagery is something to which we will return a number of times in this volume. Here, in pronouncing the mantra, the woman revived the early memory, in effect triggering a kind of posthypnotic suggestion which led her to drop off to sleep or into a form of hypnosis for a very brief time. The fact that she was already in bed, that she had only very recently awakened and was especially susceptible at that point to hypnopompic experiences, facilitated the combination of recaptured early memory and the reexperiencing of the hypnotic consequences of that memory.

The process of leading the woman carefully through this

sequence of associations proved to be sufficient to help her deal with the frightening and unassimilable experience of having gone so rapidly into a trance. She now had an alternative explanation, and no longer needed to believe that she was going mad. Since there was no crisis currently under way in her personal relationships that was specifically related to any of these events, she was able to accept the alternative possibility and her distress disappeared. In effect, her childhood image of herself is not unlike my baseball or football fantasy, which I use as an adult to put myself to sleep.

To a habitual introspectionist nothing in the way of human thought may seem alien, but to the person inexperienced in self-awareness, a vivid image, a perverse sexual idea or a death wish may seem like a bolt from the blue, so unacceptable that it is often attributed to someone else and regarded as a hallucination. There are indications from some of the literature of the so-called sensory deprivation experiments that support this position. In these experiments an individual is put into a dark room under conditions in which he cannot hear anything and has little opportunity to move or to experience feedback from his other senses. In this situation many people are struck by the tremendous increase of their private images and fantasies. The people who report the experiences that are most like hallucinations—that is, where they believe they are seeing things not actually present or hearing noises that have not occurred in reality—are more likely to have had less experience with daydreaming. A history of imagination and enjoyment of one's thought processes may indeed serve as a useful buffer against periods of reduced sensory input, confinement or social isolation.

In summary, then, self-observation suggests that the degree of awareness of a stream of thought depends to a great extent on the intensity of external or internal kinesthetic stimulation. Engaging in gross physical activity or being exposed to a rapidly changing or vivid external stimulus field inhibits one's sensitivity

to inner processes. A relatively monotonous external environment is likely to increase one's self-awareness of the complex
cognitive activity that makes up the stream of consciousness. At
the same time the emergent awareness of one's spontaneous inner
activity generates a feedback effect which is likely to evoke a new
pattern of action, emotion or fantasy.

Some Experiments on Intrusion of Thought

Another way in which we may use our introspections and
private experiences as starting points for understanding a phenomenon can involve a rather formal experimental method. I
should like to describe briefly some examples of these experiments which I have carried out upon myself, and encourage the
reader to try similar ones. Experiments like these can later be
elaborated into more extensive researches on larger numbers of
subjects.

One of the major defining characteristics of adult daydreaming
that I have employed has been to describe it as a diversion from
the course of an ongoing motor performance or a more directed,
task-oriented sequence of thought. Since the majority of people
point out that most of their daydreaming occurs just before
sleeping when they are relaxing in bed, it might be interesting to
study one's mental processes under conditions of drowsiness
while at the same time attempting to maintain an ongoing
complex or formal stream of directed thought.

The first step of this study, based on earlier research by
Silberer, called for me to wait for a period, usually in late afternoon following a heavy schedule, when I could relax on a couch
or in an easy chair. Then I would assign myself a specific mental
problem. Sometimes it would be something fairly routine, such as
a survey of debts and finances, or plans for home repairs. Sometimes the task might be more complex—I might decide to think

through in detail technical problems from the theory of psycho-analysis. In order to carry out this experiment in a fairly controlled fashion, I would set an alarm to ring. At the sound of the alarm, I would quickly review the sequence of events that occurred in the previous period of time and note these down in tabular form. While I was rather self-conscious at the beginning, I gradually became accustomed to the process and thought less and less about the "experiment" that was in progress. I wrote down the number of intrusions of unrelated thought, blank periods or attention to external stimuli. I classified the interrupting thoughts in terms of degree of visual or other kinds of imagery and also recorded the amount of symbolic content, the relative personal or impersonal references in the interrupting thoughts, and finally the apparent strain or effort required of me to maintain continuity of the task I had assigned myself at the outset.

This was a rather complex experiment to try on oneself and while it was engrossing for a period of time, it is not something I have been eager to repeat. I have, however, been able to use the format in experiments with larger groups of people.

The impression I gained from this fairly extensive personal experiment was that under relaxed, slightly drowsy conditions, one's brain is not geared to producing an orderly sequence of thought. Personalized visual imagery intruded upon me quite regularly. A shift toward imagery was more likely to occur with complex impersonal material than with simple material and in the former case there was also a greater trend toward symbolic transformations of the material, that is, metaphorical kinds of thinking.

By far the simplest line of thought to maintain was a memory sequence. Once initiated, a memory sequence seemed to run its course almost automatically, while theoretical thought of future planning seemed to call for more conscious effort. My experience of this unrolling of a memory was somewhat analogous to that of the early phases of learning a motor skill such as riding a bicycle. The awkwardness and conscious effort at the outset of learning is in sharp contrast to the relative ease, integration and almost automatic flow of motor activity once the skill has been acquired.

The metaphorical images occurred when I was dealing with rather abstract problems. Comparing Freud's and Sullivan's theories of the ego and self system, at one point I was trying to formulate the psychoanalytic conception of the neutralization of energy or the formation of countercathexes. Suddenly I became aware that I had drifted into an elaborate image of a kind of giant mechanical amoeba extending pseudopodia which kept turning back upon their source.

The experiment I have described was carried out in the late 1950s. Since that time there has been a great increase in psychological research on the nature of imagery and the ways in which various kinds of language or imagery materials are stored in the brain. Most of the research now seems to suggest that there are at least two major systems for material to be coded and stored for later retrieval, a verbal-linguistic code and an imagery code. The former has somewhat different characteristics and greater advantages for the memory process and for learning than the latter, but both seem to be important collaborators when it comes to our most efficient learning activities. Very likely the assignment of new material we are confronted with to a verbal coding category makes for relatively efficient recall, if we can be satisfied with a concise statement. On the other hand, if our need or the demand of the situation is for a very complete account of an event, then we are more likely to have to draw on our visual memory system to explore the scene in detail. A well-known example is to ask someone how many windows he has in his house. Unless they have recently had to buy screens and therefore had to count the windows and store the number *as a number,* most people do not have that information on hand. The only way they can answer a question like that is to visually imagine themselves in each of the rooms of their apartment or home and count. Without a capacity for visual imagery, this kind of task would be almost impossible to deal with.

Most current research in psychology still focuses primarily upon understanding the nature of the individual image rather than the train of thought, and it is my hope that this volume and some of the experiments described here will stimulate more active attempts to study the ongoing stream of thought as well as the role of the individual image in the learning process. My own introspections would suggest that a good deal of the stream of thought and of our daydreaming patterns involves extensive and, in a sense, subtle and often unwitting planning for the many kinds of situations that will confront us in the future.

The Transition to Dreaming

The implication of what I have been proposing in this chapter might be summed up in the phrase "to thine own self be true." To the extent that one's own experience, not just viewed as a general reaction but examined in a more formal sense, offers data which is at variance with research reports, then the generality of these scientific studies is called into question. Personal experience systematically examined or reported can scarcely provide a basis for *decision* in science but it can raise serious questions about the generality of available group data and can suggest new hypotheses that can take such phenomena into account.

Probably the most exciting development in the behavioral sciences in the period of the 1950s and 1960s was the discovery by Nathaniel Kleitman and William Dement and various collaborators of the cyclical nature of the sleep process and of the possibility that measures of the electrical activity of the brain (EEG) and of the concurrent rapid eye movements of the sleeper could be used to determine the evidence of ongoing dreaming.

The data from the electrophysiological studies of sleep found no evidence of rapid eye movements at the outset of sleep and no indications of dreaming until perhaps three-quarters of an hour after the onset of sleep.

I had often noted I dream immediately upon falling asleep. I knew this because of external evidence of the lapse of time that had occurred. For example, my wife and I have observed that on occasions when one or the other of us has fallen asleep before the other while we are conversing at bedtime and then is suddenly aroused, he or she will often make an incomprehensible retort to the other's remarks. What has happened is that the one who has fallen asleep has had a brief dream and upon being suddenly awakened has made a response not to the unheard conversation but to the stimulus material in the dream.

Thinking over the situation of the relation of dreams to sleep in other situations, I recalled that often I might fall asleep during a dull administrative meeting or lecture and awaken abruptly while the meeting was going on, almost invariably with the recollection of a dream. I had occasionally dropped off to sleep at a social gathering or party when it was late at night and I had had something to drink. I might actually fall asleep in midsentence, awaken abruptly and make a bizarre comment, notice the puzzled looks on my friends' faces, and hastily seek to tie in the unrelated remark to the previous waking flow of conversation. Phenomena like these seem to me indistinguishable from the usual night dream in richness of content and in other qualities that are usually scored when experimenters attempt to deal quantitatively with night dream material.

I began making numerous inquiries and found that many people reported that they, too, had had dreams under similar circumstances. Yet the evidence from all the electrophysiological studies of dreaming was that people showed no eye movements at the onset of sleep or during siestas or brief naps. There seemed to be a contradiction between the reports current in the late 1950s that the eye movements in a dream were identical with waking eye movements and that the so-called REM (rapid eye movements) that are so crucial a part of evaluating the sleep cycle represented normal "looking" responses.

I next tried a more systematic self-observation. It had been a regular practice of mine to take late-afternoon naps, particularly on days when I had a heavy or late-hour schedule of patients. I therefore began setting my alarm to awaken me at various predetermined random intervals to ascertain whether or not I could recall a dream. Immediately upon being awakened by the alarm I made a note whether or not I recalled a dream, and if possible, wrote out the content in sketchy form.

My findings were quite clear. I recalled a dream after all but one awakening. Clear recollection of the detailed content was less common after short intervals but I found no relationship between clarity and interval of sleep. Contents of the dreams that I did record were typical of my usual dream patterns. The material generally proved susceptible to analysis in terms of personal problems, unresolved issues and the usual symbolic characteristics of dreams. As far as I could tell, there was rarely any continuity with events or thoughts immediately preceding sleep. A major finding was that vivid dreaming did occur within minutes or seconds of my falling asleep, since in the three- and five-minute intervals some time must have been consumed before I actually was asleep. For example, in one dream I was traveling on a moving sidewalk and kept trying to get on another one but always seemed to be heading in the wrong direction. Then I was at the New York World's Fair trying to get to the General Motors stairway but finding myself going up and down on General Foods!

Subsequently I served as a subject wired up for EEG study during afternoon naps. In those experiments, awakened fairly early in the sleep cycle, when I was in stage one but without any evidence of rapid eye movements, I recalled rather vivid dreams.

In one instance at the laboratory of Dr. Montague Ullman of the Maimonides Hospital in Brooklyn, I was awakened shortly after falling asleep and with no evidence of eye movements on the polygraph. I reported a dream that involved the vivid appearance of a woman, an Igorot whom I had once photographed in the Philippine Islands. She seemed to be approaching me menacingly in a crouching position with hands extended. I recall the dream vividly and in color but there was no indication on the EEG record of any ocular motility.

These experiences suggest that there may be a much greater amount of fairly continuous associative activity going on in the brain than was recognized by the early dream researchers. A number of studies directed by Dr. David Foulkes and various collaborators on mental activity at sleep onset made it clear that a good deal of dreaming does occur. A very interesting finding, which gives me some comfort, was that there are important individual differences in who is likely to report dreams at the onset of sleep. Foulkes found that those who were already more given to introspection and who indicated less anxiety and more psychological self-awareness were more liable to dream at the outset of sleep. That is, they showed no eye movements and yet carried on vivid dreaming. Persons who had indications of emotional distress were more likely to report their most extensive dreaming during the rapid eye movement stage later in sleep.

In concluding this section I would like again to urge upon the reader a similar acceptance and interest in ongoing thought processes. Just as any novel experience may engender doubt, the exploration of our own daydreams, fantasies and stream of thought may be frightening to some people. This need not be the case. One can take pleasure in this self-awareness and discover new possibilities about one's own capacities for imagery and the novel integration of memories and images.

CHAPTER 3

Normative Studies of Daydreams: Who Daydreams, When and Where?

Until about twenty years ago, what we knew about the prevalence of daydreaming came entirely from the kinds of individual reports I provided in the previous chapter or from accounts by psychoanalysts, psychiatrists or psychologists describing the daydreams or fantasy patterns of specific patients. Literary interpretations by stream-of-consciousness writers, while obviously touching home with many readers, nevertheless were derived from the introspections of highly gifted and self-conscious artists who were not at all typical of the ordinary man and woman. In the United States there was a certain negative connotation associated with daydreaming. It tended to be viewed as a bad habit of children carried over into adult life, a likely sign of emotional disturbance. In the very first questionnaire used to screen out neurotic individuals from the United States Army in World War I, Robert S. Woodworth made sure to include items such as "I daydream frequently." European psychologists were less likely to be concerned about daydreaming patterns.

Let us start by collecting some very basic information on the range and scope of daydreaming in the general population.

People's tendency to guard their privacy and to avoid the embarrassment often associated with admitting fantasies may of course be expected to limit the effectiveness of asking directly about daydreams. During the 1940s and 1950s psychologists placed great emphasis on getting at the daydreams and fantasy lives of their patients and of the general population through projective methods. These techniques, of which the two most famous are the Rorschach ink-blot test and the Murray Thematic Apperception Test, call for the presentation to subjects of ambiguous scenes or pictures, for which associations are then obtained. In the case of the Rorschach ink blots the emphasis has been primarily upon analyzing the more formal qualities of the response. The associations to the blots are scored on the basis of their form or their color or on the attribution of motion (M score) to the inert figures. Rorschach associations involving humans in motion has been shown in quite a large number of researches as well as in clinical use to be a good indication of the imaginative capacities of an individual and of the quality and complexity of his inner life.

The Thematic Apperception Test calls for the subject to look at pictures with ambiguous scenes—a boy staring at a violin, for example—and to make up stories based on these scenes. Here the emphasis is on scoring the stories for the primary motive pattern of the individual. The work of investigators such as David McClelland of Harvard University has indicated that careful examination of the stories told by large numbers of individuals will give us clues as to the strength of certain motivation tendencies such as achievement or power strivings.

I myself worked extensively in the area of projective techniques with both these instruments. Nevertheless, when confronted with the task of developing an approach to daydreaming as a specific human phenomenon I felt that the projective techniques were not entirely satisfactory. It seemed to me that psychologists had been overly cautious about simply asking people directly about their daydreams and fantasies, on the assumption that everyone would be so defensive and inhibited that the results would be of dubious value. It is certainly true that many patients in psychoanalysis exhibit defensiveness. Often enough, individuals are not aware of how much they are hiding about their private fantasies. But direct methods might help to answer such questions as:

1. What is the frequency of daydreaming in various samples of the normal population?
2. What types and content of daydreaming are in evidence among normal individuals?
3. Are there differences in the frequency or content of day-dreaming as a function of the sex, age, cultural background, educational level, marital status and various other environmental characteristics of normal individuals?
4. Are there particular patterns of daydreaming that go together? That is, is daydreaming a general phenomenon that everyone experiences or do individuals differ in their style of daydreaming or in their orientation toward it?

Interview and Questionnaire Methods

My first step was to make lists of all the daydreams I could find reported in popular literature, psychological and psychiatric case reports, and any other sources I could tap that referred to specific fantasies. I also drew on the daydreams of various friends and relatives and threw these into the lists. Because any attempt at carrying out very large-scale interviewing is beyond the scope and staff of most psychologists, it was most feasible to organize the interview into a questionnaire which would list a large number of daydreams and ask people to report on whether they ever had any of these and with what frequency; and to indicate the times and places they had such fantasies, the conditions that seemed most conducive to their occurrence, and so on. Some of the specific daydreams we employed in our earliest questionnaires included:

> I plan how to increase my income in the next year.
> I have my own yacht and plan a cruise of the eastern seaboard.
> As a child I imagined myself a great detective.
> I see myself in heaven and see myself transformed.
> I suddenly find I can fly, to the amazement of passers-by.
> I see myself eating and drinking unusual delicacies at a great banquet.
> I see myself in the arms of a warm and loving person who satisfies all my needs.
> I picture an atomic bombing of the town I live in.
> I see myself participating with wild abandon in a Roman orgy.

There were a large number of such statements, which were organized into a formal inventory given to a sizable number of normal individuals from reasonably well-educated backgrounds and of middle-class socioeconomic status. The scales include what might be called the structural characteristics of daydreaming—that is, where and when they are likely to occur, whether they are future- or past-oriented, what the general attitude of the respondent is toward daydreaming, how much emotionality occurs in daydreams or how vivid the daydreams are. Specific kinds of fantasies are also grouped into clusters such as Sexual Daydreams or Daydreams of Heroism, Guilt, Aggression or Achievement.

Unfortunately we have not been able as yet to extend the use of the questionnaries to very large samples of lower socioeconomic groups in our nation or to the ethnic minorities of the working class. Probably the vocabulary level of the questionnaires is a bit high for many educationally disadvantaged segments of the national population. It is a sad fact of life that for lack of funds or adequate resources, psychologists cannot reach some of the broadest segments of our society when it comes to collecting many technical kinds of psychological information.

Among the groups that have been studied in large numbers are a variety of college students from backgrounds that include substantial numbers of Columbia College freshmen as well as City College students; educators and librarians; graduate students from Teachers College at Columbia University, who came from all parts of the country; students from the University of Bridgeport, who might represent a northeastern seaboard group; and most recently, large numbers of students from Murray State University in Kentucky, a group derived from rural backgrounds in Kentucky, Tennessee and bordering states, who are attending school in a county in which not only drugs but alcohol are banned. In smaller numbers studies have been carried out by students of mine with rural Pennsylvania high schoolers and with relatively poorly educated working-class white and black subjects from the South. The indications are that these groups show patterns of responses quite comparable to those of the college-educated groups from whom most of our information is derived. Whenever possible we have supplemented the use of paper-and-pencil inventories with direct interviews of subjects. Our results seem also to suggest that the kinds of content and patternings of daydreaming we get from the questionnaires are representative of what people tell us when we question them more intensively and personally. Let us consider some of the major results that have come out of almost twenty years of administering inventories and questionnaires to large numbers of relatively normal, reasonably well educated middle-class American men and women.

Conditions Favorable to Daydreaming

Practically all the subjects report that they engage in some form of daydreaming daily. A very large number also describe their daydreams as taking the form of fairly clear images of people, objects or ongoing events. Visual imagery is the predominant modality for experiencing fantasy. Most people report that daydreaming occurs chiefly when they are alone, although there are some subjects who are likely to be aware of daydreaming almost all the time, even in social situations.

Many individuals are inclined to assume that daydreams are limited to wish-fulfilling, castles-in-Spain types of thinking, but this does not prove to be the case for most respondents. Daydreams frequently deal with planning for future actions and particularly for dealing with other people in significant relationships. Probably daydreaming occurs most often when people are preparing to go to sleep at night. It is least frequent upon awakening in the morning and during meals. Contrary to some of the psychological literature, the majority of our subjects have reported that they enjoy daydreaming and deny that it embarrasses them. A look at the large numbers of responses we have obtained leaves one with the general conclusion that daydreaming is a remarkably widespread occurrence when people are alone and in restful motor states. It is a human function that chiefly involves resort to visual imagery and is strongly oriented toward future interpersonal behavior.

If we look more closely at the content of daydreams that are reported with great frequency by a large percentage of our respondents, we see that most people's daydreams consist of projections into the future of the fairly practical immediate concerns they have in their daily life. This daydreaming cannot be equated with specifically wish-fulfilling ideation. It appears more appropriate to look upon the content of daydreaming for most of our sample as reflecting attempts at exploring the future. It is a form, as Freud suggested, of "trial action" in which individuals review a variety of alternatives, not by any means always involving satisfactory outcomes for themselves. The predominant content is practical, but a great number of respondents also have frequent daydreams dealing with sexual satisfaction, altruistic attitudes, unusual good fortune and various magical possibilities that are much less likely to occur in their individual lives. More than a few subjects have reported daydreams of relatively unconventional kinds, such as fantasies of being the Messiah, homosexual relationships, murder of members of their family, and so on. Frequent daydreamers entertain a great range of the more fantastic types of content, often running the gamut of heroic achievement, Messianic identification and sensual gratification in their inner thoughts.

Some Background Characteristics Associated with Daydream Frequency and Content

SEX. So far, our studies have shown very few major differences between men and women in the pattern or frequency of daydreaming. Women, on the whole, still reflect in their daydreams the well-established cultural stereotypes of somewhat greater passivity and nurturing tendencies, more interest in their bodies and in fashion, and little inclination to report heroic achievements or athletic feats. Women's fantasies tend more toward speculation about human relationships and reflect considerably less inclination to be directly aggressive. In at least one study there were indications that women who showed a great many achievement-oriented daydreams were also characterized by having more frequent guilt-oriented fantasies.

While biological sex differences do not appear to be of very great significance in the structure and frequency of daydreaming, there are some interesting indications from our studies that the psychological orientation toward traditional roles does make a difference in the pattern of fantasy. For example, men who in general are more inclined to be accepting in themselves of what are thought of (at least in the American culture) as traditionally "feminine" interests are also more likely to be frequent daydreamers, inclined toward a highly positive acceptance of fantasy and a more speculative and vivid inner life. Those men whose orientation is toward the very traditional masculine stereotypes are disposed to more controlled inner activity with greater prominence of sexual, heroic and achievement daydreams and more mechanical curiosity and speculation, rather than concern with human relationships, in their private thoughts.

FAMILY CONSTELLATION. An interesting hypothesis that bears on the pattern of relative maternal-paternal identification in the development of fantasy life was tested in two studies. The opportunity for identification with a benign parental figure appears to be of particular significance in child development. This identification takes place under circumstances in which a parent frequently rewards the child for controlling its movements and emotions when there is a delay in satisfying some urgent desires or impulses.

To some extent mothers in our society tend to represent inhibition of impulses and also to foster aesthetic or spiritual interests, while fathers are more likely to represent action tendencies within the family structure and also to be the agents of the external environment. Closer identification with the mother figure would therefore appear particularly likely to be related to fantasy or daydreaming tendencies. In general, the data we obtained in two separate studies supported this hypothesis. In the investigation carried on by myself and Rosalea Schonbar with female respondents, greater daydreaming frequency was reported by women who described themselves as more similar to and closely identified with their mothers than their fathers. Women with infrequent daydreaming not only seemed closer to their fathers but were more likely to list male figures or women associated with masculine activities when they were asked for the names of favorite historical or fictional personalities. A similar finding of greater maternal identification for frequent day-dreamers emerged in a study by Vivian McCraven and myself which employed men as well as women subjects.

AGE. We have as yet relatively little information on the changes in daydreaming across different life stages. Results from questionnaire studies do suggest that late adolescence is a peak period for reported daydreaming frequency, and that there is a very gradual decline with increasing age through the fifties. There are indications, however, from questionnaires administered to elderly persons even into their eighties that daydreaming and fantasy activity is still in evidence, and is not essentially different in its patterning even for very old people. Not surprisingly, the elderly seem to carry out more reminiscent types of daydreaming and spend a good deal of time reliving past experiences or comparing current life situations with the somewhat rosier cast they tend to attribute to their earlier lives. Sensitive portrayals of the fantasies and reminiscences of older adults are available in literary form in books such as Bellow's *Mr. Sammler's Planet* or in the Peter Nichols play *Forget-Me-Not-Lane*. In both these literary works we see older people still anticipating the future and by no means overestimating the past, but tending more than young people to dwell upon it.

There are several possible explanations for our finding of a decline in daydreaming with age. Increased responsibilities and the family involvements of early adult life leave fewer opportunities for solitude and therefore minimize the conditions necessary for daydreaming. Even in its more fantastic aspects daydreaming involves some orientation toward the *probable*. As mature adults move on from their late teens and twenties they are likely to be full of plans and possibilities and to be receiving training and preparation toward long-range goals. By the onset of early middle age, however, they find themselves in settled roles, with more limited ranges of career and family choices. The distant future beckons less and concerns become narrowed to more current and near-future situations. However much most men may fancy themselves becoming great football players, once one has set forth on a program of training as a steam fitter or accountant or salesman (or is already involved in the day-to-day activities of a vocation), the likelihood of a professional athletic career fades rapidly indeed. Fantasies become considerably narrowed, only a small portion persist actively, and these are generally ones that have at least some reasonable possibility of fulfillment. The research of Leonard Giambra has suggested that it is the more unpleasant fantasies which especially decline with increasing age. Studying teens through seventy-year-olds, he found that positive, "happy" daydreams persisted but fantasies of guilt, aggression or extreme anxiety declined. Expectably, older people projected less far into the future and had fewer sexual fantasies.

EDUCATION AND SOCIOECONOMIC STATUS. Our research has not brought out any clear-cut evidence that frequency or content of daydreaming is related to any great extent to either the level of education or the general socioeconomic status of individuals. Naturally one would expect that persons with some degree of leisure and with superior reading skills or aesthetic training would be likely to produce somewhat more "literary" or "artistic" fantasies as a result of exposure to a greater variety of cultural content. Much of this difference, however, has probably been changed by the availability of television to the broad masses of our society. Through the television medium the humblest of the poor and the most isolated rural residents are now exposed to far-off countries, attractive and adventurous life styles, and the possibilities of wealth and influence.

One might speculate that persons of limited education or lower socioeconomic status may be stimulated by television or movies to envision romantic fulfillments without any awareness of the intermediate steps necessary for attaining such goals. In contrast, middle-class youth, whose life is often structured from an early age in terms of a series of linked subgoals—high school, college, executive interviews, executive training, movements up the ladder—may demonstrate a more realistic type of fantasy content. A personal communication from Dr. Kenneth Clark, based on his experience with Harlem adolescents in the Haryou Project, does indeed support the above assertion. These lower socioeconomic, poorly educated black youths initially showed very high fantasy goals, which then seemed to prove frustrating, forming the basis for bitterness and despair as it became clear how little possibility of attainment there really was. Still, for any upwardly mobile subcultural group, the existence of heroic figures with whom identification is possible and who can form the basis for fantasies of attainment seems especially important.

RURAL-URBAN BACKGROUND. In one of our studies the highest daydreaming frequency was reported by persons raised in large cities, while those raised in suburbs reported the lowest. In addition, subjects from rural areas showed more daydreaming than those from small towns or suburbs. Findings like this may represent a subtle interaction of the likelihood of the free time that is necessary for practicing daydreaming and the availability of a great deal of stimulation, which provides content for daydreaming. Suburban young people tend to be tied into highly organized life styles—with schoolwork followed by riding or tennis or music lessons as well as various organized groups such as cub scouts—that permit very little opportunity for privacy, leisure or solitude. The urban youngster not only experiences through television, movies and a broad range of the arts much more stimulation, but may also find that long rides around the city on subway trains or buses may give him opportunities for the kind of privacy that is not available in the busy routine of suburban youth or in the noisy, crowded tenement, where one cannot easily find islands of quiet.

Recent studies comparing students from City College in New York and Yale University with those from Murray State University in Kentucky indicate few differences in frequency or patterning of daydreaming between the urban and the rural groups. If anything, the chief contrasts lie between the sexes. For the rural Kentucky young people the differences between the men and women are quite great—the men show more guilty, hostile and achievement fantasies while the women exhibit more of the traditional feminine patterns of passivity, dependency and social conformity. The students from the Northeast differ far less along sex lines in their personality and fantasy styles.

SOCIOCULTURAL BACKGROUND. The most striking results we have obtained in the analysis of questionnaire responses have related to various subcultural groups in American society. In one study carried out by Vivian McCraven and myself in the 1950s the subjects were categorized according to subcultural backgrounds that both parents shared—Negro, Jewish, Anglo-Saxon, etc.—as well as mixed parentage. The Negro and Jewish groups showed the highest daydream frequencies and the Anglo-Saxon subjects the lowest.

We then undertook a more extensive study to test specific hypotheses about what differences might occur among various subcultural groups. To some extent daydreaming represents one medium through which a person may explore his environment or "lifespace" without committing himself to action. It is possible that membership in an upwardly mobile social group might produce a greater tendency to daydreaming. Like the football runner looking for an opening between the shifting mass of men, persons seeking advancement in social status are ever on the lookout for avenues of fulfillment. For a social group that has attained a relatively stable or secure status, the future may be less intriguing or demanding of imaginary exploration. Charles McArthur found upper-class and middle-class American college students to be quite different when he studied their fantasies. The upper-class subjects looked more to present or past, the middle class more to the future.

In the various subcultural groups that McCraven and myself were able to survey in sizable enough numbers for statistical analysis, we predicted differences in daydreaming frequency and content among Anglo-Saxons, Germans, Irish, Italians, Jews and Negroes. In terms of immigration waves and relative assimilation or social stability in the United States, the order of these groups from the most to least secure should be reflected in a parallel increase and frequency of reported daydreaming. We therefore predicted that we would get responses ranging from most to least frequency for Negro, Italian, Jewish, Irish, German and Anglo-Saxon, in approximately that order.

In general, our results confirmed the hypothesis with which we had begun. The various groups differed among themselves in both frequency and content of their daydreaming reported on the questionnaire. The six groups, arranged in order of daydreaming frequency from highest to lowest, were Italian, Negro, Jewish, Irish, Anglo-Saxon and German. They formed an obvious clustering into two groups of three: Italian, Negro and Jewish, representing groups still relatively recently immigrant and upwardly mobile, showed very similar scores; while the other three groups, which have a more secure status in the United States, all scored much lower on the daydream frequency scale. On a parental identification questionnaire the Italian, Jewish and Negro respondents reported themselves to be least like their fathers in their behavioral preferences, and they described their fathers as being quite different from what they feel would be their own ideal self-images. These results seem to confirm the hypothesis that persons who show less identification with their fathers, or perceive their fathers as far removed from the standards they have set for themselves, are likely to report greater daydreaming activity.

It should be noted that the Negro subjects we used were all middle-class, well-educated subjects predominantly from southern urban centers. The Negro respondents showed a higher degree of relatively concrete realistic daydreams, while the Jewish and Anglo-Saxon subjects, at opposite extremes, reported the least number of materialistic fantasies. While none of the groups differed very much in the category of improbable or bizarre daydreams, the Irish subjects showed by far the greatest reference to mystical, other-worldly or otherwise "fantastical" fantasies—in general a culturally based acceptance of fantasy that is evident in the writings of James Stephens, W. B. Yeats, James Joyce and the many great playwrights and novelists of the Gaelic tradition. The Negro, Jewish and Italian subjects reported the highest frequency of erotic fantasies. The Negroes' general daydream pattern indicated considerable preoccupation with fairly concrete sensual gratifications and material security. Their pattern seemed to reflect the middle-class Negro concern with achievement of material satisfaction set forth by E. Franklin Frazier in his classic description of the *Black Bourgeoisie*. Interestingly, a recent article about the fantasy tendencies of Arthur Ashe, the finest American black tennis player, indicated that his daydreams during a match fit well with the results obtained ten years before with our Negro sample.

While no clearly definable trends emerged for the Jewish subjects in this group, the Italians, with their concern about death and afterlife, showed some of the fatalistic cultural values also reported in research on the Italian subculture by Strodtbeck. The Irish in their daydreams alternated passionate or dramatic-heroic fantasies with religious preoccupation. The subjects of German background showed no unique content, but did evidence a lower general frequency of reported daydreaming.

Finally, the respondents of Anglo-Saxon background, although daydreaming about practical plans, tended to be least willing to speculate imaginatively or to give free play to sensual interests or strong emotions; at the same time they showed a greater apparent self-satisfaction than the other groups.

The assimilation process of subcultural groups into the dominant white Anglo-Saxon Protestant American culture, as described in a fine anthropological study of American society published by Sister Woods, seems to involve a gradual decrease and blurring of the variety and richness of imagination. Though the data so far available cannot document that decrease conclusively, the relative change toward less vivid and somewhat less frequent daydreaming as groups become more assimilated and established in this society raises some intriguing questions. Does the lower frequency and variety of fantasy in the assimilated group represent a movement toward health and effective action rather than indecision and anxious speculation? Or does it, instead, represent a denial of inner richness and introspection, a movement in the direction of conformity and the elimination of individuality?

DRUG AND ALCOHOL USAGE AND DAYDREAMING. Fairly consistent in the research literatures on drug usage in high school and college students is data showing that the tendency to experiment at least with marijuana and sometimes with more potent drugs is associated with personality characteristics including a great deal of curiosity, a search for new sources of thrills and novel experiences, and a rejection of common social values. Studies by Bernard Segal and myself comparing almost a thousand Murray State and Yale freshmen indicated that most students at both institutions drank and smoked marijuana in moderation—even though the Kentucky school is located in a county that bans the sale of alcohol as well as drugs. The students who were heavy users of marijuana or hard drugs were not especially given to fantasy; rather, they were determinedly nonconformist and thrill-seeking loners, with little interest in self-awareness. The students who drank more frequently or got drunk were likely to be those with many guilty or hostile fantasies, who were seeking to loosen their inhibitions by alcohol.

We asked smaller groups to reenact their fantasies about drinking and smoking marijuana. This gave us an indication of what they had experienced and what they looked for in these situations. Marijuana use was presented as a passive, onlooking group experience with mildly pleasant sensations and images. Drinking was fantasized as involving more vigorous, uncontrolled action, some loud fun and many more negative emotional and physical reactions. Marijuana use generally seemed associated with trying to find pockets of peaceful "inner" space, alcohol use with attempts to be more extroverted.

Research of this sort suggests that if we are concerned about excessive marijuana or alcohol use in young people, we might give thought to ways of helping them develop their self-awareness and a greater acceptance of their fantasy capacities without resort to external props. Our evidence does indicate that a forward-looking achievement orientation in fantasy plays a role in limiting the necessity for drug use. A similar finding was reported by a group of investigators led by Dr. Richard Jessor at the University of Colorado, where expectation of achievement was a variable that differentiated between high school drug users and nonusers in some samples. The students who placed greater emphasis on achievement than on independence in their life situation tended to be more likely to avoid the use of marijuana. For many young people it would appear that since they remain under relative parental control while in school, the resort to drugs gives them a private freedom in the imaginative realm that they cannot find easily in their day-to-day life. Quite possibly the achievement orientation, both in fantasy and in action, may lead the group more concerned with accomplishment to find certain kinds of freedom in their daily lives because of the recognition they get from adults. Drug and alcohol use depends largely on social pressures but the importance of the individual's fantasy orientation is pointed up by these results. Experiments now under way are examining whether training in greater use of imagery can modify drug and alcohol habits.

So far we have focused attention on background factors associated with some patterns of reported daydreaming. What of the factors *within* the person that seem to coexist with the disposition to frequent fantasy behavior?

INTELLIGENCE AND DAYDREAM FREQUENCY. It is conceivable that if elements such as enriched vocabulary, reading experience and skill at combining and integrating diverse knowledge are involved in fantasy, there ought to be some relationship between daydreaming and general intelligence. What data we have suggests that any association between intelligence and daydreaming frequency is at most a subtle one. The early work of Seymour Sarason provides ample evidence that moderately mentally retarded children and adults reveal a considerable amount of fantasy activity. Whenever intelligence tests have been employed, the degree of intelligence does not especially appear to influence the reported frequency of daydreaming or any special pattern of fantasy.

CURIOSITY, CREATIVITY, SELF-AWARENESS AND DAYDREAMING. Intelligence as measured by tests tap "convergent" processes, the kinds of thinking that lead people to come to common conclusions or to give standard responses agreed upon as correct by a society. There is still another important aspect of intellectual functioning, which is based largely on what the psychologist J. P. Guilford has called "divergent" productions. These involve responses that are original, or that are flexible and free in their associative fluency.

In a series of studies I carried out with various collaborators in which we were able to get adults and children to make up stories, we then had these stories characterized for originality and judged as more or less creative by persons who knew nothing about the children or the adults. We found that daydreaming frequency is indeed associated with storytelling rated as showing originality. These findings are consistent with others by investigators who have used very different samples. For example, Ravenna Helson has been interested in studying young women with particular artistic or scientific gifts. Her researches have indicated that early frequent daydreaming in childhood is associated with later development of artistic abilities. A series of studies directed by Charles Schafer with very large numbers of high school and college students in the New York City area also yielded evidence that creative adolescents in literary fields or in art show greater openness to imagination and are also much more likely to have had imaginary companions or make-believe playmates in their early childhood than did otherwise matched groups of young people without creative achievements.

A general pattern that has emerged from these researches is that daydreaming frequency and certain styles of daydreaming are indeed linked to originality of thought and to the tendency to seek for novel experiences, at least at the level of imagination. Persons who show particular gifts in producing creative literary or artistic works, and who are also able to recall more of their night dreams and better describe their own personalities, are likely to be given to a good deal of daydreaming.

Patterns of Daydreaming

I have referred a number of times to dimensions or patterns of daydreaming. One of the tasks of scientific inquiry is to find out whether we can establish more precisely the way in which a phenomenon is measurable along a number of scales. In the study of individual differences in psychology, a major development has been the use of a technique known as factor analysis. This procedure calls for the administration of a sizable number of tests or behavioral measures to a quite large sample of individuals. Their scores can then be intercorrelated and examined to determine whether some of the tests (and presumably the human functions they measure) cluster more closely together than others. So far, over a span of more than a dozen years, at least six different factor analyses with more than a thousand subjects have been carried out using the daydreaming scales (the Imaginal Processes Inventory) we have developed. It is encouraging to note that generally speaking, the same factors do come out in each individual sample tested.

Basically, daydreaming scales seem to fall into between three and four major clusters, or factors. I shall describe each briefly here without an attempt to deal with some of the more technical characteristics involved.

ANXIOUS DISTRACTIBILITY IN DAYDREAMING. This grouping of scales includes Absorption in Daydreaming, Frightened Reactions in Daydreaming, Distractibility, Mind-Wandering and Past-Oriented Daydreaming. A person whose scores were high on the various scales that make up this particular pattern of daydreaming would be characterized by having many rather fleeting and loosely connected fantasies, usually involving anxieties and worries. Such an individual would experience an inability to attend to tasks and to stick with anything for a period of time. People who report many of these types of daydreams also tend to get high scores on psychological tests developed specifically to evaluate neuroticism and anxiety. It seems clear that for the persons who fall into this pattern predominantly, daydreaming is not a useful resource and they take little pleasure in it.

GUILTY, NEGATIVELY TONED EMOTIONAL DAYDREAMS. This pattern is characterized by high scores in scales of Guilty Daydreams, Fear of Failure in Daydreams, Hostile-Aggressive Daydreams, Hallucinatory Vividness of Daydreams and often also by Achievement-Oriented and Heroic Daydreams. The person who scores high on the various scales that make up this factor is likely to be someone whose thoughts and fantasies take on a strongly ethical tone, full of self-doubt and self-questioning. At the same time he or she might show much striving for achievement and significance through heroic activities but also considerable fear of failure and resentment of others.

A person who scored high on this scale would not necessarily be any worse off than many other people. Indeed, he or she might be likely to seek help and recognize more readily his own doubts and fears and difficulties. It is of particular interest that persons with high aspirations for accomplishment may also be prone to considerable guilt and self-doubt. Certainly it is known that very driven individuals who accomplish much in life often do experience periods of great depression and guilt manifested in somewhat dramatic forms. Such a person might score high on this daydreaming scale. My results also suggest that the persons with high scores on this scale tend to be more oriented toward traditional masculine concerns in the society; and this of course includes women respondents as well as men. Such individuals are also more likely to resort to drinking as a means of loosening inhibitions and evading guilty fantasies.

POSITIVE-VIVID DAYDREAMING. A third factor that emerges consistently in all the factor analyses is characterized by high scores on scales such as Positive Reactions to Daydreaming, Acceptance of Daydreaming, Visual Imagery in Daydreaming, Auditory Imagery in Daydreaming, Future-Oriented Daydreams, Interpersonal Curiosity, and other scales which suggest ideational interests, an active thought life and the use of daydreams for solving problems. This "happy daydreamer" factor seems to represent a more generally positive approach to one's own fantasy activity, characterized by an enjoyment of daydreaming and its use for anticipation of the future and for self-distraction without any pathological implications.

Sometimes a fourth factor emerges in certain samples, which on further inspection is linked with this one. It is characterized by primary emphasis on controlled thoughtfulness and objectivity in fantasy orientation. In most instances this factor tends to overlap with Positive-Vivid Daydreaming, reflecting a considerable acceptance of one's inner life and an ability to use it for planning and a variety of forms of effective functioning. Where the Controlled Thoughtfulness cluster does come up somewhat separately from the Positive-Vivid Acceptance of Daydreaming factor, one gets the impression of two adaptive manifestations of a high acceptance of inner life, the one characterized more by freedom, flexibility and nonconformity in fantasy and an interest in people, and the second distinguished by an emphasis on control, curiosity about the physical world and natural events rather than people, and a greater emphasis on orderliness and objectivity of thought.

The analogy to C. P. Snow's contrast between the "literary humanist" scholar and the physical scientist-engineer comes to mind. Both extremes represent responsiveness to internally produced cognitive experience which are quite different from the extrovert's push for direct perceptual and physical contact with the environment. In all our studies with personality scales and the daydreaming scales, we do find a clearly independent factor, which can be called Extroversion. This represents a factor that is separate from the tendency toward fantasizing or attending to one's own inner experience. A person high on the Extrovert factor would be characterized by great searching for direct physical experiences, for active social engagement and for direct manipulation of the physical environment. This is not necessarily the opposite of the capacity for daydreaming and it is conceivable that a person could score high on several of the factors that emerge in one of these batteries of tests. In general, however, persons who score high on the Positive-Vivid factor or the Controlled Thoughtfulness factor tend to translate a great deal of their experience into ideational form. They are willing to take the time to elaborate mentally many of the experiences they confront and are also quite curious about people or the complexities of natural phenomena.

SOME BEHAVIORAL MANIFESTATIONS OF DAYDREAMING PATTERNS. It seems reasonable to ask whether people's reports on questionnaires about their daydreaming patterns really reflect differences among them in other situations. Since we can't get "inside" their heads, how do we know that what they answer on paper has any accuracy? Scientific psychology takes this question seriously and has devised various methods of approaching an answer. For one thing, we know that, at least according to statistical checks, people are consistent in how they fill out questionnaires. We also know that when we interview smaller groups, whose inventory scores on daydreaming are available, they present similar descriptions of their fantasy styles. For example, Dr. Barbara Hariton's research (described in Chapter 7) checked out through intensive private interview the questionnaire answers women had given about their daydreams during sexual relations. Dr. Steven Starker had persons who were especially high and low scorers on the three patterns of daydreaming keep records of their night dreams for several weeks. When these dreams were scored by judges for characteristics similar to the daydream patterns, the results indicated considerable consistency in style.

Other approaches have involved laboratory procedures, some of which will be described in subsequent chapters. These studies indicate that persons who report a good deal of positive daydreaming on the questionnaire will also report more extraneous thoughts while concentrating on a demanding task. As time goes on the daydreamers may begin to miss more cues if the task is boring, apparently preferring to attend to inner fantasies. High-scoring daydreamers are more likely to shift their eyes to the left when reflecting, and are also more likely to give elaborate and vivid answers to questions about their recollections or fantasies. Computer analyses of their accounts of extraneous thoughts during a task indicate that Positive Daydreamers use more metaphors or analogies. Their imagery is not only more vivid by their own account during special concentration; it actually prevents them from noticing pictures flashed at the very spot on which they are focusing their images.

We still have a great deal to learn about what difference it makes in daily life to be a person who daydreams a great deal in general or someone who represents a particular style of fantasy: Anxious, Guilty or Positive-Vivid. The data presented in this chapter should make it clear, however, that daydreaming is a common, natural phenomenon, broadly experienced by large groups of people. Certainly one can no longer assert that daydreaming is inherently pathological or an indication of psychological deviance. This point needs to be stressed because many individuals are inclined to be frightened by their own fantasies or by the interpretations given them by clinicians who are unaware of just how natural daydreaming is. The large-scale surveys now suggest that to be human is also to be subject to daydreaming.

CHAPTER 4

The Stream of Consciousness: Experimental Studies of Daydreaming in Relation to Attention and Cognition

The recent upsurge of interest in tennis provides us with a good introductory example for studying the relationship of daydreaming to the processes of attention and concentration. Clearly the main rule of tennis is to keep one's eye on the ball. Any slight shift of attention away from it will lead to a complete miss or a poorly timed reaction. An anticipatory glance in the direction where one intends to hit the next shot may be enough to spoil effective execution of the play itself. A glance from the opponent or a distracting sound from the audience are other external stimuli that will tend to get one's eye off the ball. But there are also internally generated experiences that produce the same effect, although in a manner less obvious to the onlookers at a match.

Here are some quotes from the experiences of some of our finest tennis players.

The mind of Arthur Ashe is wandering [wrote John McPhee in *The Levels of the Game*]. It wanders sometimes at crucial moments such as now—in the second set of the semifinals of the first United States Open Championships, at Forest Hills. . . . With the premium now maximum on every shot, Ashe is nonetheless thinking of what he considers the ideal dinner—fried chicken, rice and baked beans. During matches, the ideal dinner is sometimes uppermost in Ashe's mind. Graebner, like other tennis players, knows this and counts on it. "He'll always daydream. That's one of his big hangups. That's why he escapes to the movies so much. But in a match he won't dream long enough. I wish he would do it longer."

Ashe's daydreams generally are of food but also include things such as parties, earlier experiences he's had, and particularly girls, whom "he dates in three colors." "This is my way of relaxing. Other people call it lack of concentration. Which is true. But I do it by habit, instinctively."

Here is Stan Smith (as reported in the *New York Times*) describing his reaction, during the Wimbledon finals, after he had made a strong shot and John Newcombe had fallen down trying to reach it.

Then he began to clown around as if he had broken his arm . . . and maybe I entered into the spirit of it. I stuck out my hand as if to say, "Thanks, old buddy. If you want to default the rest of the match, I accept it."

I started daydreaming. I guess thinking what I'd say and do at the presentation of the trophy. I thought about the Wimbledon ball that night, when the men's champion and the ladies' champion traditionally dance the first dance together. I lost all my momentum, and also lost the match.

Lest we limit this only to men, here is a quote (also from the *Times*) from Chris Evert following her loss in the semifinals of the International Match to Billie Jean King, who had come from behind to defeat her. Miss Evert said that after winning the first set and then leading strongly in the second she began to lose her concentration.

"I started thinking about what I was going to do after I won," said a disappointed Miss Evert. "I was thinking of playing Evonne." She was referring, of course, to Evonne Goolagong, the

Australian teen-ager who was Chris's leading rival at that point in tennis history.

One need not dwell further on tennis. It should be obvious to the reader that fleeting fantasies and daydreams intrude themselves upon us throughout the course of many situations in which we are actively engaged in performing tasks that require attentiveness ranging from normal regard of the physical environment to intense concentration.

Lest one get the impression that daydreaming during most waking situations is inevitably dangerous or maladaptive because of its distracting effect, let us adopt a broader perspective. One way to think of our physical environment in relation to the tasks we have to perform and our ability to steer ourselves around in it is to view it as representing an array of signals to which we have different priorities for responding. Some signals demand instant response or disaster may follow—as in the case of a red light at a dangerous corner. Most of the signals in our environment are redundant and we have a chance to pick them up a second or third time around without any serious difficulties. It therefore seems likely that in many situations we can manage to engage in a good deal of awareness of our own ongoing thoughts, fantasies or expectations, many unrelated to the task at hand, without great risk or loss of time or effort. Our brain even seems geared for managing this process by the mechanism of what has been called the short-term memory system. As material becomes available in the environment that we need to attend to and organize, in order eventually to deal with it or store it in our memory system, it seems to be held for a few fleeting seconds in a kind of suspension so that we can very briefly replay it before it is lost forever. Think of the situation in which you have been listening to a piece of music on the radio that you find very enjoyable but can't identify. You'd like to know the name of the piece or who the performers are but just as the music ends, the doorbell rings and you start up to answer it. Suddenly you realize that they're announcing the name of the music. There is a critical matter of seconds within which you can hear almost echoing in your brain the announcer's identification of the piece and who performed it. If you pass that critical couple of seconds you never seem to be able to retrieve what was said, and will have to wait for another performance to identify the piece. Because the information-processing capacities of man are extensive and complex, it seems better to regard the stream of thought and our daydreaming tendencies as part of that overall process, rather than simply as a kind of distracting intruder.

The Interaction of Environmental and Internal Sources of Stimulation

During the 1950s psychologists devoted a great deal of attention to an area of research that might be called the study of sensory deprivation. Under the impetus of the theoretical analysis of the brain offered by Dr. Donald Hebb of McGill University in Canada, a great many investigators set up experiments in which individuals were kept in environments that limited drastically the possibilities for them to receive input through any of the major sensory modalities—vision, hearing, touch or smell. What was particularly interesting was that individuals confined under such conditions for a lengthy period of time were inclined to report an increased awareness of images and fantasies. Accounts that they actually experienced hallucinations were somewhat exaggerated and perhaps overpopularized. What was more frequently the case was a great increase in "daydreams, fantasies and pseudo-somatic delusions."

In effect, the studies demonstrated that when man is denied stimulation from the outside, he either produces more inner stimulation or perforce *attends* more actively to the ever-present stream of his own imagery or fantasy. The *amount* of external stimulation itself may not be as critical as man's need for what psychologists Dwight Fiske and Sal Maddi have called the need for *varied* experience. When one's environment is grossly limited either in material available or in variety of content, one may begin to shift attention inward. This tendency has been recognized by engineers working to reduce industrial accidents or to increase productivity in factory work. A monotonous environment can lead the workers to shift their attention away from moving machinery to other stimulus sources in the shop, with a consequent increased danger of accidents. Sometimes they may also engage in joking or teasing with their co-workers and lose their concentration; then either the quality of the work suffers or, again, there is a greater chance of accidents. As long ago as 1929, two British researchers on industry called attention to the fact that daydreaming might actually keep workers alert during otherwise monotonous tasks, because they would be less likely to look around the room when they were providing their own "internal" novelty.

INTERNAL AND EXTERNAL STIMULUS SOURCES. Let's assume for the moment that we can designate two major channels of stimulation available to a human being—the first, the external environment, and the second, the inner dimension of his short-term memories, the elaborations upon events perceived and events drawn from long-term memory storage, and associations and combinations of old memories with recently perceived events or with images just aroused. Under most circumstances it is likely that the response to the external stimulus source will take priority over a response to material drawn from the long-term memory system. When wide awake with eyes open, a man will ordinarily be far more responsive to the changing pattern of external stimulation— shouts of children at play, a flickering of light, the passing roar of a train, the suddenly loud blare of a switched-on stereo set, the movements of a fly on the wall—than to his own inner associative stream. External stimuli may be more insistent and vivid compared with those drawn from memory. Normal adaptive behavior also demands greater attention to the environment if we are to survive.

Actually, most normal behavior undoubtedly calls for some rapid switching between the two channels and possibly also some of what is called "parallel processing." Most researchers in the field of cognition now believe in general that the act of perceiving an external stimulus cannot occur effectively without some matching of this stimulus with material from long-term memory, a process that takes a certain amount of time even though it seems almost instantaneous to us in the natural situation.

Most people report the greatest frequency of daydreaming to occur just prior to sleep. Under those circumstances, as one settles down for the night, consciously excluding varied *external* stimulation by shutting one's eyes and covering oneself with a blanket, there occurs an upsurge of awareness of inner activity. The increase of imagery and fantasy at this time may be so vivid and varied or affectively arousing as to maintain alertness even when sleep is much desired.

Folk experience has suggested that this arousing effect of varied *inner* experience may be counteracted by sharply restricting the variety of such activity. We accomplish this ordinarily by techniques such as "counting sheep," which limit thoughts such as those about the important unfinished business of our lives that would impel us to action and undoubtedly keep us aroused. Counting sheep may not be effective if the internal activity involves anticipation of very important events that will need to be attended to in the morning, or frightening thoughts about dangerous consequences to come because of certain acts left undone. The technique that I described in an earlier chapter of playing out a private baseball or football game in order to induce sleep has an advantage over counting sheep. There is at least some degree of interest in the game itself. By being able to concentrate for at least a little while on the game, one can prevent the intrusion of all those concerns and anticipations that might inhibit sleep. In my case it takes just a minute or two of interested attention to the game to stifle the leakage into my consciousness of more urgent concerns, by which time I have established a rhythm that leads almost at once to sleep.

SOME EXPERIMENTAL STUDIES OF THE INTERPLAY OF INNER AND OUTER STIMULATION. Let us look more closely at how we devise experiments to tap the ongoing stream of consciousness by using this notion of the different priorities assigned to internal and external sources of stimulation. In experiments developed by Dr. John Antrobus and myself, the individual sits in a darkened room in what would be considered a moderately sensory-reduced situation. He is required to pay attention either to sounds fed into his ears through earphones or to lights flashing before him, depending on the specific experiment, and to perform a task requested of him by pressing a button. In effect, then, he has an extremely limited external environment which the experimenter controls because it consists primarily of flashing lights or alternating sounds that the subject has to evaluate as they are presented to him with great rapidity. This assumes he is actively involved in the task; and we can easily judge that involvement by the accuracy with which he detects the signals that are part of the experiment. In most of our experiments, as monotonous and tedious as they seem, it was possible by financial incentives to get subjects to perform at a 90 percent accuracy level for very long periods of time. The situation we employed is similar to that faced by a radar or sonar operator in an airport or on an oceanographic expedition.

In one experiment, an observer was seated in a small darkened and soundproofed booth. Before him was a small light that flickered continuously, on for one second and off for two seconds. The subject was required to tap a switch whenever the light flashed just a little more brightly than usual. For every series of fifteen minutes of continued light presentation, there were six "signals," randomly interspersed, to which the subject would have to respond by pressing his switch. Since the task was a visual one and we wanted to reduce external stimulation, subjects were seated in a darkened room and had limited opportunity for movement; and "white noise," a steady but not unpleasant hissing sound, was fed into their ears by earphones.

Here, indeed, was a sharply restricted external environment, in which the subject's basic outside world consisted of the flickering light. What of his "inner" environment? This was controlled by setting up two alternating conditions for him—one in which inner activity was varied and the other in which inner activity was extremely monotonous. For the former condition the subject was required to carry on orally a continuous free association throughout the ninety minutes he sat in the booth detecting the visual signals. He could attend as much as possible to his own ongoing varied stream of thought without restraint. The reason he was asked to talk out loud was so that we could ascertain by recording whether he was complying with the instructions and also examine the pattern of associations produced. He himself could not hear what he was saying because of the "white noise" in his ear. In this sense the situation was somewhat analogous to normal activity of an interior monologue carried out simultaneously with the performance of a motor and cognitive task.

The alternative condition that each subject went through attempted to limit internal activity to a narrow range. Here he was simply asked to count out loud from one to nine continuously for the full ninety minutes. Again we could keep track by a tape recording of whether or not he was complying with the instructions. By counting sequentially over and over again through the hour and a half he stayed in the booth, he sharply limited the amount of varied complex internal thought processes he could have, or so we felt. The results of this experiment were intriguing. It turned out that those subjects who limited their internal environment were much more likely to report themselves as having become very drowsy. Indeed, there were indications that on a number of occasions they actually fell asleep, since there was a sharp drop in their counting, evidence of regular breathing and a sudden decrease in finger tapping to detect signals. It seemed very clear that the varied activity of free association kept the subjects more alert and in a better general emotional state than did limiting their internal activity to routine counting.

There was, however, a curious finding that begged for further analysis. On an overall basis, even though the "counters" tended to fall asleep at the switch they did not perform the overall task significantly more poorly than when in the "varied talk" condition. The monotonous counting task, by providing less competition and distraction during signal detection, led to a good level of performance, though as time went on the lack of variety induced drowsiness and sleep. After a nap of a few seconds, the observer might well snap out of it and catch up on signal detections, even surpassing his own performance when he was required to engage in varied talk.

In a second experiment to check this out, Antrobus and I carried through much the same kind of study. This time, to make sure that the counters were staying wide awake we piped into their ears lively brass-band march music instead of the white noise. This "oompah" sound certainly seemed to maintain a lively state of arousal as measured by the scales of alertness that were administered to all subjects at the end of an extended watch. Under these conditions, with alertness artificially maintained, the subjects in the limited internal environment condition of counting actually turned out to be better at signal detections than when they were engaged in varied internal activity and free association.

Our data suggest that subjects who managed to sneak in some

daydreaming while they were counting during the experiment reported less drowsiness and managed to perform better. Those subjects who sneaked in daydreaming *on top of* the free-associative speech condition did show a deficit in performance.

If we take a look at these results in relation to many of the daily requirements of living, which involve what psychologist D. E. Broadbent has called "understimulated tasks," then we can see the positive benefits that come from attention to fantasy. At the same time, maintaining greater arousal and alertness by internally oriented attention covers up the fact that we pay a price by missing some external cues. Since our environments are indeed so redundant in cues, missing a cue once in a while is not serious if our overall attitude is one of alertness and good spirits. It is only as the task becomes increasingly more complex or as we are already extremely alert that the shift of attention to internal processes can be shown to lead to a significant deterioration in effectiveness of performance.

A further series of experiments by Dr. Antrobus and myself with various co-workers in our laboratory has sought to establish more carefully the conditions for increasing or suppressing attention to internal processes. By interrupting subjects every fifteen seconds and getting their reports in the form of either a "yes" or a "no" response or an account of extraneous thought content, we can establish the frequency of what we call stimulus-independent mentation under various conditions.

Without going into technical details of these experiments, let me summarize some of the major findings. We have learned that it is not really easy to eliminate attention to internal activities even under conditions in which a subject is receiving auditory signals at the rate of one every half second, matching these signals against previous signals, pressing a button to indicate whether the signal is a high tone or a low tone, or the same or different from a previous tone, and then receiving the next signal and evaluating it at once in the same fashion. Remember that subjects maintain an accuracy on the order of 90 percent for detecting fifty to one hundred signals in any given "watch."

We find that we get a relatively irreducible minimum of about 10 percent of reports of stimulus-independent thoughts. Usually it is considerably higher than that level. We find that we can reduce the number of reports of task-irrelevant fantasies by increasing the *rate* of presentation of signals and the *complexity* of the task or by increasing the *monetary penalties* for an error. Despite this, we still get some degree of spontaneous thought. One clue we have as to how one manages to produce thought that is unrelated to a task while at the same time carrying on the task quite accurately comes from experiments which suggest that subjects pace themselves rhythmically in order to allow themselves some leeway for attending to task-irrelevant material. If we break up the natural rhythm of presentation so that signals come at random speeds rather than regularly every second, the amount of task-irrelevant stimulation falls off drastically. We can also demonstrate certain mathematical relationships between the amount of information the subject has to process in any given task and the amount of task-irrelevant mentation he shows. There are indications that some of the time, people can carry on thinking about private events *at the very same time* that they are accurately detecting signals, but during other phases of an experiment we see clear indications of what is called sequential processing, that is to say, skipping rapidly back and forth between attention to the external situation and attention to ongoing ideation.

What are some of the circumstances that are likely to increase attention to one's ongoing stream of thought? In one experiment carried out in late 1964, we arranged for subjects to be sitting in a waiting room just prior to going in to participate in one of the signal detection tasks. A radio was playing. Suddenly an announcement came on. It reported a dramatic escalation in the Vietnamese war. This of course excited great interest in the waiting college students we were using as subjects. Once they went into the booth to start their signal detection procedures, they showed a great increase in frequency of task-irrelevant thought, as might be expected. When we inquired about the content of this thought, much of it had to do with fantasies about the consequences of their recent information—the dangers of a wider war, of being drafted, of losing one's boyfriend to the army, of being made a prisoner of the Communists. Though many of the fantasies were not entirely related to the immediate situation of being drafted and were somewhat unlikely to occur, they were all anticipations of possible consequences of this new information. The most curious factor in this experiment is that despite the great increase in attention to private thoughts during the task, accuracy was not interfered with very much. This would suggest that we all possess much greater capacities or "channel space" for the processing of both internal and external signals than we use much of the time. Under pressure we can increase the range of our information-processing capacities.

Establishing that a person can carry out the complicated response of accurate signal detection in a situation like this, while at the same time paying a good deal of attention to his ongoing stream of thought or producing some fairly extended fantasies or daydreams, has been one major outcome of these laboratory experiments. We have also learned that attention to *positive* fantasies during one of these extended watches can help pass the time, as well as serve effectively for anticipatory and planning responses. In one experiment it was found that those subjects who reported many positive emotions in their daydreams during a lengthy signal detection task also revealed at the end of the watch that the time had gone very rapidly. Those who reported *very little daydreaming,* or fantasies and thoughts associated with *unpleasant emotion,* indicated that the time had dragged and thought that they were in the booth a much longer period of time than was really the case. In still another experiment, subjects were given an opportunity either to sit quietly in the booth for long periods of time or to activate the signal detection experiment by pressing a button, thus giving themselves something to do while sitting in the darkened chamber. We found that persons who reported in general more *positive* kinds of daydreams, more daydreams of a *personal nature,* and in general more *imaginative* and more *interesting content* in their fantasies tended to be the ones who, given the choice, preferred to sit in silence rather than engage in detecting signals. In other words, they had developed a means for providing themselves with an interesting environment and varied internal stimulation and so could tolerate long periods of quiet.

When we approach this issue from the other standpoint, that is, comparing subjects who say they have a great deal of predisposition to inner thought and fantasy with those who are very little inclined in that direction, we find similar differences in their signal detection performance. Both groups are able to perform equally well initially. As time goes on, the high-fantasy subjects begin to show more of a decrement in signal detection. Their priorities for processing and enjoying their inner activity seem to be great enough so that they are willing to let their attention shift away from the external task even at the cost of losing a little money. Quite recently it has also been possible to program a computer to analyze the content of subjects' task-irrelevant and task-relevant thought during one of these tasks so that we can examine more precisely the nature of the stream of thought in process. Eventually this method should give us a better insight into the way associations are chained.

Imagery and Signal Detection

The vast majority of people report that most of their imagery is visual in character. If this is the case, then what is happening to our reaction to the *outside* visual stimuli when we are engaging in a private visual image? The late Dr. Sydney Segal developed an extended series of experiments to determine just what happens when an actual picture is flashed in the very place where a subject is projecting a private image: the chances were quite good that the external cue would not be recognized at all. This phenomenon has practical importance. A pilot coming in for a landing will be anticipating well in advance certain patterns of lights or geometric shapes in the landing area. This anticipation involves the projecting of an image. The image could slow down slightly his recognition of the actual external cue for which he is looking.

An experiment using Dr. Segal's imagery and signal detection format was carried out by Dr. Vincent Fusella in our laboratory. The subjects were either high or low scorers on the Positive-Vivid Daydreaming scales and also on a measure of sensitivity to private experience. Fusella found that generally speaking, high scorers tended to report that their images were significantly more *vivid* than those of persons who scored low. More than that, however, they actually did miss more of the pictures that were flashed on the screen while they were engaged in projecting their own vivid imagery at the fixation point. This was the case even though, when not engaged in imagining, they showed no inferiority at all in their ability to spot faintly presented images on the screen. The indications are that people who reported on a verbal inventory that they engage in a great deal of vivid imagery demonstrated in the experimental situation that their self-estimate was indeed correct.

Independent experiments by Dr. Segal as well as by Dr. Antrobus and myself made the important findings that if we are primarily involved in attending to *visual* images and fantasies, we are less likely to be accurate in detecting external *visual* cues. If, on the other hand, our internal processing is primarily oriented around *auditory* fantasies, that is, imagined conversations or music, then we will not show any special difficulty in detecting external *visual* cues. The same principle holds if the internal material we are processing is *visual* and the external signals we seek to detect are *auditory*. Such experiments suggest that a private image in a given modality uses the same brain structures or pathways as does the processing of an external stimulus in a given modality.

EYE MOVEMENTS, PHYSIOLOGICAL REACTIONS AND DAYDREAMING. Can our eyes provide a clue to what is going on "inside the head"? This question leads to many interesting speculations regarding indications of ongoing thought. How do we know if someone is engaging in a daydream while sitting near us in a social situation? Are there any regular body processes, including eye movements or changes in breathing rate or blood pressure, which are typically associated with fantasy activity? Do different kinds of thought show different patterns either of eye movement or of physiological reaction? Are there any ways we can detect whether someone is paying attention to us in the course of a conversation or is letting his mind wander?

In a delightful episode from the Sherlock Holmes stories of Sir Arthur Conan Doyle, there is a good example of how eye movement and facial expression can provide clues to private thought. Dr. Watson is seated with Holmes in their apartment. He has fallen into a "brown study" when Holmes interrupts by making a statement that seems to answer a question Watson had just been asking in his own mind. It is as if Holmes had read Watson's mind. Naturally Holmes denies any occult powers, but rather proceeds to point out he had been watching Watson's eyes move around the room from a picture to space on the wall, then back to the picture. Certain emotions had registered on Watson's face as well, and he had touched an old war wound. The pattern of eye movement had led Holmes to track the sequence of Watson's thought until at the end, with his other observations,

he felt sure that Watson must be thinking about the ineffective-
ness of war as a means of solving human problems.

While the tracking of one's eye movements may lead to some
cues about private thought, the process is by no means as
"elementary" to psychologists as it appeared to Sherlock Holmes.
Since eye movements are so rapid and so many occur in a short
space of time when one is wide awake, eyes open, in a complex
environment, the technical problems of setting up experiments to
study the relation of thought to eye movement are great. I should
like, however, to describe a few studies we have carried out which
have attempted to approach this problem and to determine the
relationship between ocular motility and ongoing thought processes. In one experiment by John Antrobus, Judith Antrobus and
myself, we asked our subjects, who were young college women, to
recline on a lounge in an otherwise bare and darkened room.
There were some shadows, light changes, street noises, and the
audible rumble of a Fifth Avenue bus. We made no attempt to
eliminate such natural sounds or visual stimuli in the interest of
keeping the situation relatively like one that might prevail in
ordinary daydreaming situations. The subjects were wired up to
a polygraph to record their brain waves as well as vertical or
horizontal eye movements. The women were asked what was
happening whenever there were either long periods of no eye
movement or extended periods of active eye movement. Specific
episodes were also assigned which called for them to imagine
certain events with eyes open or closed: they were to think about
a man on a trampoline, visualize a tennis match, think of arithmetic progressions. Of special interest were the instructions for
one episode which was to allow them to "engage in a daydream
of the fulfillment of a secret wish, one you haven't told people."
Subjects were encouraged to revel in the fulfillment of this wish.
The next time around they were encouraged to revive this image
of the secret wish but this time to attempt to suppress it from

consciousness on the assumption that their mind could be read. Here they had to suppress actively a developed image.

The results of these studies were on the whole rather clear-cut. The reports the women made which the raters judged to be more "daydreamlike" came after periods of *no eye movement*. More active, objective thought was characterized by a greater amount of ocular activity. When the subjects reported that they were producing *internal* visual images, other than their simply looking around the room very little eye movement was in evidence. A good deal of eye movement of course accompanied their reported examination of the physical environment. When the young women were engaging in the private elaboration of their secret wishes, there was relatively little eye movement. In their effort at suppression of the secret wish, there was a considerable amount of rapid eye movement. When a person is wide awake it appears that in order to engage in a daydream or elaborate visual fantasy he must somehow suppress attention to the external environment. Presumably the same brain structures or neural pathways are employed in processing elaborate fantasies or images from long-term memory as are employed in paying careful attention to material in the physical environment. In order to carry out an elaborate fantasy one must, therefore, often enough *fix* the eyes and somehow or other blot out new information from the external world.

Another experiment, carried out with young male subjects and with a somewhat different format, provided further support for the hypothesis that eye movements were greater during suppression of thought than during active fantasy. The suppression seemed to be related to attempts to shift content rapidly or to look around the room, if the eyes were open, as a means of cluttering up the "channel space" available for processing the fantasy material.

Subsequent research in our own laboratory has further confirmed the finding that a person engaging in an elaborate daydream is likely to keep his eyes relatively still. This is different from a situation in which a person is trying mentally to mimic a situation that would naturally require a great deal of eye movement. Subsequent studies in our laboratory have repeated this finding and research carried on by investigators such as David Marks in England and Eric Klinger at the University of Minnesota have also supported this reduction of eye movement during imagery and fantasy.

In an attempt to pin down more carefully the mechanism underlying the limited eye activity during fantasy, Dr. Stanley Greenberg, Dr. John Antrobus and I devised an experiment whose subjects were put in a situation in which their visual environment consisted almost completely of a screen on which moving vertical stripes were projected. This procedure produces the *optokinetic nystagmus reflex*, which is characterized by regular tracking movements of the eyes across the screen in the direction of the movement.

It was our hypothesis that a person would have somehow to shut out the effect of the moving stripes in order to dwell on a private fantasy. It would seem likely that by staring ahead fixedly at a particular point, one might block out the effects of movement in the immediate visual field by letting the eyes go out of focus. For this experiment we had special lenses ground for each subject which would, in effect, *prevent* him from shifting his focus to infinity, and maintain his focus directly at the stripes. We theorized that under conditions in which the subjects *could not* shift their focus, they would have much greater difficulty in blotting out the moving stripes and, therefore, in engaging in some form of elaborate daydreaming or fantasy.

It turned out that there was indeed a very marked decrease in tracking eye movement when the subjects engaged in fantasy and daydreaming activity. For our male subjects in the experiment this "gating out" of the external visual environment was accomplished by the shift of focus as we had hypothesized. The female subjects, however, seemed to be able to blot out the stripes even when their eyes were forced to focus directly on them. This would make it likely that the brain structures related to blotting out an external stimulus were more "central" than the more peripheral mechanism of retinal focus used by the men. This intriguing finding begs for further exploration.

In other studies we have in general found that a person lost in extended concentration on his own fantasies or thoughts is likely to show very little obvious physiological reaction. His heart rate remains relatively low and he shows no great changes in respiration or palmar sweating. It is only in the shift from one line of thought to another or from one task to another that one sees an upsurge of various signs of autonomic responses, including, also, a great deal of eye movement. We sometimes call this the "concertgoer's effect" because it is similar to what one experiences in a fine performance of classical music where the audience is relatively hushed and concentrating intensely on the performance. It is only as the music terminates or a particular movement ends that you get breathing, shuffling, movement and conversation.

BRAIN HEMISPHERE DOMINANCE AND EYE SHIFTING. One of the exciting things about scientific research is the possibility of discovering new ways of looking upon human beings in the course of exploring a problem from a fresh standpoint. It had long been suspected, but with very little supporting evidence, that the two sides of the human brain were somewhat different in their functions in relation to processing of information. Only very recently, on the basis of observations of human beings in whom the connection between the left and right brain hemispheres had been severed through accident or surgery, was there indication of support of this differential development of the two hemispheres. This encouraged experimenters such as Sperry and Gazzaniga to carry out a variety of experimental studies with animals that made it clear that there are indeed somewhat different functions controlled by the two sides of the brain. It also had been pointed out by a clinical psychologist named Day that people seem to be fairly consistently left or right eye shifters when they are engaged in reflective thought. Since the mechanism for a shift of the eyes to the left is controlled by the right side of the brain, and vice versa, the direction of a shift might be a clue as to what kind of thought process an individual was engaged in, and what style of thinking was particularly dominant in his personality.

Evidence accumulated during the last three or four years seems to suggest that the left side of the brain is more specialized for what might be called verbal or logical thinking, for quantitative forms of analysis and for more formal or controlled and logical cognitive operations. The right side of the brain seems to be associated with more imaginative and intuitive forms of thinking, with the recognition of melodies and with more emotional forms of expression. Research carried out by Paul Bakan at Michigan State University provided intriguing evidence that male subjects could be classified fairly consistently as either left or right eye shifters on the basis of their responses to what are called reflective questions, that is, questions that call for a fairly extended search of one's memory, in contrast with minimal-search questions such as "What is your name?" or "What is the color of your eyes?" Bakan found fairly definitely that those of his subjects who were consistent left shifters tended to be more emotional, imaginative and aesthetically oriented, and also more capable of showing extended *alpha rhythm* in their brain waves, a pattern usually associated with relaxed and dreamlike waking states. Subjects who were consistent right shifters and presumably had greater dominance in the left hemisphere of their brain tended to be more logical and analytical in their orientation, more objective in their thinking and better at mathematical kinds of processes.

Bakan's work came to my attention at a time when Dr. Bonnie

Meskin and I were engaged in setting up a series of investigations about the nature of eye movement during a face-to-face interview. We had started out with the intention of studying in a more natural situation one of the processes we had investigated in the laboratory, as described above: how can you tell if a person is engaged in a fantasy or a daydream or an extended personal reminiscence when he is awake and in a social situation? We have all had the experience of talking with someone only to find that we are not being heeded.

Basically, our experiment was an attempt to track down this phenomenon more precisely. We made the assumption that in human contact the face of another person is the single most intriguing and meaningful stimulus in our physical environment. This notion derives from extensive work by Professor Silvan Tomkins of Rutgers University, who has developed an important theory about the major role that facial expression plays in the communication of emotion and in the feedback to the person himself of his own ongoing emotions and motives. If the face of another person is the major source of our reinforcement, then it is necessary to shift our eyes away from that face if we want to engage in an extended reminiscence or fantasy. Since the shift of a smile to a scowl or the slightest change in the twist of a lip can affect us dramatically, we are less likely to be able to concentrate on private imagery if we focus our eyes upon another person's face. We therefore hypothesized that the amount of shifting of the eyes a person has to do while answering questions from an interviewer will depend on how extensive the answer has to be in terms of its dependence on a search of the memory system or on visual imagery, and also on whether or not the interviewer and the subject are face to face.

We found, first of all, that when a person was asked a relatively simple question that required a minimal search of his memory system there was indeed considerably less shifting of the eyes away from the face of the interviewer, or from the frontal plane when the interviewer was not present. In at least one of our experiments, the characteristics of the room itself clearly influenced the pattern of eye shift. Generally, the presence or absence of the interviewer made a very great difference in whether or not the subject shifted his eyes during the processing of fantasy or reminiscent material. This certainly seemed to offer support to Tomkins's theory.

To our surprise, we found that we could indeed classify our male subjects into those who showed a predominance of either left or right shifting in response to a large number of questions. We found that the subjects who were primarily left shifters tended also to give more imaginative and elaborate responses to the questions that were asked, reflecting what we would call a more extended search of their long-term memory systems or a more vivid fantasy content. These subjects also tended to score higher on our scales of Positive Daydreaming, such as Visual Imagery in Daydreams, Future-Oriented Daydreams, Positive Reactions to Daydreams, etc. The men who were predominantly right shifters tended to give relatively terse answers to the questions, and showed certain other systematic differences in the pattern of their performance that suggested support for the notion that there were indeed long-standing style differences that might be related to the different functions of the brain hemispheres. These experiments, therefore, clearly seem to indicate that eye shifting and fixation at a blank wall may not only be a consequence of the need to clear channel space for the processing of a fantasy or visual image, but may also reflect the particular kind of brain process at work. Presumably some individuals who are frequent daydreamers have developed the right side of the brain more extensively for use in vivid imagery as a behavioral resource.

Recently Dr. Judith Rodin and I studied the eye shift patterns of obese and normal-weight young people in a similar face-to-face format. There is a good deal of evidence that overweight individuals are "externalizers," persons who are strongly drawn to attend to cues in their environment. This accounts for why they overeat when food is present but are less hungry when there are no food cues around. In our research we found that overweight subjects showed less visual imagery in their daydreams but were unable to resist reacting to visual cues directly in front of them. They tended to be right-direction eye shifters when asked to reflect on a memory or a fantasy. If one or two people were sitting in front of them, they had to either shut their eyes in order to think or move their eyes to the ceiling or a blank wall. So drawn were they to external cues and so given to thinking in verbal rather than visual terms that they, like the Leprechaun in *Finian's Rainbow,* might say, "When I'm not facing the face that I fancy, I fancy the face I face!"

Some Theoretical and Practical Implications

LIMITED PROCESSING CHANNELS AND EYE MOVEMENT. I have suggested that the stream of thought is a relatively continuous process that is part of the way the brain works to maintain memories and have them relatively available when they are needed for matching of new percepts or for helping a person solve problems and recall past events. For an individual to get around in the physical environment, however, it is necessary that a major portion of his attention ordinarily be devoted to the new sources of stimulation in the external environment, and that these bits of information be processed efficiently. Probably there is limited channel space in our consciousness for carrying on action or a conscious mental task without finding shifts of attention to unrelated fantasies and anticipations disturbing.

While we have some evidence from our research that task-irrelevant mentation can be carried out at the same time as (that is, in parallel with) performance of visual or auditory tasks under some circumstances, it is likely that much of this activity is carried out more sequentially. This implies rapid shifting back and forth of attention, noticing the external situation and then switching to the material from the long-term memory system represented by the stream of consciousness.

In a lovely song based on Goethe's *Faust* which Schubert wrote as a teen-ager, young Gretchen is at her spinning wheel day-dreaming about her lover. In the background, as she sings, the piano keeps up an accompaniment that simulates the movement of the spinning wheel. Her fantasy reaches its climax with her words "And oh! His kiss!" and the spinning music stops abruptly. The sensitive Schubert knew full well that there are times when our thoughts are so powerful that we cannot go about even automatic actions.

In daydreaming, of course, we are constantly aware of being awake. Our processing of stimuli from the physical environment (unless we lean back and shut our eyes for a period of time) goes on, to some degree. Our waking fantasies therefore tend to be less vivid and are not, of course, taken as "real" in the same way that nocturnal dreams are.

One technique we have learned in order to engage in day-dreaming is finding ways of driving out the external pull—the visual environment—by fixing our eyes straight ahead and letting them go out of focus. There may be other mechanisms our brains employ, as yet unknown, that also play a part in helping us blot out stimulation from the environment. We don't yet know, for example, how we blot out auditory information, but we certainly do it very well. Anyone can think of instances in which the statement of another person in the course of a conversation stimulated a private and extended flow of thought. Suddenly one becomes aware that a good deal of the other person's subsequent remarks has passed unheeded. This can, of course, be very awkward and embarrassing. We have all learned little devices for trying to disguise to others the fact that we have not been fully attentive. We allow ourselves to nod and smile. Sometimes we are detected only by the fact that a question has been asked to which we have not responded, but have continued instead to nod, showing the wan ghost of a smile.

Our evidence also indicates that a person can dream without eye movements. Persons born blind who never have visual content in their dreams do not have eye movements during sleep. As far as waking behavior is concerned, however, we have little evidence that a great deal of eye movement is necessary for vivid or effective fantasy. Rather, the reverse seems to be the case, and attention to both auditory and visual internal material in adults seems to require the fixation of the eyes for a period of time.

We still have the problem of reconciling this notion of fixation of the eyes with the findings about eye shifting and its relation to personality characteristics and to presumed dominance of the left or right hemisphere of the brain. This is an area only at the beginning of research exploration. I would propose that a great deal of eye contact and shifting of eyes in social situations depends on the nature of the relationship between the people and the expectation of how one is to look at another person; recall in this context the point I made earlier about the human face communicating relatively more information than almost any other stimulus source in our environment. If we want to engage in any kind of extended processing of material from our long-term memory, it is usually essential that we shift our attention away from the face of our interviewer.

I have made a practice of watching the faces of people being interviewed on television talk shows or in the course of television news broadcasts, and the regular shift of the eyes away from the face of the interviewer is a common occurrence. Good actors build this eye shift, perhaps quite unconsciously, into their performance. In one of the best scenes in the movie *Lovers and Other Strangers,* an Italian father at a wedding begins to reminisce about his early experiences with girls and marriage. The actor, Richard Castellano, talks in the stumbling and somewhat inarticulate fashion of the character being portrayed, and allows his eyes to shift for long periods of time away from the face of the other person, and to remain fixed to the left while he reviews these early events.

Presumably the shift away from the other face ought also to be in a systematic direction, depending on what the content reviewed is to be. If it is primarily verbal, the shift away ought to be to the right; if it is a review of visual images, the shift is presumably to the left. While we have some research evidence in support of this differential direction, we have not yet studied how consistent this is across large samples of the population and how it interacts with the personality of the individual and the characteristics of the physical environment, including what other kinds of stimuli are in the room to the left or right of the speaker.

Let me insert a romantic note here. Why do most people close their eyes when kissing? Isn't it likely that if they keep their eyes open they will be forced to notice other things around the room, which then have to be processed? Perhaps their attention will focus on some of the close-up details of their partner's skin— pores, or a pimple—that will interfere with the tactile and taste sensation that makes up the kiss. With eyes shut, one is free, at the same time as one enjoys the fullness of the kiss, to elaborate in fantasy on implications such as future kisses, other more satisfying events, or even people one would rather be kissing. What one can see with eyes open while kissing is not likely itself to be sexually arousing. In fact, a person whose eyes stay open during a prolonged kiss is not fully caught up in the act and maybe looking around to distract himself or herself or to escape from the situation.

SUPPRESSING THOUGHTS AND FORGETTING. How do we stop thinking about particular things or blot out unpleasant or painful fantasies and memories? Some of our research evidence suggests that there are people who can erase thoughts either by moving their eyes back and forth very rapidly or by imagining a dark night scene and perhaps vague light in the distance, and focusing on that.

I recall once making an interpretation to a patient that seemed to touch home at once. Her face flushed and tears welled up in her eyes. I waited for an appropriate reaction, and instead noticed that her eyes began darting back and forth in very rhythmic fashion. After waiting a reasonable amount of time, I asked what was going on. She smiled rather apologetically and said, "I'm counting the books in your bookcase behind you." Obviously she had not yet felt ready to go further with the implications of the interpretation, despite its immediate impact on her, and preferred to shift her attention by engaging in a little obsessive ritual.

There is, then, a defense which involves reliance on the external environment: taking in information from the outside as a means of avoiding playing out any extended thought process or studying a situation that confronts one. This process provides a clue as to how the defense mechanism of repression operates. When confronted with a series of unpleasant situations, the more extroverted or outgoing individual may simply shift attention rapidly around the room or toward different persons, with the result that there is little opportunity for the critical distressing imagery to reverberate long enough in the short-term memory system to be stored. This makes it likely that for such a person there are simply fewer memories available in the long run. Rather than a repressive mechanism that forces the person to forget material already stored, there is the possibility simply that less material gets assigned or ticketed for replay at all in his memory system. There is clinical evidence that the more extroverted hysterical patients are poor in recalling many kinds of events and also have a vague and undifferentiated capacity for describing situations.

Even when we have stored material, we must replay or rehearse it actively from time to time, in order to increase the likelihood that it will be recalled, and also to increase the number of associations of this material with current life situations. Systematically avoiding rehearsal may serve to reduce the chances that one will recall specific traumatic events or the implications of events that have important consequences for us that we do not wish to face. As Scarlett O'Hara says at the end of *Gone With the Wind,* "I'll think of it all tomorrow."

Another way of avoiding thought is through the repetitive recall of certain phrases which, in effect, also clutter up channel space. Someone who goes about habitually singing to himself the words of certain popular songs, or who has a series of private obsessional rituals and phrases that go round and round, may be able to avoid rehearsal of some of the memories or anticipations that are fraught with major significance in his life.

To recall our dreams or to savor our own memories and fantasies requires a certain stillness and self-acceptance. Dreams are best recalled, for example, if one lies quietly upon awaking and reviews the content with eyes still shut. Dr. Ernst Schachtel has pointed out that we forget dreams not so much because of resistance, as was originally thought, but because "'the extroversive attitude of waking' is in marked contrast to 'the introversive attitude of dreaming.'" The antagonism between motor activity and dream recall brings to mind Proust's words that he could recapture his former being only *"dehors de l'action, de la jouissance immédiate"* and that in such a moment he did not budge, lest he lose the refound memory of the past. Taking a dip into the waters of the stream of thought unquestionably takes a certain amount of courage and the willingness to renounce the comforts of the shore.

CHAPTER 5

The Function of Daydreaming: Drives, Motives and Emotions

Of what use are our daydreams? Are they reflections of our basic tissue needs that are currently unsatisfied, such as hunger, thirst or sex? Do they represent attempts primarily to escape from an unpleasant reality into a never-never world? Are they symptoms of severe neurotic disturbance reflected in replays of long-standing childhood frustrations? Are they expressions in more adult form of early imagery associated with childhood masturbation? Can we reduce at least temporarily the tension associated with unsatisfied sexual aggressive drives by daydreaming about fulfillment?

The questions raised here represent some of the proposals that have appeared in the speculative literature about daydreaming, particularly on the part of clinical investigators. In approaching the subject of the function that daydreaming plays in human experience we touch on some very basic theoretical issues in all psychology. In trying to get at the functional role of daydreaming in the personality system we have to confront some of the fundamental questions about the nature of all human motivation.

Theoretical Models and the Purpose of Daydreaming

THE PSYCHOANALYTIC THEORY OF THOUGHT AND DRIVE GRATIFICA-
TION. One of the methods scientists use in trying to pull together
diverse strands of observations and give unity to a particular area
of study is to develop what is called a theoretical model. A particular model often reflects the major thinking, philosophically
and methodologically, of the period in which the investigator is
working. In this sense, the theoretical model developed by Sigmund Freud, and followed until relatively recently by most
psychoanalysts, stems from Freud's fascination with the physical
concepts of hydraulic energy being developed in the physics of
the late nineteenth century. Freud also reflected in an important
way the implications of Darwin's linkage of man with other
animal species. Freud's theory was therefore based upon a model
that assumed that man, like other animals, was essentially driven
to action by the arousal of basic instincts built around the satisfaction of the hunger, thirst and sexual drives. Using the hydraulic energy model, Freud believed that drives were periodic
and rose and fell as a function of opportunities for their discharge through satisfaction. Following his exposure during
World War I to the horrible extent of violence of which man is
capable, Freud added to his list of human incentives aggression
as a basic instinctual drive. While this concept of an instinct of
aggression was less accepted even among psychoanalysts, common
usage in clinical work still tends to view both sex and aggression
as characterized by the kind of internal build-up and release that
Freud proposed as the basic motivational cycle in human beings.

In effect, the model that characterized psychoanalytic thinking
until the 1960s implied that all thought or imagination grew out
of suppressed desires. While psychoanalysis today is in a state of
considerable change from this energy model, the fact remains
that for more than half of this century the primary theoretical

position that related to the nature of daydreaming and fantasy thought stemmed from the basic model of psychoanalysis, which was stated in perhaps most formal terms by the great integrator of psychoanalytic theory, David Rapaport, in 1960.

As elaborated by Rapaport from Freud's early proposals, the basic model of psychoanalysis is depicted in terms of the arousal and satisfaction of the hunger drive in an infant. A hungry child, in the absence of immediate gratification through the breast or the reassuring presence of Mama, automatically hallucinates the image of breast or bottle, since what is wished for in the infant appears at once, in what Freud called primary process thought. The image itself, in its hallucinated form, has a temporarily satisfying value, and the child gradually learns that it need not thrash around in violent restlessness or fruitless crying. By imagining the arrival of Mama the child experiences a partial discharge of the original aroused drive and is capable of restraining gratification-seeking movements for a longer period, until the mother does appear. This momentarily drive-reducing quality of imagination becomes the key to the later development of the ego, which in the psychoanalytic system is the basis for a variety of defensive and synthetic functions that eventually characterized what Freud called secondary process, or mature thought and action tendencies.

This model implies that much of our daydreams and fantasies, as well, of course, as our night dreams and indeed many of the more extensive characteristics of all human thought, are reflections of our fulfillment of a limited number of drives, primarily the tissue-related sensual or sexual needs or the cyclical aggressive drive within us. In his classic paper "On the Poet and Daydreaming," written in 1907, Freud said that "Happy people do not make fantasies, only unsatisfied ones do." Even highly socialized daydreams, such as seeing oneself as a great national leader, or as a saintly individual serving the poor, or as the recipient of a trophy for an athletic achievement, are probably reducible to basic sexual or aggressive tendencies that have to be defended against by being expressed in more socially acceptable forms.

An important concept that follows from this early psychoanalytic view of the nature of fantasy is *catharsis*. This term was adopted by Freud from Aristotle's famous theory of the function of tragedy in the theater. When we view on stage the representation of an important goal or conflict situation in our lives, we partially reduce some of the energy associated with the original aroused drive, and this permits us to tolerate the frustration a little bit better. Watching the powerful unfolding of Oedipus's discovery that he has killed his father and married his mother helps us, at least temporarily, discharge some of our own nagging sexual and aggressive tendencies relating to our parents. Similarly, watching wrestling or boxing matches or the roughness of professional football may also serve to release some of our pent-up aggressive tendencies, at least partially.

This same catharsis principle has, of course, been widely used in psychotherapy, with both adults and children. In many forms of group and individual psychotherapy as currently practiced, patients are encouraged to express violent emotions through weeping or through angry denunciations of the therapist or other group members. Most of these methods represent extensions of the basic implicit notion of bottled-up instincts that need some form of vicarious satisfaction, lest they either create severe psychological or psychosomatic symptoms, or lead to socially unacceptable overt expressions of sexual and aggressive tendencies. Daydreaming in this model has a kind of safety valve quality for the adult. It is a holdover of childish, wish-fulfilling thought that is still permissible to the adult as a means of partially discharging some drives. Since most of our thoughts inevitably reflect either sexual or aggressive energy, our daydreams, in this psychoanalytic viewpoint, represent attempts at denying or avoiding open expression of these fundamental drives by symbolic, displaced or socially acceptable variations.

The more recent developments in psychoanalysis of what is called ego psychology have led to a very serious and revolutionary reexamination of many of the assumptions of Freud's hydraulic energy model of motivation. Modern ego psychology pays a great deal of attention to the social input in human experience as it interacts with the psychosexual development of the child. Many psychoanalysts today are more inclined to emphasize broader concepts such as basic trust, the development of autonomy in the child, the importance of affection and identity, rather than to focus on most behavior as expressions of oral-incorporative or anal-sadistic fantasies.

But despite the changes implied in ego psychology, much of the writing about daydreams and fantasy processes by clinical investigators (most of whom have been strongly influenced by some variant of psychoanalytic thought) still leans heavily to the drive-related and catharsis notions I have summarized above. There are, in addition to their psychotherapeutic implications, very significant social implications of this view of the function of fantasy. If vicarious experience (whether in the form of private daydreams or as packaged daydreams presented in movies or television) serves as a discharge for pent-up sexual and aggressive energies, then exposure of all of us to considerable sexuality and violence in the popular media is probably fairly useful in keeping us from raping or killing indiscriminately. Is, then, the concern about portrayals of sexuality or violence on television needless? This is an example of the kind of issues that flow from a particular theoretical position such as is implied by the catharsis theory.

COGNITIVE-AFFECTIVE MODELS OF THE FUNCTION OF FANTASY. Psychologists, even those strongly oriented toward the earlier behaviorist approaches, are increasingly inclined to emphasize man's role as an information-processing creature, rather than as one who is motivated chiefly by a set of biological drives closely related to survival and reproduction. Research in psychology has placed greater emphasis on the cognitive or knowing processes and the human capacity for imagery as playing key roles in learning and adaptive behaviors. In trying to devise theoretical models for describing human behavior, psychologists are resorting more and more to some of the concepts derived from computers and from information theories, as well as from more complex feedback or self-regulating, cybernetic types of organizations.

A model of personality that has the special advantage of tying man's information-processing characteristics closely to his emotional structure has been set forth by Dr. Silvan Tomkins, whose work on the role of the face in emotion was cited earlier. Tomkins suggests that man has evolved a fairly differentiated set of emotional reactions which permit him to become aware of his own varied moods and to communicate these to others through facial expressions and bodily posture. The emotions, which include surprise, fear, interest, anger, sadness, shame and joy, are aroused by particular patterns of information that the organism has to process. For example, if a person is confronted very suddenly with a great deal of novel information that he does not have time to assimilate and match up to established memories, he will respond by showing the startle reflex or by becoming quite terrified. But if, instead, he is confronted by a moderate amount of new information which is more gradually assimilable, he will react by surprise or the positive emotion of interest. After a quantity of highly unusual or difficult-to-assimilate information has been dealt with, and there is therefore a reduction in novelty, the individual will experience joy and manifest overtly a smile or laughter. If very complex and difficult-to-assimilate material persists over a long period of time, an individual is likely to experience a great deal of anger. But if the material is not especially complex and novel and can be matched up in part, yet is still not readily assimilated, there may be a continuing experience of sadness or distress.

Suppose your doorbell rings and you open it to find yourself confronted with a gorilla. It is likely that you will respond with a startled reaction or with terror because this is a most unexpected and difficult-to-assimilate set of information. Since man is an image-making creature and is constantly anticipating through fantasies or imagery what will happen in the future, you very likely went to the door picturing a salesman or a needed repairman or the delivery of a package. Instead—the gorilla! If you slam the door shut and then cautiously open it again, and the gorilla says, "Trick or treat," you realize it is Halloween and your response almost certainly will be a smile or a burst of laughter and perhaps a generous gift of candy. If, on the other hand, the gorilla stays there and indeed tries to force its way in, you may be unable to make sense of this experience, to assimilate it into anything that you can deal with readily, and are likely to become either terribly angry and try to attack the gorilla if you have a weapon about, or terribly distressed and start screaming.

The same principle of the relationship of information processing to the arousal of emotion can be applied to private fantasies, to recall of memories or incidents from the past or to other thought processes that are not observable by others. For example, a man is asked for the key to the office washroom by one of his co-workers. As he reaches into his pocket for his keys, he suddenly realizes that he has taken the car keys with him and that his wife was supposed to use the car that day to take the children to the doctor. This realization may produce a startled reaction and then, as the information persists without his being able to do anything about it mentally, he may respond with anger and pound one fist into the other. His co-worker waiting there for the washroom key will be utterly amazed by the strange behavior of our protagonist. Suddenly the frustrated husband may realize that there is a spare car key his wife knows about which is always kept hidden in the garage for emergencies like this, and he can now assimilate the unfortunate incident of the car keys into a well-developed mental schema. This leads him to smile or laugh out loud, again to the utter puzzlement of his fellow worker. What I have described is, therefore, a complex sequence of behaviors that take place privately with a considerable feedback of information and strong emotion, but without any specific arousal of a biological drive.

I have gone to some length in describing this alternative model and view of man because I believe it can help us understand something more about the way to look at the function of day-dreaming and fantasy processes in human behavior. Our day-dreams and fantasies are not merely bland events that occur to us. Many of them, as our questionnaire study and interviews suggest, are characterized by a great deal of negative emotion, anxiety or anger or guilt, in addition to joy. The private make-believe play of children as well as many more elaborate adult fantasies are frequently accompanied by smiles, a sense of delight and anticipatory glee. While the psychoanalytic model would generally suggest that fantasy activity is derived from conflict, and is also a childlike way of thinking (the word "regressive" is still widely used by psychoanalysts in discussing daydreaming thought), the cognitive-affective model does not emphasize the role of conflict in ordinary daydreaming. This approach increases the likelihood of viewing it as having positive or arousing charac-teristics and also makes no statement that it is necessarily a regressive phenomenon.

Experimental Studies of Drives: Affects and Fantasy

STUDIES WITH PROJECTIVE METHODS. I have already mentioned some of my own research on the behavioral correlates of the human movement (M) score in interpreting the Rorschach ink-blot technique for describing personality structure.

The significance that Rorschach attributed to the human movement response was that on the one hand, it was supposed to reflect inhibited motor activity in a person who gave many such responses, and on the other hand, it was supposed to indicate a strong tendency for inner experience and imagination. In various experiments carried out by the distinguished developmental psychologist Heinz Werner and others, it was shown that altering one's body position affected the way one perceived motion in the environment. Werner also found that people who exhibited very little overt movement for one reason or another, or were blocked in such movement, were more likely to perceive movement either in ink blots or in some experimental demonstration. Working with various collaborators, I also carried out a series of studies with the Rorschach ink blots, to determine if persons who were forced to inhibit their overt movement would show an increased tendency to see people in motion on the blots, and whether people who showed a great deal of motor activity were likely not to see very much movement on ink blots. In general, our whole series of studies suggests that people who turn out to be rather controlled or inhibited in their movements or in their ability to stay less active during solitary forced waiting periods, or who are more deliberate in their problem solving, are also likely to produce associations involving movement to the ink blots and to be more imaginative on the basis of various measures of fantasy tendency.

One way to measure imaginativeness is to have people tell stories to ambiguous pictures such as those that appear on the Thematic Apperception Test (TAT), developed by Professor Henry Murray of Harvard University. One can measure the "transcendance" of these stories as an indication of imagination. One picture consists only of a boy looking at a violin. Suppose a subject tells a very elaborate story about parents forcing the boy to study, his resisting and running away to join the circus, and then having a whole series of subsequent adventures. One can score each of the elements introduced into the story that is not actually on the picture, as an indicator of the imaginative tendencies of the respondent. Using measures like this, it is possible to show that people who give M responses to the Rorschach are likely to exhibit high transcendance on the Thematic Apperception Test, and may also be people rather controlled or slow in overt motor activity. In addition, the Rorschach M response can be shown to correlate significantly with the self-reports of frequency of daydreaming made to a questionnaire like the one described in the previous chapter.

At first glance it would seem that the research with projective methods does support the implications of the psychoanalytic model: that someone showing a good deal of fantasy would be less likely to be expressing drive activity overtly, since some of the energy would be discharged in the fantasy. But a more careful look at the very large number of studies that have now accumulated fails to support this interpretation. For one thing, when people have been actually subjected to some type of drive deprivation, as of hunger, thirst or sex, one does not find any increase in projections of these drive states onto projective test materials. Indeed, there is sometimes a decrease in imagination about the desired object after a period of deprivation.

In addition, people who are known to be consistently aggressive or impulsive ought not to show much overt aggression in their fantasy products, while those people known to be consistently inhibited and little given to aggression ought to show much more evidence of aggressive fantasy. This, too, does not prove to be the case. Rather, the evidence is that persons who are consistently aggressive or rambunctious express this tendency directly in their imagery on projective methods. More controlled people may show just as much aggressive fantasy on tests but will generally also indicate qualifications of this tendency, such as awareness of the consequences of hostile acts, or guilt or fear about such expression. Individuals given to overt acts of violence or attack are more likely simply to express the aggressive content in fantasy without any qualifications.

Therefore, these results do not support the notion of a drive-reducing function of fantasy, at least on the basis of projective techniques. It would appear that one has to take a broader view of the role of fantasy, and see it as a general response possibility which is available to many people who also may be controlled or inhibited in a variety of social situations. Furthermore, it is possible to show that there are many people who are capable of a great deal of imagination as manifested on the Rorschach and also a good deal of emotional expressiveness. Such people are vigorous and active as well as imaginative, and seem to be able to choose the times to express either one or the other possibility effectively.

STUDIES OF EXPERIMENTALLY AROUSED EMOTIONS AND DRIVES. I have mentioned the implications of the drive-reduction theory of psychoanalysis for fantasy and its impact on catharsis in psychotherapy. According to the catharsis theory, a fantasy expression of hostility manifested in play reduces the aggressive drive for a child who dares not express it openly. No self-respecting child guidance clinic today is without toys or punching bags or the popular Bobo clown, a weighted giant balloon that bounces up again and again as children punch it.

Here is a true story that grew out of our frequent use of the catharsis notion in child psychotherapy. A student therapist whom I was supervising reported that his eight-year-old patient had spent hour after hour the previous week pounding away at a Bobo clown, saying, "Take that, Mrs. Jones!" On inquiry he revealed that Mrs. Jones was his teacher at school. The following week he started all over again pounding away at Bobo, but this time he said, "Take that, Mrs. White!" Asked about the switch, he simply said, "Mrs. White is my new teacher. Mrs. Jones dropped dead last week of a heart attack." My student and I had sudden visions of voodoo rituals, fostered by child therapists all over America in the name of catharsis theory.

Some ingenious experiments initiated by Seymour Feshbach twenty years ago opened the way to scientific studies of the drive-reduction theory of fantasy. The bulk of accumulating evidence seems contrary to the catharsis notion. An entire series of experiments by Leonard Berkowitz of the University of Wisconsin has made it clear that individuals who are exposed to aggressive scenes in movies and then given opportunities to behave aggressively in various experimental situations will show an increase in such aggressive activities, depending on how the experimental situation is defined for them. In other words, the way a social situation is presented may be even more important than so-called drive arousal in determining the subsequent aggressive behavior of individuals.

A rather complicated study using some of our own questionnaire procedures, carried out by a group of investigators at the University of Washington in Seattle, indicated that college students who were insulted and aroused to anger might reduce their subsequent aggressive tendencies toward the experimenter if they had an opportunity either to write fantasies to TAT pictures or merely to engage in daydreaming. However, the reduction in aggression was not simply the manifestation of a reduced drive, for it was possible to show that many of the people engaging in subsequent daydreaming turned the anger back upon themselves and, because of the chance for fantasy, apparently reexamined their situation and thought there was perhaps some merit to the criticism of the experimenter. The complexity of the situation is also indicated in some studies carried out by Richard Rowe and myself, in which, for example, we arranged for a number of college students to be confronted with a surprise midterm examination. Immediately afterward some were given a chance to engage in daydreaming while others were given an additional task to perform. On the whole, the data from these studies do not support any simple hydraulic energy view of drive reduction.

Let us take a closer look at some experiments that tried to test the power of the two alternative models of the relation of daydreaming to drive or affect that were described at the beginning of this chapter. The first experiment, using a previously developed format, was carried out by Dr. Renee Paton at the City University of New York. A group of college students first took the Imaginal Processes Inventory and then later in the semester were put into a situation in which they were subjected to a series of insults while performing a task. Immediately afterward, one group was given a chance to look at pictures that were generally full of aggressive material (such as battle scenes) while another group that had been insulted was shown equally interesting pictures containing no violence. The groups were then encouraged to engage in fantasies and to report these to the experimenter. Subsequently they were given questionnaires that made it possible to determine how angry and aggressive they felt toward the person who had insulted them. There were, of course, additional groups who served as controls: a group with no opportunity for fantasy activity after being insulted, and a group that was not insulted at all. These control groups made it possible to be certain that the insult did indeed arouse the anger of the subjects, as was evidenced by the fact that without an opportunity to engage in fantasy the insulted group showed a high level of subsequent anger compared to the group that had not been insulted.

The crucial element of this experiment has to do with whether the opportunity to engage in fantasy following the arousal of anger (or presumably the drive of aggression, if one accepts the Freudian position) will lead to a reduction in the amount of aggression expressed toward the insulter. More specifically, if there is an aggressive drive that is aroused and if fantasies related to the aggressive drive reduce that drive, then one would expect the greatest drop in aggression following insult and fantasy to occur if the subject has produced angry and hostile fantasy material, rather than nonviolent ideation. On the other hand, if one adopts the cognitive-affective theory then one would propose that the effect of the fantasy activity following insult would be primarily to divert the subject from the high level of persisting tension and provide him with an alternative mode state that would reduce the likelihood of his showing anger subsequently. In this case, therefore, one would expect that the persons who showed more neutral and nonviolent fantasies would show a greater drop in subsequent aggressive tendencies toward the insulter than did those who showed aggressive fantasies. Consistent with this position would be the notion that both kinds of fantasies might still produce a greater reduction in aggressive tendency than would no opportunity for fantasy at all.

Dr. Paton's results seem to support the latter hypothesis. It turned out that both groups who had an opportunity to fantasize showed less aggression toward the person who insulted them than the group who had no opportunity at all. But there was a rather sizable difference in the drop in anger, depending on the conditions. Subjects who had the chance to engage in primarily neutral fantasies showed a greater reduction in subsequent anger than those whose fantasies were primarily aggressive and violent. It seems pretty clear from this study that the effect of the fantasy is indeed one of diversion and a shift of mood, rather than some kind of relatively automatic reduction of a certain quantum of drive energy, as the old Freudian theory might have proposed. Incidentally, those subjects who showed a good deal of daydreaming on the questionnaire administered initially turned out to produce much more imaginative and interesting fantasy material in response to the pictures they were shown. This would support the view that the questionnaire measures of fantasy do indeed tie in with other indications of imaginative tendencies.

A second experiment at the City University of New York, carried out by Dr. Ephraim Biblow, gave groups of nine-year-old children tasks to perform while an older child kept disrupting their performance and so made them rather angry. One group of angered children was given an opportunity to see an aggressive television movie immediately after they had been frustrated. Another group was given a chance to view a scene from the film *Chitty Chitty Bang Bang*, which involved fantasy and interesting content, but no violence. After viewing the films, the children were allowed to play freely with a variety of toys and games that were in the playground. Observers recorded everything the children did, and later rated their behavior on measures of various emotional states and indications of aggressive behavior.

The children who were shown the nonaggressive film subsequently behaved much less aggressively than did those shown the more aggressive film. This finding was further supported by the evaluation of the emotional reactions of the children. It turned out that the children who were low in initial imagination and somewhat more aggressive in tendency would often become more angry and distressed when shown the aggressive film and were inclined to increase their aggressive tendencies somewhat. Children who were shown the neutral film generally appeared happier and showed positive emotional states during their subsequent play. There was, of course, a control group in this study, which was not given an opportunity to engage in imaginative behavior, and this group showed the increase in anger following frustration, but no reduction, since there had been no opportunity for diversion through fantasy.

I have cited these experiments in some detail to point up the way in which psychological research can begin to resolve questions that have been drawn from clinical and theoretical speculations over the years, but could not have been decided on the basis of individual clinical experiences. When experiments such as these are added to the accumulated body of other formal studies in this area, the weight of the evidence seems to line up against the idea that daydreams or fantasies show a so-called catharsis value, in the sense that they can actually reduce someone's tendencies toward violence or aggression. The same would seem to be the case for opportunities to view films or television shows or to read literature that is violent. The fact that persons who engage in fantasy may subsequently show reduced aggression seems more explicable on the grounds that their resort to imagination provides them with a form of diversion, and changes the focus of their attention from the single-minded intent and violent goal they might have had after being insulted or frustrated. When aggression is presented as justified in a movie, angered subjects are likely to increase their aggressive tendencies subsequently. Looked at from this point of view, the vicarious fantasy of popular media, or private fantasy, may have the dual possibilities of increasing aggressive tendencies under certain situations and of suggesting the appropriateness of certain kinds of aggressive behavior. All this raises serious questions as to the value of catharsis ideas or hydraulic energy models of the kind so widely employed by psychoanalysts and a great variety of clinicians, who urge on their patients the importance of expressing "bottled-up" aggression through games and fantasy or through shouting at each other in encounter groups.

What I am suggesting, therefore, is that daydreams do not have any *automatic* relationship to the arousal or reduction of aggressive tendencies or even to the arousal or reduction of a specific emotion such as anger or anxiety. Much seems to depend upon the habitual way in which individuals have learned to use their daydreams in various stressful or difficult situations. Probably, also, a great deal depends on the context and social meaning of the situation.

Fantasy or daydreaming is perhaps best viewed simply as a kind of capacity or skill in us that is part of our overall repertory of behaviors. We will tend to use fantasies or daydreams in ways that depend on our own background of experience with them during our development. For many people who have not had much experience in daydreaming or paying attention to their fantasies, or who have been encouraged by family experience to avoid such tendencies, the occurrence of frustrating circumstances or an exposure to vicariously aggressive fantasies may affect their mood and lead them toward a single-minded focus on the specific hostile image, and this focus, given the opportunity, may be translated directly into action. Other persons, whose backgrounds are such that they have enjoyed fantasy and have learned to use it in a variety of settings, will be able to deal with an insult or frustration by playing it out more extensively "in their mind's eye," or by shifting their attention to more pleasant fantasy activities. They are likely to be less prone to direct aggressive action. They may consider alternative recourses to a violent response to frustration, or reexamine their past and conclude that some of the insults were justified, determining to try to do better in the future. Quite possibly they may simply shift to an escape type of daydream and find themselves enjoying their reverie—feeling not quite so angry as they did a few moments before, and with little likelihood that they will engage in a direct attack on someone else. This is quite different from reducing a drive. I would expect that many people who had been insulted, but who had diverted themselves through fantasy from the mood of anger, would feel just as angry and as inclined to aggression as they had at the first encounter if they were again confronted with the same insult. Indeed, they might feel even angrier, realizing that this was the second instance.

Emotions, Daydreams and the Popular Media

Some readers may feel I have not given as much importance as I should to the role of sex and aggression in human motivation.

Certainly, a great many of our daydreams involve sexual fantasies, anticipated rendezvous, hoped-for seductions or memories of previous sexual encounters. A good deal of daydreaming may also include thoughts of harming others or of gaining revenge. But there are many other kinds of daydreams, shown by our questionnaires to be of great frequency, which do not fit so neatly into these two categories. Some, of course, involve expression of one's basic competencies and capacities for social or vocational achievement. Many others reflect rather simple and direct needs for luxuries, freedom from insecurity, and the ability to overcome some of the nagging complexities that confront us in day-to-day life. A great many daydreams during the bleak winter months have to do with nothing more complicated than relaxing on pleasant warm beaches beside the blue sea. What I am suggesting is that to try again and again to reduce the great richness of our fantasy lives to fundamental drives such as sex or aggression, or to the working out of the complexities of a specific family relationship stemming from early childhood, seems artificial and much too confining, and does disservice to the great range of human interests. It seems to me much more useful to view daydreaming as a way by which we can explore a great range of future possibilities without necessarily committing ourselves through action to irrevocable consequences.

Daydreams may even be more than just wishful explorations. They may indeed be useful. Some, of course, simply divert us and lower the level of tension and distress occasioned by a frustrating or anger-provoking circumstance. Others may provide us with an alternative environment to one that is boring or contains within it reminders of failures or insults. But to some extent, daydreams also represent rehearsals for future actions. They may suggest new and alternative ways of dealing with situations. Even our more fantastic daydreams may illuminate the humor in a situation or point up the incongruity between our current reality and our hopes, thereby giving us a chance to decide on a more effective approach to a life situation. In the course of fairly extensive fantasizing we may also encourage ourselves to further action in the pursuit of a particular goal. In this sense our daydreams can actually have motivational characteristics; they can encourage us to try new kinds of experiences, or at least to look for ways of reaching some compromise approach to these wishes.

In summary, then, it is difficult to draw any really final conclusions about the functions of daydreaming without a good deal more careful research into the kinds of problems I have raised in this chapter. It seems likely that daydreaming is in a way *just there*—it is a capacity, just like our capacity for language or our capacity to develop various motor skills, which has evolved in human beings as a part of our behavioral repertory. It can unquestionably serve to help us in long-range planning, but it also has more immediate values in steering us effectively through life, and in enriching our momentary capacities for enjoyment of certain experiences. Much of our pleasure, as we all realize, comes in anticipation of events; well before we attend the concert or ball or honorary occasion that we have looked forward to, we find ourselves experiencing a thrill from fantasizing the event. It would seem that our task is really one of learning more and more about this basic capacity for creating images and playing with the future, and then finding ways of increasing our ability to use these skills effectively in a great variety of situations.

Part II

CHAPTER 6

Childhood Origins of Daydreaming: Make-Believe Play and Early Fantasies

How does daydreaming develop? Is the process evident in the thinking of children from the earliest age, or does it show a particular evolution as do other types of motor or cognitive skills through the years? Most psychologists who have paid careful attention to the origins of thinking in children believe that daydreaming evolves out of the make-believe or pretend play that all children seem to show somewhere from about the second year of life through ages seven or eight. As the great Swiss observer of children, Jean Piaget, reported, most children seem to express their thoughts out loud up until the beginning of the school years. By watching them at their make-believe games, we find clues to the nature of early childhood imagination and fantasy.

Let us take a closer look at some examples of imaginative behavior in children. The spontaneous play of children in a nursery school or during recreation in kindergarten shows us striking differences in the pattern of play. Some children are sitting amid blocks they have piled together into a structure holding toy soldiers or plastic figures, and are having the figures interact in a rather complicated game punctuated by shouting voices. "Help! Help! Batman, come quick!" Then, with a change of voice, "Robin! I'm on my way!" "Bang! Wham! Zap!" This is accompanied by much up and down movement of the objects and the knocking over of some of the blocks in the course of a fantasy battle between Batman and the forces of evil.

Other children may be engaged in a make-believe game that involves cooperation between at least two participants—as in playing school or running a pretend candy shop. Sometimes a larger group of children will work out a more elaborate adventure, usually in an outdoor setting, where they become pirates and explorers or cowboys and Indians.

Parents are sometimes unnerved by overhearing their children talking to themselves. Walking by a child's room in the afternoon, one can hear inside the sounds of singing, snatches of conversations—some in different dialects or different speech patterns to represent different characters—or various sound effects, like airplane engines or the screech of sirens. As far as we can make out, these are perfectly natural developments in the growth of the child. Writers such as Robert Louis Stevenson and Mark Twain have provided us with charming examples of the kind of imaginative play that so enriches the early years. Here, for example, is an excerpt from *Tom Sawyer*, which, as every reader knows, is full of incidents in which Tom and Huck Finn pretend that they are pirates or adventurers of various kinds. This scene takes place at the time that Tom is reluctantly painting the picket fence.

> Ben Rogers hove in sight presently. . . . He was eating an apple, and giving a long, melodious whoop at intervals, followed by a deep-toned ding-dong-dong, ding-dong-dong, . . . for he was impersonating the *Big Missouri*. . . . He was boat captain and engine bells combined, so he had to imagine himself standing on his own hurricane deck giving the orders and executing them. . . .
>
> "Stop the stabboard! Ting-a-ling-ling! Stop the labboard! . . .

Let your outside turn over slow! Ting-a-ling-ling! Chow-ow-ow!
. . . Done with the engines, sir! Ting-a-ling-ling! *Sh't! s'h't! sh't!*"
(trying the gauge cocks) .

As the astute observer of children Erik Erikson has noted,
". . . my clinical impression of Ben Rogers is a most favor-
able one . . . on all . . . counts; organism, ego, and society.
For he takes care of the body by munching an apple, he
simultaneously enjoys imaginary control over a number of highly
conflicting items (being . . . steamboat . . . captain . . . and
. . . crew) ," and at the same time Ben is well aware that Tom is
painting away at the fence.

The variety of make-believe play in children ties in with many
of the significant growth areas and conflict situations that develop in the course of childhood.* An intriguing collection of
children's fantasies presented by Dr. Rosalind Gould points out
many of the ways in which the natural play of children reflects
major issues that will become even more prominent as the children move into the broader structure of adult society. For
example, she has recorded two boys who start out by saying that
they hate women and then decide that the only women they
would marry would be princesses because they are "prettier" and
"because they have jewels and gold." Soon the boys set about
digging in a pretend fashion in an effort to find a princess.
Young Olivia comes by to learn what is going on, tries to tell
them that she has a bridal dress at home, and keeps hanging
around hoping that they will view her as a princess. It is to no
avail. The boys plunge ahead with their "digging for princess"
task and even when Olivia presents them with a "real live ear-
ring, from a princess" (actually a piece of paper) , the boys
simply chase her away and go on with their fantasy search.

There has been extensive use of the natural play of children
for psychotherapeutic purposes. The psychiatrist David Levy

* I have dealt at considerable length with the whole area of make-believe
play in an earlier book, *The Child's World of Make-Believe.*

formalized many of the techniques used in play therapy today, and introduced special doll families with which children could play out representations of the conflicts they experienced in relation to their parents or siblings. The make-believe play of children is a valuable clue to areas of difficulty and conflict that may exist either as a normal part of growth or in response to grossly pathological family circumstances.

As children grow older they gradually internalize their make-believe games, and learn to play them out privately or through the use of their own imagery. Here is an example from day-dreams of nine-year-old children as transcribed by their classroom teacher:

My favorite daydream is that sometimes I feel that I'm a princess in a palace dreaming of wonderful things. Dreaming that Prince Charming is coming to my father's palace. I'm dreaming I'm in the grass in the garden picking flowers then a witch puts me into a spell then I can't speak or hear. That's why I don't speak at times. The witch washes my mind so that I can't remember a thing. That's why I am always at the garden picking flowers. The witch says that I can't speak, hear, or remember anything until a prince kisses me. I am there picking flowers and the people from the town get worried and everything. Then one day a prince comes to the palace and sees me in the garden and comes to me and says hello but sense [sic] I can't hear I move to pick up a flower and I saw a man's foot. I looked up and smiled and he smiled back. He looked at me with a glowing and sparkling eye because he found me so beautiful. Then he kissed me, and I spoke and heard and remembered everything. He married my [sic] and we lived happily everafter. It was a wonderful daydream.

And another:

My favorite daydream is that my father and I were on a whaling ship, we were going to hunt Moby Dick, the whale who killed my mother and brother. My father and I went to get him. I said if I catch him I'll kill him and bring his head home. Then I would throw darts at him. We were afloat. We spotted a whale but it was not Moby Dick. After forty days we spotted him. We took a cannon and blasted his eyes out. I did what I said. Then I visited my mother's and brother's grave every day.

These two daydreams present an interesting contrast. The first one certainly suggests the beginnings of sexual interest in the young girl and may also be seen, from a psychoanalytic standpoint, as providing a clue about the so-called latency period, the stage of puberty when children are likely to repress many of their interests in the opposite sex. Cast in the framework of a fairy tale, this daydream has charm but does not suggest gross pathological problems or severe disturbance. The second daydream has a much more disturbing tone and almost certainly reflects deep feelings of loss and anger in the boy. In fact, the narrator of this daydream did suffer severe family deprivations which, while not specifically related to the whale's story which he must have heard earlier, before he developed the fantasy, he has incorporated into a powerful image of bitterness and attempted restitution of his loss.

There are certainly instances of children whose general quality of daydreaming and make-believe play seems to reflect severe emotional disturbance and psychopathology. Some examples will be discussed later in this book. Since many parents are frightened about make-believe play and fantasies as they occur in young children, it is worth taking a closer look at what we actually know about these processes and how they may gradually lead into daydreaming. There is surprisingly little scientific information in these fields. We have to rely a great deal on the accounts of individual clinical psychologists or psychoanalysts, and these accounts are necessarily obtained from disturbed individuals. That is why it is particularly important that we pay more careful attention to the spontaneous make-believe play of normal children and try to study some of the imaginative tendencies of children in more formal experimental research.

Some Theories of the Origin of Daydreaming

Attention to children's play is a recent development. Indeed, there was little tendency to view childhood as a special developmental stage until the eighteenth century. Early theories of children's play came from writers such as the famous German poet and playwright Friedrich Schiller, who proposed that children have surplus energy that has to be worked off since they are not called upon to use their energy in daily work. The Dutch anthropologist Karl Groos, who wrote the first—and still extremely impressive—work on the play of children back in 1901, emphasized the fact that for the child or the immature animal, play is the necessary form of early training in behaviors essential to later survival. In this sense, much of the fantasy play of children built around adult roles—caretakers, teachers, warriors or other adventurers—can be viewed as the initial practice of skills that later will be necessary for effective adult living.

The psychoanalytic theories of the nature of fantasy stress the origin of daydreaming and make-believe play in the child's attempt to deal with conflicts between its instinctual strivings and the demands of reality. Play and fantasy games represent in particular attempted solutions to the problems of sibling rivalry or the Oedipus complex in the working out of the family romance. Play also represents manifestations of the various oral, anal and phallic sexual orientations of the child. A classic account of children's play viewed from a psychoanalytic perspective is presented in Erikson's observations that little girls' play with blocks tends to produce rounded enclosing spaces, while boys are more inclined to build towers and pointed sharp spaces.

Piaget's view of children's play is an interesting contrast to the psychoanalytic view. His approach is cognitive—that is, it emphasizes man's role as an information-processing organism, rather than as one which is endlessly seeking to discharge instinctual energies that build up inevitably after discharge to the point where they again demand release. For Piaget the development of make-believe play comes out of the sequence of the two major activities that are an inevitable part of the normal growth experience. The very young child seeks, on the one hand, to *accommodate* itself to the external environment. That is to say, it tries to grasp objects that move or to follow them with its eyes; it attempts to imitate the movement of parents when it is a little older and is mobile; it strives to repeat the sound and phrases of the adults around it and eventually to provide a reasonable imitation of adults' communication and movement. The second major characteristic of growth is the endeavor by the child to *assimilate* these attempted imitations into its limited range of memories, its *cognitive scheme.* This is the basic task of establishing an internal control over one's behavior by developing a set of memories which in effect store within the organism the important sights, sounds and movements of the outside world.

It is in this attempted assimilation that we see the beginnings of make-believe play. The child left alone tries to repeat actions and behaviors of the adults. It does so against the very limited background of previous knowledge. Therefore what emerges, at least for a while, sounds to us strange, bizarre, amusing or cute. Consider the example of a little boy I know who came home from his first day at nursery school rather chagrined. He had enjoyed playing there, he said, but was very disappointed when at the end he asked his teacher if he was now a lawyer and she replied that he wasn't. "I remember Daddy saying that he went to school and became a lawyer," said the child. Clearly the simple phrase this child was imitating from his father was related during the assimilation phase to a very limited context of experiences.

Viewed from this perspective, imaginative play becomes one of the important ways in which the child gradually integrates the complex external environment into a set of organized memories. The frequent repetitions, play and replay, that characterize children's activities are of still novel experiences. In keeping with Tomkins's theory of emotion, the new material a child deals with is attractive and arouses the positive feelings of surprise or interest. When the material finally is matched to a well-established memory, there occurs the strong emotion of joy. And indeed, much make-believe play is associated with positive emotions, as we have found in a number of formal researches.

Since the child talks out loud in make-believe play, his words provide him with additional verbal stimulation, to which he responds even further. Gradually, however, it becomes necessary for him to conform to the demands of society, which, on the whole, frowns upon talking out loud. Here the role of the family is probably critical in the extent to which it will tolerate different degrees of open make-believe. Soon the child enters school, where the demands of learning require attention to the teacher. Children are therefore increasingly forced to internalize their communications.

The information-processing emphasis which has been growing among psychologists interested in the psychology of childhood and particularly play does not preclude the concerns that psychoanalysts have shown with conflict and anxiety in childhood fantasies. The child must also try to make sense of confusing family relationships, and his observations of anger, violence or quarreling in the family. To adults the arrival of a new baby is an event anticipated for months, its implications largely well understood and easily assimilated into their complex cognitive structures. For a three- or four-year-old child such a new arrival, coming, it seems, almost from nowhere, is a puzzling event indeed and not easily integrated; so the child's fantasy play will frequently reflect all kinds of material relating to the arrival of a newborn baby. Obviously some of this will represent jealousy and rivalry, but much will simply reflect an attempt to fit into the child's cognitive schema this strange new creature and the mystery of its arrival.

Certain bizarre or strange events also become part of children's fantasies. Often enough adults engage in actions that are directly—though not intentionally—frightening to children. We have all seen relatives and older peers tease younger children by taking advantage of their limited understanding. A man may put his fingers over a child's nose and say, "I am going to pull off your nose," and then display a closed fist with part of the thumb exposed through the fingers. "Here's your nose, right in here!" says the cheerful old uncle. For the young child this displacement of its own flesh from a body that the youngster has only begun to see as all of a piece is terrifying indeed. Though the family may laugh at the child's reaction, the real fear of episodes like this is reflected in later make-believe play and the attempt to assimilate the strangeness of "now you see it, now you don't" phenomena. Children often have terrors of being flushed down the toilet or of being seized by demons or goblins if they are not obedient. At a young age they cannot be sure such possibilities do not really exist; and it is out of this kind of confusion that the symbolic and mythological figures that people children's play, their games of pretend or street rituals, and even their dreams, first take shape.

Children's fantasies develop not only through their direct attempts to imitate adult behavior but through vicarious influences such as the stories told to them by adults, books that are read to them or that they later read themselves, and—of increasing importance for man during the twentieth century—the tremendous power of popular media like movies and television. Athenian youth learned of the hierarchy on Mount Olympus and of the vast array of gods, demigods, nature spirits and legendary heroes by word of mouth or by memorizing long sections of the *Iliad* or the *Odyssey* or, on special festival days, by viewing the plays of Aeschylus or Sophocles. Today the panorama of legend, actual history and a new kind of fantasy world is opened to vast masses of the society through television. While we may no longer take supernatural beings and their intrigues quite so seriously, we not only find ourselves aware of such traditional themes through television, but add to them current materials based on the lives and intrigues of our present aristocracy of public figures, celebrities and movie stars, as well as the endless stream of commercials that become part of our language and associative stream.

Imagine for a moment the complexity of information that a young child who watches television four or five hours a day must assimilate. Green Giants, Mr. Cleans, Peter Pans selling peanut butter, snarling cougars atop automobiles, comical but menacing monsters that threaten one's lawn but are driven away by fertilizer companies, little demons that pound away inside one's head only to be chased away finally by aspirins—all these provide novel images that have to be fitted into the limited cognitive schema of a child. Who knows? Where poets once included images of Pan piping through woods or Icarus falling into the sea in a vain attempt to fly to the sun, our fantasists of the future may draw on images of fat Al Hirt trumpeting the merits of Miller beer or gray-flannel-suited businessmen falling from the heavens to land in Hertz rental cars.

An important implication of the cognitive or information-processing model of daydreaming, which has been finding increasing support among psychologists, is the possibility that the model can encompass the great complexity of human motivation, interests or social experiences. Where psychoanalysts in the past have sought to *reduce* the content of daydreams or make-believe games to a relatively limited number of major themes, such as the Oedipus complex or phallic or anal preoccupations, or (if one is an Adlerian) power strivings, or to basic inherited archetypes which presumably represent all mankind's common mythology (Jung), a cognitive view need not be concerned with such a narrowing. Instead, its emphasis is more upon how experiences are organized, under what circumstances they are learned, and the role of the current stage of the child's psychological capacity in dealing with material presented, as well as opportunities for modeling on and interacting with parents, peers and the broader social milieu. Daydreaming and make-believe play in children are probably best regarded as manifestations of a basic cognitive capacity that develops naturally at certain stages and persists to the extent that it receives encouragement and reinforcement from circumstances in the child's environment.

My own research and that of various colleagues and students suggests that even in three- and four-year-olds we can discern the beginnings of strong individual differences in modes of using make-believe as a way of dealing with the world. By adolescence these predispositions to resort to fantasy as a resource are well established and may play an important later role in the life style of the individual.

Some Experimental Studies of Imagination in Children

Of the literally dozens of experiments in the area of daydreaming and imagination with which I have been involved, the most enjoyable have undoubtedly been studies with young children. While any psychological experiment has an element of risk in the sense that people will never do quite what one expects them to do in a formal research setup, the unexpected is expectable when children are the subjects. Our clinical literature and folklore are full of complex theorizing about children; but direct observations of youngsters in different settings with very careful recording of their actual behaviors, rather than inferences about their inner experiences, are rare indeed. The result is that psychologists until quite recently have known very little about the spontaneous ongoing activity of children, and this makes each new research effort something of an adventure. Let us take a closer look at some examples of studies with children in relation to the issue of make-believe and imaginative play.

EARLY MANIFESTATIONS OF MAKE-BELIEVE PLAY. Piaget's observations of his own children, as well as studies by Groos, point up
the fact that even before the age of two signs of imaginative play
can be perceived in children. Here, for example, is a quote from
Groos recounting the monologue of a little girl a little less than
two years of age overheard while she was in her bedroom.

> Go Grandma and buy a pretty doll Grandma for me under the bed
> for me to play the piano . . . get up cling, cling-ling-ling. Grandma
> comes up the steps. Oh, oh, ah, ah, ah, lying on the floor tied up no
> cap on Theodosia [the doll] lie on the bed, bring yellow sheep to
> Theodosia, run, tap, tap, tap, for Lena. Strawberries, Grandma,
> wolf lie on bed. Go to sleep darling Theodosia you are my dearest;
> everybody is fast asleep. . . . A cat came in here, Momma caught
> it, it had feet and black boots on—short cap, band on it. Poppa ran,
> the sky—Grandma gone—Grandpa resting.

A study carried out at Yale University by Drs. Greta Fine and
Ann Branch used the technique of offering different kinds of toys
to two-and-a-half-year-old children and encouraging them to
play with them. They found evidence at this age of a good deal
of pretend play. It was also clear that toys that were less well
structured and less obvious in function lent themselves somewhat
better to make-believe play under certain circumstances. Extremely interesting sex differences in styles of make-believe play
were already apparent by this age. Boys tended to more adventure-oriented games while the girls were already into nurturant
or caretaking behaviors. It seems very likely that from the very
earliest age our parenting habits foster sex differences in the style
of play.

A series of studies carried on by Dr. Dorothy Singer and myself
has involved extensive investigations of nursery school children
between the ages of three and four in various nursery settings,
using some of the techniques and measurements we have described. It is apparent that when children are put in what is

called a free-play situation—where the teacher simply withdraws to the rear and serves mainly to observe and break up disputes—they show a considerable amount of imaginative play. There is an ebb and flow to this kind of play and it seems best carried on by very small groups of children. Three is often a crowd; it is difficult for more than two children to get any sustained make-believe games going at such an early age. The children were generally consistent in the amount of make-believe play they showed over a period of time, although the nature of a given situation influenced make-believe to a great extent. For example, the play yard setting with its open spaces and its large structures such as sliding ponds and Junglegyms seemed to be more conducive to boys' types of make-believe. Despite the fact that girls when interviewed reported that they had a much greater amount of make-believe play at home, the boys exceeded them in this setting, largely because the kinds of running and adventure-oriented games they preferred could take place more easily here. Girls who tried to get into some of the games were rebuffed by the boys and tended to pull back somewhat. Inside the nursery school, the girls' make-believe was likely to center around games such as tea parties and playing house.

A very important aspect of make-believe is the occurrence of an imaginary companion. Parents sometimes are upset by indications that their children have nonexistent friends, either in thin air or in the form of teddy bears or bits of blankets or perhaps merely a stick to which they regularly address communications. All findings indicate that such imaginary companions are quite common in children. Up to one-third of all children report an imaginary playmate. Some of the studies of creative young people, that is, individuals who have shown genuine accomplishment in various artistic fields, report a greater frequency of imaginary companions in childhood. For our scoring of predisposition to imaginative play in the nursery school or kindergarten setting, therefore, we ask children about make-believe friends as well as about their favorite games and whether they "see pictures" in their head.

On the basis of our interviews and testing, we were able to ascertain that by three and four there were indications that children already differed in their tendency toward make-believe play. There were also indications, which were supported by a number of studies of older children, that those children who show a predisposition to imaginative play are less likely to be overtly aggressive, or to attack other children during the course of play. This does not mean that they don't show a good deal of aggression in the make-believe itself, but rather that they are less likely to get involved in fighting with other children except in self-defense. This finding is especially true for boys, who show a greater range of aggressive behavior. From the earliest ages we have observed, girls tend to be relatively little inclined to direct fighting. The children who show consistent make-believe play also manifest a good deal of positive emotion—much smiling and indications of liveliness and elation. Further, they are somewhat more inclined to be able to concentrate.

If one thinks about it, it seems reasonable that because of the very nature of the story line, a make-believe game will induce the child to stay more or less in one place and follow through a sequence of behaviors with some consistency. The practice in concentration that comes from playing make-believe games may have benefits for the child later, when it becomes necessary for him to pay attention to the formal instruction of the teacher in the school setting.

In research carried out with kindergarten children in New York City's Harlem, Dr. Joan Freyberg found considerable evidence that children predisposed to imaginative play were able to enjoy their ongoing play much more. With a co-observer, she made careful recordings of the children at play, which demonstrated that those whose spontaneous play was full of fantasy elements seemed to enjoy themselves more, and to be better able to concentrate. The children who were little inclined toward make-believe were likelier to mope around the play area. They were rarely able to get started at anything and often appeared sad or apathetic. Occasionally they would interrupt others' games and snatch away a block or toy and run off, but they remained basically unable to develop any ongoing sequence for themselves. A very similar finding among kindergarten children from an upper-class private school was reported by Dr. Mary Ann Pulaski.

In still another research using the methods we have described, Dr. Ephraim Biblow worked with nine-year-old boys and girls. Here it was very apparent that the more imaginatively predisposed children were not only likely to play more fantasy games spontaneously but also more difficult to arouse to anger and aggressive behavior when they were frustrated. When they did become angry and showed their annoyance at an older child who was spoiling their game, they were less likely to attack him directly.

To say that children predisposed to imaginative play are not overtly aggressive does not mean that they are not active and energetic in their movements during spontaneous play. A study by Leone Lesser indicated that imaginative children in the actual play situation tended to be quite vigorous and they "bopped" Bobo clowns or shot off "burp guns" even more often than the less imaginatively predisposed children. But at the end of the experiment, when the children were offered a choice of toys as a reward for their participation, the more imaginative usually chose toys that required very little motor activity but much more fantasy interpretation (for example, a fort with soldiers or a science kit). The less imaginative children were much more likely to select toys that involved direct physical activity for its own sake: baseball bats, basketballs or other athletic equipment.

In general, then, our results from all these studies indicate that children of differing degrees of imagination tend to differ not so much in the amount of actual movement they show, but rather in the greater option that the imaginative children take for the inclusion of make-believe in their play, or for electing a variety of resources in a play situation instead of a direct aggressive expression.

CONDITIONS CONDUCIVE TO MAKE-BELIEVE PLAY. Under what circumstances are children likely to play more imaginatively? One obvious consideration is the physical setting, as we observed in the nursery school in which certain types of large-scale toys and open spaces tended to be more conducive to imagination in boys than in girls. Architects are becoming increasingly interested in designing optimal conditions for playgrounds or day care center settings, which will encourage children to play with enjoyment and offer them a greater potential for good learning experiences in the school atmosphere.

What about the toys with which children play? Dr. Pulaski's research was addressed specifically to determining the effects on children of the types of toy available to them for spontaneous play in kindergarten and first grade. Sometimes they came into a room in which all the toys were very specific in their functions—a Barbie doll in bridal costume, a GI Joe doll in army outfit, Play-Doh with forms and molds, a toy garage with automobiles, a dollhouse with furniture inside. On other occasions the children came into a room in which the toys were relatively unstructured and unspecific, such as Playskool blocks or dolls without any clearly defined function, dress-up clothes of great variety and Play-Doh and other modeling material in bulk form. The children showed a much greater richness of imagination and chose a wider variety of themes when confronted with less structured toys. The more imaginatively predisposed children, in particular, seemed to do better with less structured toys. All the children were initially attracted to the very definite objects, but the more venturesome ones lost interest in them as time went on because they couldn't be worked into a more complex game. Even the toys all the children chose later as their favorites or as the ones they would like to keep reflected a preference for the less structured materials.

How does make-believe play get started in children? In one study carried out with children age six through nine, I arranged to have a group interviewed, classified according to their imaginative capacities and then observed in a variety of tasks. The more imaginative children proved easily able to enter into a proposed game of pretending to be a space man. They sat quietly in their chairs, which were supposed to simulate space capsules, for much longer periods of time. They also proved to be more creative in the kinds of stories they made up and, incidentally, they showed an interesting difference in the colors they preferred in drawing. The more imaginative children tended to prefer the so-called cool colors, such as blue and green, whereas others more often chose the "warm" colors, red or yellow.

When we asked about their experiences with their parents and in the family setting, the high-fantasy group reported that they spent much more time in play that had make-believe elements (including storytelling as well as games) with their parents. They tended to have a clear-cut identification with at least one of their parents. They also tended more often to be either the oldest child or the only child, or to have fewer older siblings than the children who were in a low-fantasy group. A number of other studies have confirmed the finding that children who have fantasy companions are likelier to have spent time as children alone, by being either only children, first-born children or children enough separated in age from others in the family so that they were less likely to play directly with their peers. A group of housewives, interviewed by Barbara Hariton, who reported much daydreaming in their lives also tended to be first-born or only children.

Without question, the kind of stimulation available in the child's environment plays an important part in the development of imaginative tendencies. In Dr. Freyberg's study of a group of poor children in New York City, she interviewed the mothers of children who differed in imaginative tendencies. The mothers of the more imaginative children reported spending more time with their children playing some variety of imaginative game, or at least condoned such play in the child; also, there were generally fewer people living in these households. Again it would appear that the availability and interest of a parent, and also the opportunity for some degree of privacy, make a difference in the development of imaginative tendencies.

A study carried out under my direction by Mrs. Bella Streiner compared the imaginative behavior of children who were blind more or less from birth and others of the same age and general background who could see. Blind children certainly do show imaginative play and also report dreams—though of course without visual images. Nevertheless, there was considerably less complexity and elaborateness in the dreams and fantasies of the blind children. The sighted children had available to them a greater variety of stimuli through television and through the visual senses. This environmental richness seems to lead to much more complex and elaborate kinds of fantasy activities.

Here are the make-believe stories of a trip to an airport told by two children of comparable age and background, one sighted and one blind. The blind child's story focused on the little boy's reaction to the plane, his having a nice trip and the fact that he enjoyed going places with his mother. The sighted child described an adventure in which the pilot was knocked unconscious when the plane hit an air pocket so that the parents had to fly the airplane back to the airport. The parents taught the children to fly, the children became famous pilots in the war and shot down many planes. They were rewarded by receiving two personal jet planes as gifts from the Air Force.

The blind child's fantasy appears to be a more direct reflection of recent experiences, while the daydreaming content of the sighted child represents a complex pattern of interwoven associations leading to a final story that is on the whole more original and also often more abstract in its implications. In only one respect did the blind children in this experiment show a greater trend toward more imaginativeness than the sighted children. Almost all the blind children reported that they had an imaginary companion, invariably a sighted person who served to some extent as a guide in fantasy for the blind child.

INCREASING IMAGINATIVE PLAY. Since it seems clear that environmental stimulation of various kinds plays a role in fostering imaginative tendencies, it is natural to ask in what other ways we can increase the level of imaginative play in children. In the Harlem kindergarten, Dr. Freyberg found that six hour-long weekly training sessions in make-believe play led to a very clear increase in the amount of imaginativeness shown by her experimental group in the course of free play in the schoolyard. Dr. Freyberg used some very simple props, such as pipe cleaners and sticks, with blue crepe paper to represent an ocean. She would set up an ocean voyage game as the focus of a particular session, giving each of the children a chance to participate, to try out different roles and different voices, and to imagine different adventures. Observers noted how much more fun the children from the experimental group were now having in the schoolyard because of their fantasy games. The experiment included a control group of children who received an equal amount of attention from the teacher, but in activity built around mechanical construction games that had no imaginative component. The control group showed no comparable increase in spontaneous make-believe play or enjoyment during free periods.

Working with somewhat older children, Dr. Sybil Gottlieb of the City College of New York tried to see if boys and girls in the fifth and sixth grades and in junior high school would respond to the modeling of a teacher in relation to their production of imaginative material. The experiment called for the children to watch movies that were purely abstract movements of forms and shapes without a definite story or meaning—experimental films by Norman McLaren which were, in effect, like abstract expressionist paintings come to life. Following the showing of the movie to a particular group of children, the teacher would either provide a very literal description of what happened on the film, a somewhat realistic account of the background of the film, or a very imaginative story that had little to do with the film beyond the fact that it was fanciful and elaborate. Dr. Gottlieb found that the younger group of children tended to follow whichever direction the teacher set. Those who heard a literal or realistic narration from the teacher after seeing the first film offered roughly equivalent kinds of fantasy material after a second film was shown to them. Those who heard the most imaginative story tended to give considerably more fanciful material in the response to the second film. There was less imitation of the teacher in the junior high school. For these youngsters, their own inclination to imaginative play was the significant factor in subsequent reactions.

All in all, the results indicated that the teachers had a clear effect on fantasy in the younger groups but that as children grew older their own predisposition toward fantasy played an increasingly important part on the kind of fantasy patterns they developed in response to the model. Here, of course, we are dealing with fantasy in make-believe as expressed in storytelling and creative productions, in contrast to the direct and spontaneous make-believe play of the younger children.

TELEVISION, IMAGINATION AND AGGRESSION. The television viewing that is a regular part of the lives of almost all youngsters in our society is a very important influence on them. In effect, the characters on television have become the imaginary companions of a whole generation of young people. The recent report of the Surgeon General's Commission on Television and Social Behavior pointed out the possibility that for very young children predisposed to aggression, exposure to aggressive material on television increases considerably the likelihood that they will show aggressive behavior in spontaneous play. This possibility presents a serious issue. Even if only 10 or 20 percent of children are predisposed to be overtly aggressive a good deal of the time in their spontaneous play, their exposure to aggressive material on television and the subsequent increase in violent behavior they may show constitutes a sizable mental health problem for the society.

Biblow's study described in the previous chapter offers one clue to an approach that might be beneficial in counteracting some of the dangerous effects of television. Biblow found that the more imaginative children, that is, those who scored high initially on our measures of fantasy predisposition, also turned out to be the children who showed a reduction in aggression after viewing both aggressive and neutral television shows. It was the children *low* in imaginative potential who tended to be more aggressive spontaneously in their play, and who showed a small *increase* in aggressive tendencies following the viewing of the aggressive film and no particular change after viewing the neutral film. If we can reach this low-fantasy group in our society and provide them with opportunities to increase their level of make-believe and fantasy, we may have a wedge into cutting back on the likelihood of socially undesirable consequences of television viewing for a segment of the child population.

Television programing itself may be able to help accomplish this. If particular television shows can induce increased make-believe or fantasy play and are programed for that purpose, the children who view them may subsequently increase their own spontaneous imaginativeness, and therefore be less susceptible to imitating the violence they see on other programs. They simply carry the aggression over into play and work it into the story lines of games in which they will not directly hurt other children. Research by Drs. Aletha Stein and Lynette Friedrich at Pennsylvania State University came up with an intriguing finding: nursery school children who viewed a program such as "Batman" were inclined to become *more* aggressive if they were initially inclined toward fighting. On the other hand, those viewing the program "Mister Rogers' Neighborhood" tended to become less aggressive and more socially cooperative in their behavior.

Dr. Dorothy Singer and I carried out an investigation with a group of children at the Pinafore Day Care Center in Shelton, Connecticut, under the sponsorship of the Child Study Center of Yale University, with the cooperation of Fred Rogers and his staff from the "Mister Rogers' Neighborhood" program. We were interested in determining what combination of circumstances might be most effective in increasing the level of imaginative play, enjoyment of play, concentration and various other positive emotional reactions in children in the course of nursery school spontaneous play, as well as in reducing their aggressive reactions. We observed the children systematically over several weeks, using a number of independent raters and observers, and then set up the following conditions (in addition to a control condition during which the children were simply observed on two separate occasions without special intervention other than ordinary nursery school supervision) : One group of children watched a half hour of "Mister Rogers" (a program they could not ordinarily view in their area) every day for a little more than two weeks. A second group of children watched "Mister Rogers," but this time in the company of an adult who served as a kind of intermediary between Mister Rogers and the children, much as a parent might when viewing together with a three- or four-year-old. When Mister Rogers demonstrated flying activities to children, the adult might encourage the children to imitate the movements. When certain other activities were carried on in the story line of Mister Rogers' "Neighborhood of Make-Believe," the children were encouraged to go along with fantasy material. A third experimental condition involved no television viewing at all but rather direct training in imaginative play presented for a half hour daily by an adult. This curriculum began with training the children to try out small-scale imagery and fantasy exercises; then gradually more complex story lines were developed to increase the scope of the make-believe in a given session. Simplified play materials like hats and other props were employed but generally on a very limited scale, so that the children were encouraged to rely on external devices only as a starting point for more elaborate and more flexible kinds of make-believe play.

The children were observed closely as they watched television or as they participated in the make-believe training, and were rated on the various measures—imaginativeness, positive emotion, etc.—so that we could get some notion as to the pattern of their reaction to different "Mister Rogers" sequences and to the kind of training they were receiving. Finally, after the conclusion of the TV viewing or training sessions, the children were observed in the course of spontaneous play activity over a two-week period. General indications were that all the children exposed either to television or to the training tended to improve the level of their imaginative play. The increase in make-believe play was by far the greatest for those children who had the live teacher providing training. Those whose teacher sat with them as they watched "Mister Rogers" on TV were next highest in improvement. Both groups not only showed more imagination in their play; they also seemed happier and livelier. The whole atmosphere of the school had a brighter cast and parents reported to us that children seemed to be much more playful and imaginative at home.

Some Implications and Further Research Directions

The picture that emerges from these investigations of the imaginative play of children suggests that the growing child is active, curious and extremely inventive. In the course of the assimilation of novel materials he has witnessed or overheard in the environment, he confronts interesting and emotionally arousing possibilities which form the basis for his make-believe games. In almost all children between the ages of one and a half and three, a great deal of encouragement from adults or from environmental conditions is apparently necessary to sustain a tendency toward sociodramatic play. Initially this support is likely to come from a close relationship with the mother or with any adult who takes the time to play imaginatively, to tell stories and to foster a variety of "as if" behaviors in the child.

Probably the greater tendency of only children and older children toward imaginativeness or the development of make-believe companions has to do not only with the fact that they may be lonely and use these companions in an adaptive fashion, but also with the *privacy* that makes it possible to practice such activities. Other children tend to disrupt and interrupt ongoing make-believe games. In a group of children engaged in free play one sees rapid movements back and forth. Some children get a game started and are quite caught up in the different roles they have assigned to one another, and then another group swoops down, intervenes and snatches away props or toys. The sequence is interrupted and perhaps never continued.

Most of the evidence on the way aggression develops in children suggests that frequently it is a consequence of imitation of the parents. For example, a study by Dr. Leonard Goldberg of the City University of New York found very clear evidence, in measuring the aggressive tendencies in a large number of children, that the most significant single factor in a child's overt violence was the aggressive behavior of the father. If the mother and the father were both aggressive individuals, there was an even greater likelihood of the child's being overtly aggressive. In those instances where children showed a good deal of imaginativeness in their behavior or fantasy capacity, they were less likely to be overtly aggressive in a spontaneous fashion. Of course, they would often fight back if directly attacked. Imaginativeness, therefore, may be an important additional resource that helps children cope with observed aggressive behavior, tolerate frustrations and put up with the necessary waiting and delays that are part of ordinary experience.

Further, engaging in pretend play seems to help children develop the beginnings of what the famous neurologist Kurt Goldstein called an "attitude toward the possible." That is, the make-believe world encourages an ability to differentiate between the immediate real world and the possibilities of reviewing the past or playing out things in the future without the commitment of action. There is even some reason to believe that the child's ability to engage in make-believe play helps him to make a sharper distinction between what is real and what is fantasy. An imaginative child can move back and forth between these two realms comfortably, whereas the child less disposed to imaginative play may take fantasy situations, such as television scenes involving violence, and confuse them with reality, imitating them directly by hitting other children or by resolving conflicts through physical assault.

The act of engaging in make-believe play from the very earliest ages also involves some degree of organization of one's experience into sequences that have beginnings, middles and ends. While the story lines of children between two and three are of course skimpy, by kindergarten one can observe quite well-worked-out plots which, even with their magical features and happy solutions, require a modicum of organized thinking that can only benefit the child later in socialization and in the school learning situation. Striking results supporting this view were obtained by Dr. Sara Smilansky in Israel.

It is extremely important to recognize that imaginative play is a normal development in the growing child. We have noted that our society, and many parents within it, tend to be somewhat distressed by and suspicious of fantasy and make-believe, thinking them characteristics of the "sissy" or indications of potential mental disturbance. On the basis of our observation of large numbers of children engaging in imaginative play, we see little evidence that these assumptions have any validity. On the contrary, these children seem to be happier and more curious about the world. They are more energetic in their day-to-day behavior and more capable of dealing with frustrations in a constructive fashion. It seems to me that an important direction for future research in the curriculum of day care training, and also in the development of approaches to helping parents in the important task of raising their children, should deal with the many ways in which the adult can help the child sustain his natural tendency toward imaginative play and foster it into avenues that ultimately lead to a rich and enjoyable cognitive growth.

CHAPTER 7

Daydreaming During the Adolescent and Adult Years

Somewhere between the ages of six and thirteen, the child internalizes make-believe play and carries it out more and more in the form of private imagery. Although Piaget has stressed the disappearance of make-believe play by around the age of eight, my own experience and my interviews with teen-agers suggest that the fading away of open fantasy activities is much more gradual. Such make-believe games persist into adolescence. Readers are urged to think back themselves to some of the kinds of games they played either alone or with friends in the early teen years. Using playing cards or a commercial game, or simply bouncing balls in the street, many boys develop a series of baseball games replete with announcements of the play in the style of popular broadcasters, even including occasional mimicry of commercials. Girls in late puberty may continue to play out fantasy games sociodramatically around romantic subjects. Many young people have admitted to me that they enact these imaginative games, and still with a certain amount of talking aloud when they have sufficient privacy. In a review of Philip Roth's wild fantasy about baseball, *The Great American Novel*, Christopher Lehmann-

Haupt wrote in the *New York Times* that the book reminded him of his youthful bathtub fantasies. In the solitude of the bathroom, he, in common with other boys in early adolescence, would find himself replaying verbally incidents in current baseball situations, creating new players and leagues not unlike the kind that I described earlier.

Inevitably social pressure forces the internalization of such make-believe play. Either fantasy play continues in the form of actual performances of stories or scenes from plays or movies, or it becomes the stuff of the daydreaming that, in our society, we link so closely to the adolescent period of development. In early adolescence another boy and I used to put on dramatic performances for our sisters and other younger children in the apartment house where we lived. Generally we played episodes from Sherlock Holmes. Since the other fellow had an aquiline nose and possessed a deerstalker's cap, he always got to play Holmes, and I was forced to be either bumbling Dr. Watson, sinister Professor Moriarty or, often, the Hound of the Baskervilles.

The more common manifestation of daydreaming in adolescence is reflected in the popular image of the teen-ager curled up in a chair staring off into space, engaged in active contemplation of future heroics or romances. The moodiness of adolescence which so bedevils parents certainly seems in part attributable to the fact that the adults' injunctions to get at homework or some household chore are interrupting elaborate private sequences of pleasurable or anticipatory fantasies. If a young girl is lost in a richly colored vision of how she will meet the young high school football star at a dance or party, the sudden order to "do the dishes" can easily evoke an angry snarl.

Some of the research carried out by my own group of investigators has suggested that adolescents report much more frequent daydreaming than do young adults or respondents from the older age groups. In interviews with college students, freshmen say that their daydreams had reached a peak of frequency within the period between fourteen and seventeen and that within the first weeks of college, fantasizing has already begun to show a decline. A study by Dr. Sybil Gottlieb of the fantasies reported by junior high school and elementary school children was described in the previous chapter. Dr. Gottlieb also examined the themes of the fantasies produced by children in these age groups. At upper elementary school ages (between ten and twelve), the vast majority of boys and girls had fantasies that involved some degree of adventure or lively action. By thirteen and fourteen, most boys and girls had shifted in the direction of romance, sex and achievement. This change in themes appears to reflect the overall pattern of interest as the child moves into the phase of life intermediate between complete dependence and the assumption of the adult roles expected by society.

While there seems little question that much adolescent daydreaming has a truly fantastic quality and involves many possibilities that are unlikely to materialize in the life of a given individual, there is good reason to believe that most daydreams in this period are preparations for future behavior. In 1961, Drs. Percival Symonds and Arthur Jensen of Teachers College, Columbia University, collected the fantasies of adolescents in high school and then followed them up by obtaining information from the same young people a decade or more later. The dominant themes of the subjects' adolescent fantasies were major features of their current adult thinking. Indeed, some of the fantasies might be said to have come true. Many vocational choices made by the grownups had been anticipated in their daydreams ten years before.

The tremendous emphasis on pop culture to which adolescents are exposed through the media and the recording industry undoubtedly fosters certain conformities in daydreaming. The proliferation of love songs, though reflecting some of the natural developments of the society, probably increases the interests of younger children in such areas. Popular songs are also replete with references to adolescent fantasies, and bear titles such as "You Tell Me Your Dream, I'll Tell You Mine," "Daydreams," "What a Day for a Daydream," "These Are the Dreams of the Everyday Housewife." Not only the songs but the singers become the focal points of adolescent fantasies as each generation chooses its favorites. The crooners of the 1920s, '30s and '40s have been replaced by the pop and rock stars of the '50s, '60s and '70s, but the process of idealization of and identification with these figures seems very much built into our culture.

The identification of our young people with movie and television stars as well as popular singers and musicians may be viewed as a part of the growth of a sense of separate identity, which is an important stage in maturation. One part of this stage has to do with the development of independence from parental domination. This does not mean that adolescents are turning their backs completely on their parents. Rather, it is the first step in looking to the outside world for possibilities of ways of behaving alternative to those that predominate in a given nuclear or extended family of delimited cultural milieu. The adolescent tries to find a new basis for independence from involvement with parents but in actuality he or she is not yet free or ready to be truly independent. The first step, therefore, is a kind of searching out, through make-believe and trial action, for new ways of talking, life styles quite different from those of the parent, and also new long-term possibilities for future success or excitement.

While some degree of conformity is imposed by the power of popular culture, there are still great individual differences in the structure and content of daydreaming in adolescence. Our own research suggests that some young people are given to a great range of fantasies which include some truly bizarre or unlikely imaginary sequences, as well as considerable planning; while others are more oriented toward objective or mechanical and impersonal daydream patterns. A mechanically gifted adolescent may imagine himself constructing equipment or thinking about how to "soup up" a hot rod. He might carry the fantasy further and see himself showing off his newly reconstructed car to friends or to a special girl. Traditional sex roles have already manifested themselves in different qualities of content of adolescent daydreams. Many decisions in life have not yet been made for the adolescent, and in a sense this leaves room for a high proportion of wish fulfillment in fantasy. The gap between possibility and probability has narrowed somewhat in adolescence, compared to early childhood with its imagined heroic adventures, space flights and outstanding athletic achievements. But the gap is still a big one and there is room for a great deal of wide-ranging hopeful make-believe in the period between thirteen and eighteen in our society.

In a sense, the same accommodation-assimilation process that Piaget emphasized in toddlers' development is still under way. Just as the growing child has to develop increasing capacity for logical operational thought, the adolescent is faced with a much greater complexity of social competence, which he learns to manage through imaginary role playing. Early dating is a case in point. The precocious eighth-grader who is already "going steady" may not actually be more sexually developed or interested in the opposite sex than the bookish thirteen-year-old who has no overt social expression. Often early dating reflects two factors. In the first place, sexual inclinations as part of normal maturation are likely to exert more pressure on the child who has an initially limited repertory of interests and cognitive capacities. For this child, the adult world's heavy emphasis on sexual behavior, fostered through advertising, parents' overidentification with children and, of course, the recording industry, is more likely to seem a chief source of interest and pleasure. The adolescent with a greater cognitive exploratory tendency may already have carved out a greater diversity of behavioral activities—athletics, intellectual achievements, musical skills, hobbies—which provide attraction and joy. For these children increased internal glandular or social pressures for sexual behavior seem less dominant in the motive hierarchy.

A second factor influencing early dating or socialization represents a difference in internalization capacities. The adolescent who cannot provide himself pleasure through internal fantasy, contemplation or manipulation of daydream images is compelled more directly to an overt imitation of the adult pattern. He undoubtedly has sexual fantasies at times, but he may be ashamed of these on grounds of various cultural or early family experience; or—and this point has largely been neglected—lacking experience in fantasy play, he may be unable to expand his fleeting images enough to make them really interesting. Even masturbation, which clearly should provide specific pleasure, may appear less satisfying to an adolescent who lacks the capacity to elaborate imaginatively on romantic situations and sexual partners. The pressure toward direct sexual experience is greater for the extroverted adolescent. Adolescent impulsiveness may provoke situations that lead to increased pressures from the adult world and hasten early marriage, for which the young person may not really be prepared.

The example chosen has stressed sexual activity, but it can apply equally well to other forms of pressure on the adolescent for adult imitation. For example, his natural strivings for competence and autonomy may produce a pressure to drive a car. Here again, the adolescent with greater breadth of interest and a capacity for fantasized self-stimulation may feel this urge, but it will be only one of a great variety of interests and may be internalized in a more complex daydream pattern. The youth lacking these alternatives may move more directly to actual involvement with cars. Sometimes this can provide positive benefits because he develops mechanical skills and motor abilities. But he may also risk the anger of adults and endanger his own life because his awareness of the risks of driving does not match his already mature motility skills.

A study carried out by Drs. George Spivack and Murray Levine at the Devereaux Foundation selected middle-class adolescents who had a history of conflict with parents, school and legal authorities and compared them with young people of equivalent intelligence and socioeconomic status, who had no history of delinquency. On one measure that involved fantasy, the delinquent group showed limited ability to spell out intermediate steps necessary to bring them effectively to goals they had selected. They also expressed less awareness of the consequences of transgression of social norms or legal codes. The nondelinquent adolescent, on the other hand, though equally interested in the transgressions, was much more likely to describe the pros and cons of a situation and was also capable of looking for loopholes to accomplish these goals. The delinquent group, when studied by means of the Rorschach ink-blot test, showed a consistent poverty of idea elaboration. As Spivack put it, "Their thought world appears as a rather barren place."

In the light of our discussion in the previous chapter of the importance of parental stimulation of fantasy play, it is interesting to note that the delinquent adolescents studied here showed a constriction in both future and past time perspectives. They knew little of their family tree and background or about the kind of work their fathers did. They made unrealistically hasty estimates of how long it would take for certain events to occur in the future. There had apparently been surprisingly little interaction between these young people and their parents, and little shared discussion of adult concerns, past or future, which might have stimulated the differentiated imaginative response as one aspect of the accommodation-assimilation pattern.

One important area in which daydreaming occurs widely during adolescence is during masturbation. The work of Kinsey and more recently Masters and Johnson has given us increased information about the frequency and variations in masturbation as a part of adolescent development, but there has not yet been any systematic research on the role of private fantasy during such activity. Clinical information and informal interviews suggest, of course, that fantasies play a very important part in this phase of sexual maturation. One might expect that the pattern of day-dreaming associated with masturbatory activity would offer important clues to major conflicts and doubts within the individual, as well as provide a basis for subsequent sexual choices. In a study of women's erotic fantasies by Dr. Barbara Hariton, there were indications that the fantasies wives produced while actually engaged in sexual intercourse with their husbands often had begun in early adolescence and on some occasions were associated with masturbation. There are also some clinical indications from studies with men that a particular activity that had accompanied early sexual arousal—perhaps the reading of a pornographic story, or the viewing of an explicit kind of sexually oriented material in magazine foldouts, movies or on television—had become the basis for subsequent sexually deviant practices. A patient who required his wife to wear black silk stockings every time they had sexual relations was studied while under the influence of Sodium Pentothal. He revealed that his initial sexual arousal had come during a seduction by an aunt, who had put her stockings around his mouth to prevent him from crying out and alerting his parents, asleep in the next room.

More commonly, the experience of being aroused by the sight of someone in a movie or a magazine will lead an adolescent to fantasize during masturbation on a similar individual, who later will become the symbol of a sexually desirable person. I knew of one man who grew up as the only Italian American in a predominantly white Anglo-Saxon Protestant neighborhood. Though he was a part of the neighborhood social group, he tended to feel himself something of an outcast, and never worked up the courage to ask any of the blond, blue-eyed girls in the neighborhood for a date. Such girls became the focus of his masturbatory fantasies during adolescence. When he married he chose a young woman from an Italian-American background, dark-haired and olive-skinned. Yet despite the fact that their sexual relationship was mutually satisfying, he could never feel that she was really exciting to him. A few years after marriage, he encountered, at an alcoholic business party, a fair-haired girl who responded to his overtures, and before he knew it he found himself involved in an extramarital affair that destroyed his marriage. In retrospect he realized that the blond with whom he had taken up was much more inhibited in the sex act than his wife had been, and she proved to have so many unpleasant characteristics that they eventually broke up. Even then he could not easily overcome the feeling of excitement her physical appearance generated.

Sexual fantasies in adolescence undoubtedly reflect some of the defensive and conflict-laden areas in personality growth. Some young men report that they dare not think about the "nice" girls they know while engaging in masturbation. For those young people who have been brought up to believe that masturbation or sex has sinful qualities, such thoughts would be doubly defiling. Instead, such men often introduce into their fantasies either women whom they can categorize as "tramps" or women of a different race or socioeconomic class.

We see some of the same kind of thinking reflected in the medieval paintings of sacred and profane love and in many of the themes of legends and stories. In Scott's *Ivanhoe* there is the contrast for the young hero between the blond Rowena and the dark-haired Jewish Rebecca, who must eventually be killed off. In Wagner's opera *Tannhäuser* the hero is caught between his sensual love for the goddess Venus, who still lives deep in the woods of Germany, and his more sacred attraction for the virginal Elisabeth.

It is very likely that masturbation fantasies, though rarely discussed openly except perhaps during psychoanalysis, do find expression in literature and erotic films. Many of the sexually charged scenes in novels or movies may be reflections, probably partially unconscious, of the writer's early sexual daydreams. One might speculate that popular mythology about the great sensual appeal of black men or women for whites, and the reverse of this, to some extent, for blacks, reflects sexual fantasies in which there is a defensive shift away from those closer to one's self during masturbation. A neat twist of this theme occurs in the film *Cotton Comes to Harlem.* Here the sex-kittenish black mistress of the villain seduces the white policeman who is guarding her in her apartment. No sooner is he undressed in her bedroom than she leaps out of bed and escapes out the door, leaving him to pursue her down the hall, guarding his genitals with his drawn gun. One wonders, indeed, how much of the terrible vengeance wreaked on black men by the dominant whites of American society because of ostensible sexual overtures toward white women has stemmed from the whites' practice of fantasizing sexual relations with black women during masturbation.

A question that needs answering is whether those men who are able to resort to elaborate daydreams and thus enjoy masturbation more are therefore less likely to move as actively toward direct sexual fulfillment in periods in their lives when sex may be difficult to obtain without force or payment. It would also be interesting to know whether there are differences between men who are able to produce their own pictures in their imaginations in order to become sexually aroused, and those who have to rely for arousal chiefly on erotic photographs in magazines.

Anthony Campagna of Yale University has been studying masturbation and sexual fantasies in college freshmen. He has found four distinctive fantasy patterns associated with masturbation. One style of daydream involves direct thoughts about girls one knows and rather conventional sexual positions. A second, more linked to broader daydreaming tendencies, involves imagining elaborate story lines but relatively "normal" sex—e.g., "I am a movie producer with many starlets available to sleep with" or "I am an Arab sheik with a harem of girls." A third pattern involves fantasies of a wide variety of more deviant sexual practices, including sadistic or masochistic images. Finally there is a group of fantasies that involve images only of body parts or of faceless, anonymous women or prostitutes. The young men who report the last pattern are more likely to report a good deal of guilt or inhibition about sex.

The pain of adolescence may stem in part from the fact that the fantasies of this period are being increasingly tested against reality and must be given up within a relatively short time. Within a critical span of two or three years many options in life are closed forever. A girl may have fantasies which include an image of herself as particularly beautiful, as a fashion model, a successful popular singer, the most dated girl in school, the steady of a very desirable boy. She may see herself as the unassailable virgin until marriage, the wife of a brilliant scientist, the wife of a dashing movie star, a devoted mother of a fine family, a dynamic career woman. Between the ages of seventeen and twenty many of these dream balloons are likely to be punctured; in fact, the whole delicately balanced structure may collapse when commitments are made and a very different life appears in the offing.

The adolescent who has a variety of fantasies but is able to sustain some by the hope of achievement or by actual successful experience can give up others with little distress, retaining enough of them so that fantasy itself is not a frightening dimension of behavior which must be avoided thereafter. In clinical work with adolescents I have observed that one can obtain the confidence of a young person and elicit fantasies. If one then can explore with the patient his or her areas of competence or potential reward as they relate to some of these fantasies, the bitter and painful relinquishment of *all* fantasy (often associated with depression or impulsive "acting out") can be avoided.

If a young person has had many cultural opportunities and

extensive contact with parents or other adult models, who have fostered a good deal of reading and provided educational experiences or travel opportunities, he or she may have developed a relatively differentiated fantasy life. Such a person is likely to distinguish the degree of reality in different possibilities, and to develop in the fantasy repertory a set we call "means-end awareness," which is so essential for effective planning. Dr. Kenneth Clark has told me that an especially painful factor in the life of the Harlem adolescent is that television and movies, and the *somewhat* improved economic possibilities for blacks, sustain an increased variety of fantasies into adolescence. When, too often, the reality of ghetto and slum turns these high hopes to ashes in the mouth, bitterness and resistance to further introspection often follows. Where real possibilities exist, however, as evidenced from parents' or teachers' attainments and from reading or travel, the incorporation of reality into the adolescent daydream actually sustains fantasy and, by feedback, aspiration; the inner experience serves to buffer the stress of adolescence.

Adolescent daydreaming has other functions in addition to anticipations of future roles. To some extent it continues the assimilation process from earlier childhood, and it also provides defenses and approaches to coping with frightening events. The adolescent interest in horror films is an instance of vicarious fantasy expression. For the very young child the monsters of the movies and television are embodiments of those distortions and ambiguities that people the shadow world at night when the child is preparing for bed. Linked by the adults to bogeymen and other threatening figures, these monsters cannot be readily understood or grasped and therefore arouse negative emotion and terror. By adolescence, however, the child has begun to develop a more complex experience of various realities and the monsters now can be seen as unreal. Nevertheless, the memory of the earlier fright has not gone; indeed, there may still be some lingering fear and difficulty in assimilation. This makes for the excitement adolescents feel in viewing horror films, for there is still a moderate arousal of tension and then, as one recognizes the ridiculousness of the situation in relation to realities, a sharp reduction of tension, and laughter. The popularity among adolescents of the daytime serial "Dark Shadows," with its vampires and zombies, reflected this mixture of partial arousal and release. But because the program was shown at four o'clock in the afternoon, it was accessible to much younger children and in my experience it has led to many night terrors and disturbing fantasies for these children.

Adolescent daydreams also can play a role in helping one develop a sense of power and autonomy, not only over parents but in general over one's life situation. In this sense many of the more outlandish plays on reality that characterize particular daydreams, and some of the "outrageous" notions that young people bandy about among themselves, which occasionally emerge in the form of "sick" jokes, have a quality of courting danger, complication, disaster and death with impunity. In the days immediately after Pearl Harbor, some of my friends and I developed a kind of war game which we played out with much laughter. Amid the succession of defeats suffered by the Americans there was a hungering for a victory; and one of these victories was the destruction of a Japanese ship of the Haruna class by an American pilot, Colin Kelly, who was supposed to have crashed his plane suicidally to blow up the ship. In our group of seventeen-year-olds we developed a game called "Colin Kelly and the Battleship Haruna," which consisted largely of charging, arms widespread, at another member of the group and trying to bowl him over. When the war became a much greater reality a few years later and some of us experienced real combat, such a humorous form of expression and group fantasy would have been unthinkable. "He jests at scars, that never felt a wound," wrote Shakespeare.

For the adult who once wanted to be a great violinist but who has had to settle for being a vacuum cleaner salesman, the recurrence of the "violin" fantasy brings pain at the realization of its improbability where once it might have brought joy and excitement. As the adolescent moves into young adulthood, many of life's possibilities are now sharply delimited and the continuation of fantasies about impossible alternatives can become distressing. Daydreams gradually move more and more along channels of well-established commitments—marriage, family possibilities—with only an occasional fling into the improbable. Indeed, we are much likelier to rely on television to provide us with our fantasies rather than to create them ourselves.

The daydreams of the adolescent are a basic part of his growth process. If he can effect some combination of actual achievement and a continuation of a varied and increasingly elaborate but partially reality-oriented daydream life, he can move into adulthood armed with a significant skill and with an important adaptive potential.

Daydreaming Through the Adult Years

As they assume the responsibilities and commitments of maturity, men and women face a marked delimitation of life possibilities and, within their narrowed sphere of activity, a greater necessity for attending to details the adolescent could reasonably safely ignore. Because of this direct perceptual attention to detail or to very specific, task-relevant thought, even the task-irrelevant daydream the adult indulges in is somewhat narrow in scope. While diapering her baby a woman may find herself drifting off into thoughts about what to cook for supper, or how to convince her husband that they need a washing machine, or what fun it would be to go to the Couples Club dance if only she could get reliable Mrs. Ellsworth to baby-sit. She is far less likely to slip even fleetingly into fantasies of dancing the merengue with a handsome tanned stranger amid the moonlit palms of a West Indies resort.

Her husband, with his dependence on his job, will be still more limited in the scope of his daydreams. He may not be immune to quick thoughts of sexual adventures with passing beauties on the street or with women he works near, but most of his extended inner activity will crystallize around job demands, meeting economic pressures, or keeping up with household chores. He may daydream about promotion, about telling off his supervisor or about the dire consequences of a failure to perform some task properly. He is less likely to drift into an elaborate daydream of becoming a military hero, the first man to reach another planet, a great young wizard of Wall Street or a member of the Jet Set, since by now he is fairly deeply involved in his father-in-law's wholesale furniture business.

Within the narrowed sphere of the mature adult, predominant daydreaming modes have a good deal of usefulness. I think it is especially important to consider daydreaming within the context of the daily routine of reasonably well integrated adults; the capacity for fantasy may have important uses and may also increase creativity. The young worker may think of better ways of doing his job or of more interesting recreations for the future, and these may make a routine job more tolerable. The housewife may fantasize about distracting restless children on rainy days, and not only come up with some good ideas for the future but also change her mood enough so that she is less likely to scream angrily at the children.

WOMEN'S EROTIC FANTASIES: SOME CLINICAL INTERPRETATIONS. Psychotherapists have long been aware that many women not only engage in erotic fantasy during the ordinary course of the day, just as men do, but that many women have very specific fantasies during sexual relations. At this point it would be instructive to delve into the specific role of fantasy in a woman's sex life. The research on daydreaming indicates a number of alternative hypotheses. These include the likelihood that some fantasies may be drive-arousing. Some women may also just be fantasizers in general, and carry this tendency naturally into the sex act. As with any behavior, they may be inclined to elaborate or romanticize the act in some form. Much of young women's learning and thinking about sexuality begins in early adolescence or late puberty, and is associated with a good deal of romantic literature and the kind of songs of the pop culture to which girls are exposed—all of which are woven into a whole series of anticipations and expectations about sex. These fantasies often do become associated with sexual arousal and with various mental "tryouts" of sexual experience. It is a natural step for a woman already predisposed to fantasy, whose role in sex may be slightly more passive at various points and whose tempo may be slightly different from her partner's on the basis of anatomy alone, to fill in "empty channel space" with fleeting thoughts or daydreams.

A woman whom I saw in psychoanalysis for a period of time reported that throughout her married life she had a recurrent fantasy which she used to increase her sexual excitement and reach orgasm. This fantasy generally portrayed her as a prisoner of the Chinese Communists, who were torturing or menacing her and threatening to rape her. Needless to say, this daydream was entirely private. Her husband, enthusiastically making love to her, had no inkling of what was going on in her head during their passionate interchange.

A thorough analytic exploration of this patient's sexual experience and marital relationship failed to yield any evidence that she was currently dissatisfied with her husband or in any way experiencing sexual difficulties. She enjoyed him and considered him quite a fine lover, but she had developed this type of fantasy in earliest puberty and it was now simply an essential part of her sexual arousal process. Once reassured from her own examination of all possibilities that the fantasy was not a sign of gross disturbance in her, she found herself continuing it to some degree, but with less of the guilt that had occasionally emerged before when she realized after the sex act that she had introduced this fantasy at some point in the height of passion.

A newspaper account I have read told of a young woman who was a "groupie," a follower of a world-famous rock band, who had had regular fantasies during her active sex life that she was making love to the leader of the group she so admired. In her persistent pursuit of the group she finally did encounter the great star himself and went to bed with him. Even as he was making love to her she found herself *fantasizing* that she was making love to the famous star—for in fact, the real man with her was not much different from any of the other lovers she had had.

AN EMPIRICAL RESEARCH ON EROTIC FANTASIES. A study carried out by Dr. Barbara Hariton and myself attempted to gather much more detailed data on the normative basis of women's sexual fantasies, and to ascertain what support there was for the various theoretical explanations of the function of erotic day-dreams. Dr. Hariton's first step was to locate a fairly large number of normal women who were married and whose sexual relations were chiefly or entirely with their husbands. This she was able to do through contacts in suburban adult education centers. Eventually she administered scales from the Imaginal Processes Inventory and other personality tests, plus measures of erotic fantasy and sex practices, to 141 women, who were all of middle socioeconomic background and who by most criteria would be considered reasonably normal. She was also able to interview fifty-six of the women more intensively, and to confirm the pattern of responses they had shown on questionnaires through more detailed accounts of their daydreams during inter-course with their husbands.

How common is it for women to engage in fantasy during

sexual relations? Dr. Hariton's studies indicated that 65 percent had moderate to high levels of sexual fantasy while engaged in the sexual act.

The most common fantasies they reported included:

Thoughts of an imaginary romantic lover enter my mind.
I imagine that I am overpowered or forced to surrender.
I enjoy pretending that I am doing something wicked or forbidden.
I'm in a different place, like in a car, motel, beach, woods, etc.
I relive a previous sexual experience.
I imagine myself delighting many men.
I imagine that I'm observing myself or others having sex.
I imagine that I'm another, irresistibly sexy, female.
I pretend that I struggle and resist before being aroused to surrender.
I daydream that I'm being made love to by more than one man at a time.

One-fourth of the women reported fantasies of being a teaser, harem girl or prostitute while engaging in sex. Others focused more upon being with another man or in another place and playing a relatively active role in the sexual act.

It seems reasonable to conclude that at least for this sample of middle-class suburban women, the occurrence of sexual fantasies during the act of intercourse with their husbands is a widespread and reasonably common phenomenon. A similar point has been made by Nancy Friday in her recent collection of women's erotic fantasies in a popular book called *My Secret Garden*. The importance of Dr. Hariton's extensive and sophisticated statistical analysis of her data is that it permits a more scientific approach to the patterning of sexual fantasies in the selected group of women.

In Dr. Hariton's findings, one general clustering of material indicated that women who score high on the Positive-Vivid Daydreaming scales of the Imaginal Processes Inventory also report that erotic fantasy during sexual intercourse is quite common. For these women who are active daydreamers in general, the occurrence of daydreams during the sexual act is simply a natural continuation of their predisposition to elaborate and enrich all kinds of experience through fantasy.

Women who were inclined during ordinary day-to-day activities to have daydreams that would fit in the Anxious-Distractible factor of the Imaginal Processes Inventory did not report very much erotic fantasy during sex. They indicated greater dissatisfaction with their husbands and the sexual act. They were much more likely to experience pain or annoyance with the husband during intercourse, or to be listening for the sounds or movements of the children from other rooms.

A third pattern involved the use of a specific fantasy to produce sexual arousal or orgasm. For one group of these women a fantasy of infidelity was associated with active dissatisfaction with the husband. For another group the sexually arousing fantasies involved subjugation, but these daydreams were associated with considerable marital satisfaction and happiness. In both cases the fantasy was used to produce a state of arousal, but for different reasons. The women in the first group were active in sex and relatively modern in outlook but were unhappy in their marriage and used the fantasy of another lover adaptively to escape from the awareness of their ongoing dissatisfaction. The women who produced the more passive fantasies proved to have had backgrounds of rather strict moral upbringing. Their fantasies about sex in late puberty and earlier adolescence had involved subjugation in order for them to allow themselves to indulge in erotic thoughts and self-stimulation. The fantasies were now so ingrained that they were almost inevitably a part of the sexual act, even though in general these women reported good relationships with their husbands, about whom, as lovers or as partners generally, they had no real complaints.

The women who showed a generally positive daydreaming predisposition proved on further examination to be more creative and adventurous in their pattern of behavior, and somewhat more exploratory in several different areas. This pattern carried over into their response in the sexual act itself. The women whose predominant pattern of fantasy in sex was one of subjugation tended to be somewhat more restricted and conventional in their outlooks but were basically adequately adapted. On the whole it was the women who showed the least inclination toward fantasy who were the most likely to report difficulties in a variety of relationships, and particularly in the sexual situation.

On the whole, the results of this study indicate that daydreaming is best viewed as a style or a widespread personality characteristic which carries over into many areas of experience, one of which is sex. For some women it is simply another way of expanding and elaborating on any experience, and naturally emerges in the sexual situation. The early Freudian notion that the occurrence of the fantasy should reduce arousal is not supported by this data.

The feeling of some clinicians, such as Albert Ellis, is that fantasies can play a valuable role in increasing arousal. They ought to be actively encouraged for some persons who are not enjoying the sexual act sufficiently or are finding it monotonous. This view is supported by Dr. Hariton's findings that many women's sexual fantasies have the effect of increasing excitement and orgasmic possibility. In general, the results from both questionnaire and interviews suggest that while anger and interpersonal difficulties prevent the occurrence of sexual imagery, comfort, intimacy and trust in the partner are likely to encourage fantasies, particularly if they are a natural part of the woman's cognitive style.

An interesting example of how fantasy can enhance the sexual act is pointed out by Dr. Hariton in connection with the very common daydream that the woman is being made love to by more than one man at the same time. This fantasy generally evokes the image of hands touching all the parts of her body at once, or of several men lying near her and fondling her entire body. A matching fantasy some men have reported to me involves their possession of more than two hands. This "octopus" fantasy may relate to the fact that, as Dr. Hariton notes on the basis of Kinsey's work, "A woman's sexual arousal is more diffuse than a man's and she requires constant manual stimulation to remain excited. If this is so, the fantasy of being in bed with many men would serve to perform the task that the most heroic of husbands would find impossible."

Incidentally, we have almost no formal data on the sexual daydreams of men; indeed, we have little information as to whether men engage in erotic fantasies during the act of sex to any degree at all. The man's role and sexual position is often somewhat more active than that of the woman; it may leave less "channel space" available for imagery and fantasy. It seems a reasonable possibility that some daydreaming or thinking does sneak in for some men. But we simply will not know until someone takes the trouble to investigate this problem. There are indications from case studies of individuals given to deviant sexual practices that many of these originated in unusual fantasies—a somewhat different trend than seems to be the case for the women interviewed by Dr. Hariton. This entire area is still one that calls for more extensive formal study.

CONSTRUCTIVE POSSIBILITIES OF ADULT DAYDREAMING. So far I have stressed the better-integrated person's use of fantasy, to emphasize its importance within normal adult life. The position I have taken is that daydreaming is a neutral skill available for adaptive enrichment of the life of otherwise ordinary persons—as well as a manifestation in many persons of escape, evasion of responsibility, or self-dissatisfaction. Certain childhood distortions, however, remain encapsulated in the memory storage system and have not had the opportunity to be tested by reality. Thus the husband watching his wife become the center of attention in late pregnancy may be surprised and perhaps frightened by the recurrence in himself of an earlier childhood fantasy of transvestitism or parturition. A sudden awareness of anger at one's boss may revive an early fantasy of a murderous plot against a father or an older brother. Movies, plays or television shows, particularly those with family themes, also may revive early fantasies that have long been dormant. The psychoanalytic process itself represents a technique that, by having the patient lie on a couch (a position associated especially with childhood situations), establishes conditions under which the patient may become more aware of unrealistic or bizarre sexual dependency or aggressive fantasies. The practiced daydreamer may expect many odd thoughts and experience curiosity rather than anxiety about them. But many people who are not used to noticing the ongoing inner associative stream can become terrified when they are suddenly made aware of suicidal or murderous thought sequences. Such a brief fantasy, often a revival of an earlier childhood memory, can lead an individual into a new sequence of painful associations, self-doubts or fears of the action that may follow.

Recently social psychologists have been paying a great deal of attention to the ways in which people attribute causality to various events that take place in their environment or in their own immediate experience. This attribution process has important consequences for subsequent behaviors. A bettor who loses on a horse may attribute this outcome to the jockey's ineptitude, and for years he may lose money because he refuses to bet again on any horse ridden by this jockey. Some people attribute crime to racial issues, others to insufficient police protection.

Our attributions often also determine what significance we apply to our own intrusive thoughts or fantasies. In my clinical practice I have found that many people who are inexperienced at daydreaming, or have not seen the connection between their current mood and the revival of an early childhood fantasy that may have a very strange or menacing quality, become extremely anxious and fear that they may actually carry out an imagined act or become insane. A fairly careful and direct explanation of the situation and an indication of how the attribution process may be misleading them into believing that certain thoughts will inevitably lead to action has proved to be effective in relieving great anxiety and helping people to become more tolerant of their daydreams.

As a note of caution concerning the creative possibilities of fantasy among adults, I would suggest that the complex associational possibilities necessary for creative thoughts occur in dreams and fantasies almost by chance, but that the actively creative act comes in the willingness and effort to explicate such material. Too often opportunities to reflect on the novel associative combinations that come briefly to mind are lost by too hasty immersion in action. I do not mean to suggest that the mere willingness to pay attention to one's associative stream is sufficient to produce creative responses. If a person has shown a basic indifference to subtle distinctions in his environment, if he has accepted cliché meanings, or if he has lacked interest in exploring the world through reading or novel kinds of social interaction, then the pattern of associations recently stored in his memory will reflect the same constriction; and awareness of these associations will not be especially productive. Television is a much less fruitful stimulator of creative adult associations than either a real experience or an experience gained through the process of imagining oneself in situations while reading. Self-examination and skill in daydreaming are important assets for most human beings, but they can neither compensate completely for restricted and drab life experiences nor take the place of extensive reading or commitment to some cause which makes possible more meaningful experiences.

Daydreams are many steps removed from realistic possibilities in the life situations of many adults. For the psychologist improbable daydreams may offer a clue as to important early motive or need in the individual. They also may signal serious problems. It is one thing to have a wide-ranging fantasy life if one is at the same time functioning fairly effectively in one's work and in the significant human relationships. The young man whose job is primarily to sort the mail in a large company and deliver it, but who is otherwise not sociable and lives an isolated life, may take some small pleasure from elaborate fantasies of being an explorer or a great inventor. A problem arises if he begins to substitute the fantasies for active attempts to find gratifications in his life. My own experience suggests that these more extreme cases are relatively rare, although certainly they sound like the reports of the very alienated, embittered persons who function at jobs below their potential and become soured bureaucrats. The fantasy lives of such persons tend to be monotonously oriented toward unrealistically high-level aspirations in the face of drab accomplishment. The sad fates of these limited, unrealistic daydreamers should not lead us to overlook the much larger numbers of individuals for whom memories of past achievements of fantasies of a somewhat better future may ease the pains of current reality and offer some brightness in an otherwise dreary daily routine.

More than ever before, our society has built into it a vast array of opportunities for diversion through fantasy. For millions of men the Sunday-afternoon professional football games provide a vicarious daydream of achievement and empathy. For millions of women the daily comings and goings of Jackie Kennedy Onassis (as reflected in popular magazines) or the vicissitudes of Hollywood marriages play a similar role.

We also see how important for all of us are the possibilities of shared fantasy experiences, which give us an opportunity to express our private daydreams in a public way, and to find that others share similar notions and that the broader society may sanction such notions. One could, of course, make a case, as

Freud attempted to do, for the fact that religion (which he called "an illusion") may basically play this role for a great many people. In effect, fantasies of an afterlife and attempts to circumvent the reality of death through daydreams of heaven or of reunion with lost loved ones can be shared with others and, indeed, acted out in many cases with considerable social sanction, depending on the rituals of particular religions.

Membership in a political party or charitable group, or work to support or sustain the country of one's ethnic origin, also represent examples of fantasies that can be shared and for which social support exists. The popularity of many new forms of religion or cults, the revival of interest in exotic practices such as astrology or witchcraft, all provide opportunities to express private fantasies in a socially shared manner. One could elaborate at considerable length upon the implications of taking one's private fantasy and looking for others who may share it as an important step in the development of social movements. While some private fantasies of hatred and vengeance may lead individuals to increased isolation and psychotic withdrawal, or to overt acts of random violence, comparable revenge fantasies if shared by a group may lead to conspiracies or, sometimes, to constructive social movements. Often it takes the vantage point of history to help us decide whether a particular fantasy represented a new and important insight that led to a great change in society or culture, or whether the fantasy was an example of private madness (an "ego trip") that ultimately was expressed by a small group in bizarre and perhaps destructive fashion.

For the moment I would like to consider homelier examples of daydreams and their function in daily life. Sometimes a fantasy shared in a moment of stress can help people change the pervasive negative quality of their mood, leading them on to constructive action or helping them avoid the likelihood of impulsive ruinous activities. I recall a period in my own life when a series of misfortunes had occurred in close proximity. My wife and I were depressed, and we seemed unable to organize ourselves to deal with our situation. Then we happened on an article in the newspaper about a butler on a large estate on Long Island who had killed his wife and himself in a jealous rage. At the same moment we each had the same thought. Maybe we could deal with our insecurities and the painful responsibility we felt by giving up our current way of life. Here was an opening on an estate for a couple. We both loved to entertain, my wife to cook fine dinners and I to serve fine wines. What a chance for us to demonstrate our skills and yet be taken care of indefinitely by the presumably wealthy people who owned the estate! We spun out the fantasy of domestic service as a way of life, and as it got more and more elaborate and more and more secure, with trips to Palm Beach and the Riviera, we found our depression lightening and we began to laugh. Suddenly it was possible to view our difficulties in a different perspective. In this changed mood, we were no longer paralyzed and could begin to take effective action in our immediate life situation. Here, a relatively unrealistic fantasy managed to produce a significant adaptive consequence.

Though this particular fantasy was basically too absurd to be acted upon, there are many other life situations in which what at first seems a far-fetched notion may ultimately be translated into reality. Indeed, for many young women the likelihood of returning to school or going on to take a degree in law while there are young children at home seems absurd, but ultimately many have found they could actually convert these wishes into action. Important career changes for men have also begun with this type of fantasy. Though it is necessary to appraise the realistic possibilities in a situation, the novelty of a fantasy may indeed generate a serious reexamination of what one's options in life really are. Daydreaming in the adult, far from being merely an escape or a neurotic habit, provides a challenging opportunity for renewal and the exploration of new possibilities.

Daydreaming in the Later Years

While there may be small indications of a decline in fantasy behavior with increasing age, much of our research suggests that even the extremely elderly citizens of our society continue an active inner life. The work of Dr. Leonard Giambra, using the Imaginal Processes Inventory described in an earlier chapter, clearly bespeaks the continuance of complex patterns of fantasy activity in the very old. We recognize that the private thoughts as well as the communications of many elderly people reflect a much greater tendency to reminiscence rather than to reveries about future actions or aspiration fantasies. To some degree, this emphasis on earlier memories is a function of the fact that, in general, old learning is better retained than new, and there is simply much more old learning available in the life situations of the elderly. In addition, time brings to the lives of old people an increasing sameness and lack of distinctiveness in the daily routine, which makes the content of their recent days and weeks unmemorable. The relative powerlessness of many old people in the society also puts them back in the psychological situation of their childhood years, and leads them to reexperience many incidents and events that have been stored in association with childhood contexts and were not available for recall until this recent period of social limitation provided a context that could evoke them. Obviously, too, the emphasis on reminiscent fantasy in the aged stems from the fact that for very old people the future indeed lacks interesting prospects. To think ahead confronts the old with the inevitability of death, and this makes exploration of the future traumatic. Thinking about the past is clearly less aversive and more reinforcing for many old people.

A word might be said here about possible roles of long-standing fantasies in the development of the depressions or the severe emotional distress or mental illness that may accompany so-

called change of life both in women and in men. For many
people the routine of their lives has been sustained in part by
daydreams that things can somehow be different. In many
women, the potentiality of having children or of seeing themselves as sexually desirable is a critical part of the self-image.
When they confront the ultimate reality that the childbearing
age has passed or that (and this is a frequent misconception)
sexual satisfaction is no longer a possibility, this can lead to deep
despair. If their life has not been deeply fulfilling they must give
up such long-standing fantasies at this time, and either find new
ones that are appropriate and feasible or sink deeper into the
slough of despond. Though they may not undergo physiologi-
cally the same kind of change of life as do women, for many men
the awareness of diminishing physical and sometimes mental
powers, as well as decreased sexual interests or opportunities, can
demolish a long-standing fantasy of great achievement or ultimate sexual satisfaction. The process of reexamining one's situation during this stage of life can also lead to the recall from
earlier years of significant missed opportunites, or important failures of nerve, or actual crimes or betrayals. This may account for
many of the kinds of suspicions and the "tortured self-concern"
that are often described among the symptoms of involutional
depression.

But I do not wish to overstress the pathological aspect of fantasy in later life. For many older people, retired and with fewer
day-to-day responsibilities, there is now a freedom from obliga-
tory sequences of thought and action. Some cultures, such as the
middle- and upper-class Hindu societies, permit the family patri-
arch to withdraw with considerable respect into a life of contemplation and detached philosophical or religious speculation. This
is less true in western civilizations, where we tend to undervalue
our older citizens and weaken their ties to the greater fabric of
society. Of course, prominent statesmen and generals can occupy

their later years in socialized reminiscence or the writing of their memoirs; we can think of Winston Churchill, a man so much at the center of history, who in his last years kept himself vibrantly alive through writing. But most elderly persons lack such outlets, and if they are living with their families they are likely to find their accounts of the past falling on bored ears. If old people continue to have responsibility for children in the family setting, there is still some welcome for reminiscences, which become a part of the joyful interaction between young child and grandparent. But the aged person who now has the leisure and inclination for reexamining his life or for some other form of introspection, yet lacks an audience, may give in to the apathy and depression that presages senile withdrawal.

To the extent that a person has developed an active capacity for response to internal channels, for fantasy play, for speculation or self-examination, the decreased social demands of aging hold less terror. Such a person is likelier to pursue some form of intellectual activity or hobby, and may also turn more and more toward examining the broader ethical, philosophic or religious meanings of his or her experiences. Many old people continue to keep abreast of current events in a personal field of interest such as a fraternal order, church congregation, political club or professional society. Others seek a form of direct involvement by writing letters to editors or by maintaining correspondence with distant friends, or perhaps by continuing in their own areas of work as advisers or consultants. If some such commitment is possible concurrently with the generally greater social disengagement of the retired person or the very elderly individual, the future can still beckon and be represented in one's fantasies. The aged grandmother may still daydream about schooling or wedding plans of various grandchildren, provided she has been kept informed so that her fantasies are strengthened by reality. She may speculate about the long-term changes in her growing family and in so doing may provide herself with an environment whose range of possibilities is sufficient to counteract the all too familiar routine of her present situation.

The failure of our society to employ old people in a great variety of continuing useful capacities is a national tragedy. Quite apart from failing to make available their social and professional skills in diverse occupations and social welfare activities, we are also neglecting to develop techniques for dealing directly with old people in ways that will make their psychological orientation more adaptive. We could do much more in the way of helping old people to develop skills in fantasy play, speculation and commitment to some attainable goal as a means of avoiding the apathy and depression that so often accompanies age and the loss of loved ones or friends. With help, even the aged person who has never developed a taste for inner living may be more ready for this experience than he might have been in his middle years. Many extroverted individuals who were not accessible to self-enrichment experiences because of their outgoing nature in the past may be more open to useful developments of their imaginative capacities, now that the escape of "flight into activity" is no longer so possible.

I believe also that the great richness of reminiscent thought that characterizes old people is a vast untapped realm that can be employed socially and that at the same time can provide the elderly with a sense of contribution and worth. The concept of the oral history as developed by Studs Terkel is one that could be much more widely employed as a method of research in history and sociology in various settings; it can provide us with useful information and greater understanding of the development of particular areas of industry, ethnic groups, mobility within certain settings, and the development and decline of certain neighborhoods or districts. Sociologists could learn a great deal about the significance of certain customs and social organizations through extensive interviewing of old people.

The critical factor is the establishment of conditions that make it possible for the old person to continue some form of active exploration of his private world and enjoyment of his own thought activity as a means of sustaining life. Training an older person to entertain many short-term goals may very well enable him to look ahead again, and to experience the anticipatory pleasures and joys ordinarily available to the practiced daydreamer. As the sentimental poem goes:

> For age is opportunity no less
> Than youth itself, though in another dress
> And as the evening twilight fades away
> The sky is filled with stars, invisible by day.

CHAPTER 8

Daydreaming and Psychopathology

By now the reader must recognize that my approach to daydreaming has been predominantly positive. I have stressed the fantasy process as a normal human phenomenon and as a cognitive skill available for development along a variety of lines from early childhood. This emphasis has been deliberate because, as we have noted earlier, daydreaming, at least in American society, has had a rather bad name. Most early psychological questionnaires that attempted to diagnose neurotic tendencies made a point of including questions on daydreaming as indicators of emotional disturbance. In addition, much of our clinical literature suggests that daydreaming is a symptom of disturbance in children, a precursor of later serious emotional illness and an indication of loss of contact with reality. Even so astute an observer as Dr. Anna Freud has tended in her writings to emphasize the defensive characteristics of daydreaming and its escapist qualities.

Children who are restless and who will not sit still in school are often referred to as daydreamers, yet recent evidence suggests that the likelihood is that they are not engaged in any elaborate fantasies, and indeed lack the capacity for sustained concentration that seems necessary to produce a full-blown daydream. Let us take a closer look at childhood problems and the matter of concentration or withdrawal.

SHYNESS, WITHDRAWAL AND DAYDREAMING. Some of the overemphasis on the pathological aspects of daydreaming derives from clinical case histories that have been particularly intriguing and therefore have led to extensive reprinting of the material and even to fictionalized versions. These cases usually involve children or adolescents who had especially elaborate fantasy lives. The popular notion that the schizophrenic is a person who lives in a "private world" in which he or she has carved out an intricate fantasy realm is also responsible for much of this view of daydreaming. Curiously enough, early schizoid manifestations (which include shyness, withdrawal, emotional inhibitions and an active *fantasy life*) do not necessarily foretell the development of a later schizophrenic psychosis. A very important study by Wagner and Stegman at the University of Washington in Seattle found that introverted children were *least* likely to end up as schizophrenics. More often, adult schizophrenics whose early school histories were checked turned out to have been outgoing or very variable in behavior, and showed considerable hyperactivity, antisocial behavior and other externally oriented response patterns. The authors concluded that there were no grounds whatsoever for linking adult schizophrenia with an early history of "shyness," quiet behavior and daydreaming.

It is indeed true that many aspects of daydreaming in childhood or adult life can be shown to reflect emotional disturbance or difficulties in living. Certainly we have all experienced escapist fantasies which serve to distract us from unpleasant tasks that need to be done, or at least entertain us temporarily when we really ought to be thinking about stern necessities or impending matters of great consequence. Television, the movies, newspaper comic strips, even much of the content of newspaper articles themselves often serve us as forms of vicarious fantasy that help us escape from the duties we must perform. If after a difficult day at work one turns on the television to find that the choices are yet another examination in depth of a governmental crisis, a documentary on starvation in Pakistan or the relatively pure fantasy of "Gunsmoke" or "Perry Mason," it is not surprising that most people will opt for the unreal. Private daydreams of elaborate adventure or great accomplishment can provide some of the same escape and distraction for all of us.

But for a very small number of individuals there are indications that the escape to fantasy as an evasion of responsibility or as a means of suppressing awareness of current life dilemmas is an important psychological feature of their behavior. Certainly there have been instances of young children who have developed complex series of fantasy games which they can play privately and therefore control, thus avoiding the problem of confronting social relationships with peers. This turning inward can have negative consequences since a certain amount of natural interaction with other youngsters is important in developing skills, a sense of the natural flow of give and take between children, and a sense of self-confidence in social situations. The introverted child may pay heavily for this withdrawal later in life by being very shy when thrust into social gatherings. He may lack some helpful skills such as dancing or flirtatiousness. Perhaps he may react oversensitively to the raucous good humor and teasing that characterize adolescents and young adults in many party situations. Indeed, the shyness and social immaturity of such an introvert may provoke even greater assaults and scapegoating on the part of peers.

Social withdrawal is not necessarily the same thing as the development of an elaborate fantasy life. My own clinical observations and interviews suggest that it is quite possible that the development of rather rich fantasy experience may often help someone overcome the humiliations and difficulties inherent in a tendency to social withdrawal. Sometimes the private material is turned to socially valued account in the form of literature or some other artistic expression. If the fantasy material enhances concentration capacities and the shy adolescent persists in his intellectual activities, our society is likely to reward him eventually with better educational opportunities and jobs.

The manner in which escapist or compensatory fantasy can be transmuted into reality is evident in what we know of the life of a current international figure. Beginning as a chubby, owlish-appearing German refugee boy, often afraid that approaching groups of American children might rough him up as did the Nazis, this lad develops fantasies of power through identification with such successful European manipulators and power brokers as Metternich, Castlereagh and Talleyrand. As a German-speaking American soldier in World War II he is thrust into an actual position of power over a town in occupied Germany as the local counterintelligence agent, and sees one form of his fantasy come true. He moves from that point to become a leading authority in the scholarly area of the uses of power and the history of national coalitions in post-Napoleonic Europe. And lo and behold, his childish fantasy is indeed as close to being fulfilled as most human dreams can be, for he emerges as the secretary of state and director of foreign policy for his adopted country.

DISTORTION AND ILLUSION IN EARLY FANTASIES. Obviously few such fantasies beginning in escapist fashion will lead to such heights. Indeed, it is likelier that most fantasies lead only to our recognition of our limitations and failures. Probably it is best to view the pathological possibilities of early childhood fantasy as a special case of what Sigmund Freud called transference, or the attribution of childhood experiences to adult life situations. More recently Harry Stack Sullivan, one of the greatest of American psychiatrists, proposed that Freud's notion of transference be extended to what might be called parataxic distortions, the mistaken associations between often unrelated events that the child links together in trying to make sense of his world. Some of these faulty assimilations are relatively quickly resolved, in the sense that the child tries them out and is corrected by adults or by circumstances. But many are not tried out directly because of lack of opportunity, or the child's shame at expressing private notions, or simply because the material is not appropriate for direct communication until later in life.

Think of the many distortions to which all of us fall prey in areas such as sexuality or religion, in which there is a great deal of emotional investment but little truly direct and honest communication in family settings. Psychoanalytic case studies of individual children suggest in many instances how confusions of sex and aggression, which lead either to severe inhibitions in later life or to deviant tendencies such as sadism, can be traced to a young child's exposure to parental sexual relations. For the very young person the passion of the parents' physical contact and the vocalization that characterizes the act are easily misinterpreted as a struggle. The observing child may attempt in his terror either to shut out the memory of the event or to mask his awareness in a fantasy form which is associated, later, with sexual arousal and masturbation in an especially violent style.

There are a whole host of less intense or dramatic fantasies that are generated by the child's natural development in a particular family or cultural setting. Religious beliefs are often a source of distortions. The child struggles to create a concrete image out of abstract concepts such as the Immaculate Conception, or the consumption of the "body and blood of Christ" in Holy Communion. Within family groups the child is exposed to various mythologies which as adults we might term prejudices but which in the child are represented in a variety of concrete images that often persist into adult life. Thus, when families say that "we" are not people who should mix with "them" or "they're not the sort that one really ought to get involved with," children assimilate this into their limited cognitive schema in a great variety of ways often not intended by the adults. A good deal of the work of play therapists, or of psychoanalysts working with adults, involves the gradual teasing out, step by step, of many of the private fantasies and distortions that have led the subjects into gross difficulties in their current relationships.

An important issue that remains unresolved in the present state of our knowledge about child development and the role of fantasy concerns the extent to which the distorted behaviors and thoughts of adults stem from an inherent tendency to create fantasies in childhood, or whether they reflect *actual* experiences undergone in childhood. Freud first believed that most adult neurotic symptoms could be traced back to infantile seductions or other traumatic events in the family life of the individual. This notion is quite effective in the kind of quick psychoanalysis that one sees in movies such as *Spellbound,* where the hero—in the nick of time—remembers allowing his brother to fall to his death and is of course cured. But Freud came to realize that many of the early traumatic events his patients reported could not have occurred in the form presented. He revised his theory to make the assumption that all children underwent periods of elaborate fantasy related to their psychosexual stages. These fantasies were an inevitable occurrence of the growth process, and could lead to different degrees of distortion, depending on the severity of fixation at each psychosexual stage. His revised theory therefore assumed extensive childhood fantasy to be at the root of emotional disturbance, and he tended to ignore actual patterns of interaction taking place within a given family setting.

An important function of fantasy is that it represents an effort to make sense of an area of experience that has not been lived through directly to any great extent. In pubescence and adolescence it reflects the limitations of young people's experiences in social relationships and intimacy. These fantasy explorations of a great variety of possible social and sexual interactions are gradually modified as time allows some of them to be experienced directly. But many of these attempted understandings of differences between people or other aspects of human relationships, which have not been tested in real life, persist for long periods of time.

I remember with some embarrassment how my teen-age male friends and I joked endlessly about the presumed differences in the angle of the vaginal orifice in Oriental as against Occidental women. After I had read enough biological material to know this was nonsense, I was impressed at the extent to which similar notions persisted among adult men in the army.

Certain kinds of fantasies may cause people considerable personal distress. They may lead to grossly deviant sexual behavior of the type that eventually gets in casebooks such as Krafft-Ebing's *Psychopathia Sexualis*. These deviant patterns may stem from the fact that an early distortion in the child's understanding of sexual behavior has become associated with the beginnings of sexual arousal. The fantasy may have crystallized during years of masturbation or other positive private experiences. If the individual later has unsatisfying "normal" sexual experiences or is blocked by lack of opportunity or poor social relationships from sexual activity in the usual fashion, the power of the private fantasy may persist and eventually lead to some deviant effort at expression. In many cases (as in pedophilia or voyeurism) an individual may actually move into a normal heterosexual relationship, marry and have children, but still never overcome some of the childhood excitement associated with these tendencies and therefore seek outlets for them—occasionally with embarrassing results if caught. Sometimes such an individual is fortunate to find a mate who tolerates unusual patterns of sexual expression or indeed grows to enjoy them. Probably most intimate relationships that have any lasting quality involve an attempt on the part of both partners to bring their fantasies into harmony, or to tolerate each other's more unusual patterns in the interest of sharing a feeling and out of genuine affection. Nor need the expression of such fantasies be limited entirely to sexual activity. The artistically oriented individual can find an outlet through his creative product. Undoubtedly some of Portnoy's fantasies were reflections of Philip Roth's own daydreams, or those he had heard about from some of his male friends. Very likely the attraction to little girls that comes up again and again in the work of writers like Dostoyevsky or Nabokov is a reflection of some recurrent fantasies these men experienced.

I have tried in this section to review some of the ways in which daydreams may develop in somewhat pathological directions, out of the normal course of development. Let us now examine specific patterns of fantasies associated with more clearly pathological forms of behavior.

DAYDREAMING AND SEVERE PSYCHOPATHOLOGY IN CHILDHOOD. Some unusually clear examples of pathological manifestations of daydreaming have been presented by Dr. Rudolph Ekstein, in an impressive collection of cases of children undergoing psychoanalytic treatment. One example describes a girl whose grossly bizarre behavior was built primarily around her playing a single love song over and over again on her record player. She kept her room in a style that suggested she was a married woman and she associated particular objects in the room with her fantasy husband. She was full of many kinds of romantic legends and novels, and indeed sometimes seemed a living example of the young Emma Bovary. In the course of intensive analytic therapy, the young girl brought out distorted fantasies, some of which involved sexual confusion and identification with Christ. The therapist made very good use of her interest in legends and imagination, and was able to get her to examine some of the consequences of these fantasies. Thus he was able to show support of the struggle she was having about sexuality without being too direct, and without having to force her to give up unrealistic daydreams. This case ended favorably, the young woman developing eventually into an imaginative and flexible adult. In a sense, then, one might argue that though her initial fantasy of being married by the age of twelve or thirteen led her into gross social withdrawal and behavior that was bizarre by most adult or adolescent standards, the fact remains that her capacity for fantasy was serving some significant function in the face of very complex conflicts that existed in her early childhood. Indeed, her capacity for fantasy made her more accessible to treatment, and may have made it easier for the therapist to establish a rapport that led her eventually to move in a more adaptive direction. It is important to note that with the successful treatment she did not give up her imaginative ability, simply the more eccentric manifestations of her fantasy capacity.

Another dramatic example of fantasy life gone wild is that of Tommy the Space Child, described by Dr. Ekstein. Tommy had a fantasy of a time machine, which he used to explore a variety of different previous lives and cultures and which he preferred to enter rather than engage in ordinary social relationships. His academic work suffered from his preoccupations, although it was obvious that he was a highly intelligent boy. Ekstein examines in detail the various fantasies and their origins in distorted impressions derived from the life situations this child had experienced. He was deeply concerned about being neglected or deserted by his parents. In his fantasies he sought again and again to reconstruct a past that was more satisfying, gave him more power over his life situation and precluded the possibility of abandonment. Ekstein could therefore point out the extent to which the fantasy had an important constructive aspect, because it maintained a certain degree of stability in the face of adversity or trauma. Tommy's time machine was clearly a manifestation of his unconscious conflicts or past trauma, but it also represented an attempt on the boy's part to organize his conflicts in a manner that would enable him to deal with them at least to some degree.

Here, too, a rich imaginative life was utilized in the course of therapy, and the boy made a significant improvement. One might even argue that the fantasy method provided the therapist with a ready-made communication system which was more effective than direct action could have been. A child with an imaginative predisposition, like Tommy, might prove to be more open to therapeutic intervention than one who has not elaborated a verbal system or developed the means for expressing his conflicts in the imagery of play.

A very famous example of fantasy run rampant is the well-known case described by the patient herself in the sensitive *I Never Promised You a Rose Garden*. This young woman was hospitalized for her bizarre behavior during adolescence, and revealed to her therapist a complex private fantasy world with its own language. Here the vividness of the imaginary realm was so great that often the young woman drifted almost completely away from direct communication, apparently hallucinating vividly the voices of the fantasy kingdom and often responding to them in the language she had created.

With careful and painstaking work the psychoanalyst Dr. Frieda Fromm-Reichmann was able to help this young woman work through many distortions and fantasies about her family life which were reflected in this bizarre split in her experiential world. Again it is important to note that the patient could be reached effectively through the therapist's careful respect for the importance of her fantasy. Ultimately this young woman made a remarkable recovery from so severe a psychosis, and has gone on to a productive and responsible adult life. The therapy did not strip her of her imaginative capacities and these have been expressed not only in the fine autobiographical account of *Rose Garden* but in several subsequent fine novels as well.

This case bears some resemblance to that presented in somewhat flamboyant fashion in Robert Lindner's *The Fifty-Minute Hour*. The hero of the case study called "The Jet-Propelled Couch" was a young scientist who developed an elaborate fantasy world in outer space to which he became increasingly addicted as time went on. Eventually his scientific work suffered because he grew so immersed in making up symbols and languages and in imagining trips to this land where he served as a heroic figure much like Edgar Rice Burroughs's John Carter of Mars. So real and powerful was this talented young man's fantasy that at the end, when he finally gave up the system and returned to dealing with the realities of his day-to-day life, the analyst felt some sense of loss because their mutual voyages to "inner space" would not continue.

In the cases we have described, much of the fantasy still has a good deal of the quality of childhood make-believe play, though it is carried to great lengths by relatively gifted young people. When improved after treatment, all these people retained their basic ability for daydreaming and were able to use it in socially functional and relevant directions. It has sometimes been argued that exposure to psychoanalysis or other forms of therapy can stifle the natural imaginative tendencies and creative capacities of gifted people in the process of adjusting them to "reality." While this is theoretically conceivable, I have never seen or heard of an actual instance. On the contrary, there are suggestions by various writers that psychotherapy addressed to distortions and fantasies has frequently helped them unblock creative capacities. The awareness that many of one's fantasies are unreal does not make them less accessible for literary or artistic use. Certainly one cannot avoid the feeling that a wild story such as Philip Roth's *The Breast* stemmed from his realization at some point (whether in psychotherapy or in introspection) that like many American men, he was excessively fixated on that feature of female anatomy to the exclusion of more significant facets of the human relationship. Roth's story of the professor who turns gradually into a giant breast is analogous to Kafka's "Metamorphosis," in which the hero awakens to find himself transformed into a hideous insect. For Kafka, apparently, that image represented the hero's awareness of the sterility, the insectlike quality of his own existence, as Roth chose the breast as his symbol of the dilemma of the man of the 1960s.

DAYDREAMS IN HYSTERICAL AND OBSESSIONAL NEUROTICS. In hysterical neurosis, which is often characterized by a tendency toward forgetfulness, blocking and gross repression of important conflicts into physical symptoms such as paralysis of an arm or a leg, the general cognitive style of the patient tends to be somewhat more global or diffuse. That is, the hysterical personality is inclined not to be very precise about details or to think things through with detailed care. In the clinical reports of the fantasy lives of hysterical patients, rather than extensive or elaborate fantasy we get a frequent confusion between the patient's wishes and realistic possibilities.

Many of Freud's early patients were hysterical in their symptomatology. This may account for the fact that they presented him with accounts of childhood romantic behaviors that he later found were more probably wishes than occurrences. It is very likely that the hysterical neurotic does not tend to generate extensive personal fantasies and instead relies for his fantasies on popular literature. On the basis of his experience with such patients, Sullivan pointed out that it is often hard to know whether fantasies one hears are simply accounts of recent novels or movies or are actual private events. This is also the case when one seeks to administer to hysterical patients psychological tests that call for the expression of imaginative material.

A good example in literature of the mind of a probably hysterical young woman is presented in James Joyce's *Ulysses,* in the chapter modeled on Homer's episode of Nausicaä finding Odysseus on the beach. Here the heroine is a most ordinary girl caught up in mundane fantasies based on popular magazines. She pictures herself as a wife who saturates her husband's days with the homeyness of good cooking, a warm fire, a proper and nicely furnished living room and a picture of Grandpa's dog on the wall; and in this setting there is, of course, a tall, broad-shouldered and very home-loving husband. As Gerty MacDowell elaborates on her fantasy, she becomes aware that Leopold Bloom is observing her from the beach; and in the typical disso-ciated fashion of a hysteric, she tries on the one hand to be a good girl while on the other hand she flirts actively with him, raising her skirts, exposing her legs and engaging in a variety of gestures that arouse him sexually. When she leaves it can be seen that she is lame, perhaps a subtle Joycean recognition of physical disability frequently associated with hysterical kinds of person-alities.

In contrast with the hysterical personality is the obsessive-compulsive neurotic patient. This pattern of neurosis is often part of a broader style which also characterizes many normal individuals who are much given to elaborate thought and self-examination. The obsessional neurotic is frequently described as someone with an excessive conscience, in which all potentially effective action is "sicklied o'er with the pale cast of thought." Where the hysterical personality is involved with cliché and unelaborated imagery, the obsessional at his worst is constantly examining and reexamining each sequence of thought and fan-tasy, splitting each element further into smaller segments, con-stantly preoccupied with presumed guilts or self-doubts. One might therefore expect a much more complex daydream and fantasy life in obsessional neurotics, and psychological tests sup-port this assumption. In an extreme case, however, an individual may become so obsessed with detail that he allows himself very little free fantasy or inner imagery and instead prefers to im-merse himself in detailed counting or excessively precise verbal operations. The elaborate fantasy life of the more usual obsessional neurotic is often characterized by a sense that these thoughts cannot always be controlled, and he therefore makes a great effort to structure them. At its most creative, the obsessional style has been manifested in the philosophical construct of Immanuel Kant, with its incredibly detailed logical structure and its call for the highest level of morality. John Bunyan's *Pilgrim's Progress* is in many ways the elaborated private fantasy of an obsessional neurotic, in this case that of a seventeenth-century Puritan, carried to extremes in literary representation.

A famous example of an obsessive neurotic is "Rat Man," who was treated by Sigmund Freud at the turn of the century. A highly intelligent young man had been tormenting himself again and again with a great variety of recurrent thoughts. He had overheard an account of a cruel form of punishment while he was on maneuvers in the army and then found himself obsessed with the idea that his father or his sweetheart would receive the same punishment. This torture consisted of tying an individual in such a way that rats were encouraged to bite their way into his buttocks. The young man could not control recurrence of this fantasy or of others similar to it. He also revealed many thoughts involving the wish for money, which would enable him to marry the girl of his choice. This money, he felt, would come to him only through the death of his father. These thoughts, too, returned to torment him again and again.

A patient with whom I myself worked reported a recurrent fantasy in which he cut off a woman's breast, cooked it, sliced it and ate it. Generally he had had the fantasy while masturbating as a young man. His personality structure was quite similar to that of "Rat Man." In actual life he was gentle, considerate, inhibited—and a very good cook!

DAYDREAMING IN ADULT SCHIZOPHRENIA. If we turn to the psychotic forms of adult behavior and particularly to schizophrenia, we find a curious contradiction between popular expectations and the actual pattern of thought processes. Though a schizophrenic patient is generally thought of as representing a split personality, someone who lives one way in fantasy and another way in reality, this impression is not supported by the behavior of the large bulk of the patients who are classified as one or another type of schizophrenic in clinics or mental hospitals. Among the major symptoms of schizophrenia are evidences of disordered thinking, confusion in thought and behavior, peculiar verbalizations, and of course hallucinations and delusions.

While a great many persons classified as schizophrenic do indeed report hallucinations, recent research has led to serious questioning about what is actually meant by this phenomenon. Is the patient really hearing voices or seeing images, or is he possibly misinterpreting his private fantasies, assuming that they come from the outside mainly because he listened so little to the voice of his own consciousness in childhood? Except for some of the more exotic cases, such as the girl in *Rose Garden* and examples presented by R. D. Laing, most schizophrenic patients do not show a great vividness of inner fantasy or even any great complexity in their hallucinations. Nor do projective tests provide evidence of greater imaginativeness than normal people have.

Generally, hallucinations take the form of voices that denounce the patient in repetitive terms. In a sense, these inner denunciations, which often sound in the voices of parental figures, are not terribly different from the self-denunciations that obsessional patients report, except that the latter are well aware that these are their own thoughts and do not assume that they come from somebody else. There are indications that individuals less oriented toward the development of fantasy and daydreaming are more prone when severely disturbed emotionally or socially isolated (as many schizophrenics certainly are) to become aware of their private thoughts. Such persons attribute them to external sources and are therefore susceptible to the charge of hallucinating.

Bizarre behavior often stems from the patient's making a response based on his continued involvement with his parents or childhood needs. The response, inappropriate to the persons confronting him, sounds fantastic because it is irrelevant. This distortion of reality is, however, a rather concrete thought pattern and lacks the flexibility or differentiation of most fantasy behavior.

Schizophrenics as a group are socially withdrawn. A study that I carried out in collaboration with Dr. Herbert Spohn at the Veterans Administration Hospital in Montrose, New York, involved careful observation of both acute and chronic schizophrenic patients who were in a day room while a World Series game was being televised. In marked contrast to the active involvement of normal men of the same generation, the schizophrenics responded only minimally to the excitement of the game. Interviews not only substantiated this lack of interest but also failed to indicate any alternative immersion in private fantasy. Rather, the schizophrenic patients seemed simply to be looking at some point in the room, or speculating on the possibly sinister origins of the gurglings in their stomachs, examining the ash burning at the end of their cigarettes or the pattern on the curtains.

In the early phases of the development of a schizophrenic reaction we do get more indications of intricate fantasy. An individual may become aware of strong desires, which he must attempt to deny either by shifting his attention to other kinds of fantasies or by turning his private thoughts "upside down" so that they can be attributed to others.

The primary problem that shows in early schizophrenic reactions is the excessive social withdrawal of the patient and his increasing focus on a limited number of fantasies. The patient often develops elaborate expectations of what others are thinking or what they want in social situations. He may generate a complex set of private anticipations that cannot be tested because there is no ongoing social interaction. The patient's awareness of this presumed well-developed private life, which is so different from his actual social situation of minimal contact with others, forces him to see himself as very different. Sometimes this sense of difference is justified by focusing on a fantasy of being a very special person, particularly great or important but unrecognized by others. This is likely to be the case if the person has had some talent or aspirations toward scientific or creative achievement in the past. Often the awareness of fantasies too painful to be acknowledged, such as those of a homosexual nature, cause him to deny these are his own thoughts and to attribute them instead to suspicions about others or to overtures from other people. This accounts for much of the complex development of delusional systems in paranoid schizophrenia.

It is not within this book's province to go into any extensive discussion of the various theories or notions of the origin of schizophrenia itself. I wish merely to call attention to the possibility that the fantasies of individuals already moving in the direction of psychotic breakdown tend to be elaborated only in a very circumscribed area, built generally around a single topic, such as persecution by others for having a secret invention or for presumed homosexuality. Within a short time all the daydreaming and the fantasies of the individual come to focus on the particular problem, and since there is rarely direct testing of these anticipations in social situations, the fantasies are readily sustained. Since a person has had few social contacts and failed in some interchanges, his peculiarities generate reactions in turn from others in the environment, and these real occurrences further reinforce the fantasies of being special or of being rejected or persecuted.

Perhaps the most famous case of paranoid schizophrenia in the literature is that of Schreber, a German supreme court judge who

suffered a psychotic breakdown in his thirties, recovered somewhat, and had another breakdown some years later, from which
he apparently never recovered. Schreber wrote a book attempting
to justify his behavior and criticized the various kinds of psychiatric treatment he had received. The elaborate delusions that he
described in the book were analyzed subsequently by Sigmund
Freud, whose paper, based only on the reading of the book, has
become a landmark in the psychodynamic understanding of
paranoid schizophrenia. No one denies the importance of Freud's
insight that Schreber transformed his deep concern over homosexual tendencies, which he attempted to deny, into persecutions
by others or into ideas of communication or closeness with God.
New information has emerged about Schreber's childhood, however. A remarkable essay by Dr. Morton Schatzman reports that
Schreber's father was a renowned educator whose theories of
child rearing involved the strictest kinds of discipline, restrictions
on the physical movement of the child from the earliest age,
severe forms of punishment and control, and the invention of a
variety of exercises and physical devices designed to control the
posture of the child to prevent possible masturbatory activities.

It is evident that many of the bizarre bodily incidents Schreber
reported, which were viewed as delusional, were in part recollections of physical experiences he had undergone as a subject for
his father's educational experiments. Because of the tremendous
pressure put on him in early childhood, Schreber could not
admit to himself that his father was the source of these difficulties
and indeed had mistreated him. Instead, he had in effect been
trained by repeated admonitions and aversive techniques to deny
to himself the possibility that there could be any harm in his
father's intentions. Therefore, he had to seek elsewhere for an
explanation of his confused responses to the many strictures and
physical experiments to which he had been exposed. By creating
the fantasy that the tortures and bizarre experiences that he
underwent were a function of his relationship with God,

Schreber apparently sought to avoid facing his father's involvement and at the same time to develop a feeling of greater importance and power which would justify his own peculiarities. Since daydreaming or engaging in wishful or lascivious thoughts had been strictly forbidden him in childhood, Schreber was in effect forced to view some of his fantasies and wishes as coming from the outside, a result of his involvement with God.

A major factor in schizophrenia is an individual's lack of ability to control the sequence of his associations or verbal communication patterns. In attempting to talk to a schizophrenic patient, one often gets the impression that the words he is saying are interrupted by some of the kinds of fleeting stream-of-consciousness association that we all experience but which he cannot exclude from awareness or from interfering with the sequence of thought. I may in the course of a lecture to a class have a brief image of some event from my past or some necessary chore that has to be done at home or in the office, but ordinarily this will not impede the flow of communication. The schizophrenic patient cannot always prevent himself either from expressing the association verbally or from emotional reactions which seem extremely strange to others, since his laughs or scowls as he responds to a private thought or fantasy in the course of an otherwise ordinary conversation are inexplicable to the observer.

There are certain experiences we all have that may give some sense of what an acutely distressed schizophrenic might be undergoing. Supposing a young man has recently met a very attractive girl and begun an acquaintance that looks as if it may move toward a more intimate and developed relationship. He is full of plans and anticipations for a weekend they are to spend together in a ski resort. One day at work, our hero is indulging in a host of images about the forthcoming weekend, the possibility of a long-term relationship and marriage and what this may mean at this point in his life. A co-worker approaches him and goes into a lengthy discussion about whether a new form being adopted for some purpose in the company is identical to or different in small details from the previous form. As part of his job the young man caught up in his fantasies may be forced to pay attention to his fellow employee but finds himself again and again drifting off into thoughts of the weekend ahead. Occasionally he may simply not hear particular comments about this paragraph or that paragraph in the form being described to him. He may even smile inappropriately as he thinks of an event to come, thereby puzzling the person speaking to him. Ordinarily he would be moderately interested in the material being discussed. At this point he is relatively uninterested, responds rather curtly and may even show poor judgment in the advice he gives the other person about how to interpret the form.

Undoubtedly we all have moments that reflect such drifting away from an ongoing situation and an inability to pay attention because our private thoughts have greater priority. But the schizophrenic's dilemma is that he cannot turn off either the inner reflections or his attention to the external environment, and frequently gets them hopelessly mixed up. This is all the more serious when he has developed, as have many schizophrenics, long-range expectations and fantasies built around unusual patternings within the family constellation that have led him to grossly distorted anticipations of what is to be expected in human relationships. In a normal social situation a friend may not realize this; all that happens is confusion in the communication, and frequently the interchange terminates with some form of rejection of the patient, which further confirms his sense of isolation and persecution.

I earlier stressed the fact that much daydreaming requires some support from reality to be sustained over an extended period of time. In the case of the fantasies of many schizophrenic patients, only the persecutory fantasies tend to have this characteristic of external support. The more lofty fantasies are rather fleeting. There are very few patients who genuinely believe for years that they are Napoleon or Christ. It seems more likely that some individuals, desperately confused about their own identity and what they are in the world, try out a host of fantasies, almost as if they are saying, "Maybe I'm a famous movie actress, maybe I'm a glamorous person, maybe I'm some heroic figure." They test these openly in communication with others as if in the hope that some of the fantasies will be confirmed. And indeed, sometimes they are humored by hospital attendants or even relatives or friends, who think encouragement is at least one way of keeping them happy.

Those rare instances where the patient does take on an elaborate role which persists over many years still reflect the make-believe play of children. Perhaps out of great confusion in identity at an earlier point in adolescence, the youth has decided to settle for role-playing as Napoleon or Christ. This represents a compromise which withdraws him from the real world, puts him into the relatively secure situation of a hospital and gives him a certain status within that setting. I believe that often enough in unguarded moments many of these patients do realize that they are role-playing, but because they feel that they have nowhere else to go to in their lives, they stick to living out childhood make-believe.

More significant for society in general are those instances where an individual's private fantasy, indeed his role-playing of a certain personality, somehow finds acceptance by others, and may even become the focus of a full political movement. If we take the real Napoleon, for example, there seems little doubt that one of his childhood fantasies was built around the fame of Julius Caesar and as he grew older occasionally this identification led him into gross error. Despite some heroic victories, Napoleon made what was essentially a terrible political blunder in his expedition to Egypt; but it gave him an opportunity to stand in front of the pyramids and to think of himself as Caesar or Alexander the Great. He was lucky indeed to escape from this situation and return to France at a time when there was a need for his political leadership there, so that the error of his Egyptian expedition was not recognized. Hitler's thrust at Russia seems to share some of the same qualities—a revival of a fantasy of being able to outdo Napoleon in the conquest of Europe. The great tragedy of our civilization is that all too often such leaders become embodiments of many of our own fantasies, so we give them license to direct us into terribly destructive directions. The strong support in recent years for political leaders who promised "law and order" has reflected the wish of many powerless and fearful people for simple, aggressive solutions.

PATHOLOGY OF FANTASY IN EVERYDAY LIFE. I have focused in this chapter on the more flamboyant manifestations of severe stress and difficulty through daydreaming. I should like to detail now an example, which the reader can surely match many times over, of ways in which daydreams and anticipations in day-to-day life may lead to difficulties in interpersonal relationships—difficulties, at first small, which may mushroom into serious problems. Consider the instance of how a couple may build up an elaborate fantasy prior to a much-awaited event.

A wife somewhat bored with her housework or harried by bickering children awaits her husband's return from work. She constructs an eager fantasy of his loving entrance, a passionate embrace, and words of devotion and reassurance. Meanwhile, the husband has spent his day in a seemingly endless series of frenzied verbal exchanges with customers or supervisors, and constructs in his turn a fantasy of the relaxed quiet of his home, a fine dinner and the enveloping feminine warmth that awaits him. When he finally gets home, kicks off his shoes and slumps wearily in his chair, presenting a most unromantic image, the disappointed wife (still hoping for rescue) may launch into an angry recital of the day's appliance breakdowns and children's misfortunes. This account of problems and chores still to be done smashes her husband's fantasy of a quiet haven, and he may respond angrily or withdraw into television or the newspaper or make an abrupt departure to a nearby bar. The quarrel that can ensue will end in each hurting the other by recalling old grievances. Often enough, as the quarrel mounts they are likely to forget what initially prompted it—the frustration of each in their anticipatory fantasies.

Most of us fail to realize the extent and ways in which such disappointments are masked. Many of the confusions and difficulties in our daily life are rooted in plans and expectations that are not fulfilled. We often react to rebuffs with rage or sadness that generates snowballing and ominous consequences. Frequently an important feature of psychotherapy is a very careful rerunning of such sequences of events, which clarifies for the patient ways that led him to hasty or inappropriate action. Psychotherapy in marital difficulty calls for the tracing of systematic expectations in the partners, the degree to which vivid fantasies exemplifying these expectations were elaborated, and finally the sequence of behavior of each partner that dashed the hopes of the other.

In one instance, a patient with whom I was working in psychotherapy described an ugly dispute with his wife. As we traced the origin of the situation, it became clear that during a family dinner the husband's mother had gone into a lengthy discourse criticizing her daughter-in-law's running of her household. As soon as his mother began talking, the husband tuned her out, his habitual way of avoiding difficulties with her. He assumed that his wife would be able to do the same thing. Actually, the wife had a fantasy that he would intervene in the course of this dialogue, telling his mother that she was intruding, that her comments were inappropriate and that he loved his wife and thought she was doing a fine job. Instead, it seemed to the wife that her husband, impassive during this long criticism, might even agree with it. This commonplace but complicated situation took some fairly deft reviewing before the couple realized the roots of the situation. Once the fantasies were elicited, however, the couple realized that they could begin to work out a better way of relating in such circumstances and they began to try new approaches together.

Although the examples I have just cited may seem relatively trivial compared with the severe pathological conditions discussed earlier, I do not really believe that this is the case. As I have stressed again and again, a human being is an image-making creature. We all set up fantasies, of different degrees of complexity, about what we expect to happen in our lives in the future. These fantasies are very useful in guiding us in particular directions, sustaining our hopes so that we can meet particular adversities, and giving life some of the excitement that comes from anticipation as well as from memory. But at the same time they may lead us into expectations that are not likely to be fulfilled, and little by little we feel inner despair or rage. This happens particularly in the expectations of a long-term relationship with another person in a marriage. Our childhood and adolescence have been filled with thoughts of whom we ought to marry and what it will mean to be married, about the delights of sexuality in various forms and the excitements or comforts of the relationship.

People often enter into intimate relationships because they overvalue or overestimate the similarity between their fantasy and the person they are now attracted to. Hoping against hope, they persist for years in such relationships without recognizing the disparity. Many of the games or life scripts that have been described by Eric Berne reflect the degree to which people's fantasies of winning love through martyrdom or rescuing lost souls lead them repeatedly into disastrous choices in partners.

One has to acknowledge an inherently tragic aspect to the nature of human daydreams. While our fantasy capacities represent extremely valuable parts of our ability to plan and anticipate or to entertain and sustain ourselves, they may also include unfulfilled images or the frustration of disappointed anticipation. In this sense our everyday daydreams carry the seeds of psychopathology at the same time as they offer us the best of human experiences.

CHAPTER 9

Daydreaming and Imagery Methods in Psychotherapy

Early Uses of Imagery in Psychotherapy

A major theme of this volume so far has been the adaptive possibilities of the human capacity for daydreaming. I should like to turn during this chapter to the ways in which psychotherapists or psychologists interested in education have increasingly attempted to harness the imagery resources of individuals in the service of specific forms of psychotherapy or child training.

HYPNOSIS. A word must be said about hypnosis since it is still the subject of considerable confusion and mystery in the mind of the general public—a situation not helped by the fact that so many entertainers now make use of this technique on television or on the nightclub circuit. There has been a great deal of very careful and thoughtful research on the process of hypnosis, carried on by psychologists such as Ernest Hilgard of Stanford University, Martin Orne of the University of Pennsylvania and Theodore Barber of the Medfield Foundation in Massachusetts. By any of the usual physiological criteria, hypnosis is not a state really like sleep. I have been able to "hypnotize" individuals simply by sitting with them and reading the instructions for hypnosis out of a manual. Clearly no special magic or charisma is necessary for one to be successful in producing hypnosis in another person. Primarily hypnosis is a voluntary contract, in which individuals—some more quickly than others—are able to play the role the instructions demand of them and to enter deeply into a state of extreme concentration and focused imagery. Indeed, there is considerable indication that in most circumstances even a trained hypnotist cannot detect any difference between a person who is genuinely hypnotized and another who is pretending. Simulators who have received a certain amount of training can perform any of the feats that are considered so startling when done by hypnotized subjects.

A look at the relevant research literature reveals that hypnosis involves a combination of intense concentration and a blocking out of many of the external cues to which we all normally respond, with a consequent heightening of the vividness of imagery within the relatively narrow sphere suggested by the hypnotist. In effect, the hypnotic subject has generated an elaborate role that he is playing, much as a fine actor puts himself wholly into a part. This narrowing of attention and zeroing in on a limited group of private images or associations to certain external cues lends a heightened vividness and seeming reality to these images for the brief period of time of the so-called trance state. Much of the new research suggests that rather than viewing susceptibility to hypnosis as a sign of weakness, as in the familiar tale of Dr. Svengali and Trilby, it would be more appropriate to see it as one manifestation of the human faculty for a greater range of imagery and fantasy than had been generally thought possible. The kind of concentration produced in hypnosis may be essentially an indication of another human capacity for heightened but extremely selective use of our imagery functions.

IMAGERY IN CLASSICAL PSYCHOANALYSIS. Freud made active use of hypnosis in treating neurotic patients, and then gave it up for a related experimental method of imagery association. He held the patient's head between his hands and encouraged her to produce one image after another. Eventually psychoanalysis moved away from this method and toward the use of a more conversational tone, with the person lying, eyes open, on a couch facing a ceiling or blank wall and *not* looking into the face of the therapist. Recent research evidence suggests that to lie down facing a blank wall increases the likelihood that one will generate not only vivid imagery but more material from early childhood experiences. If the therapist's goal is to have the patient relive experiences, fantasies and emotions associated with early childhood, the use of the couch makes good sense still.

Quite recently at Michigan State University, Dr. Joseph Reyher has revived Freud's original imagery association method. He calls it the technique of "emergent uncovering" and has carried out experiments to show that the use of imagery associations not only evokes more emotion but also provides material that seems closer to very basic drives and conflicts within the individual. The patient is encouraged to begin by imagining anything that comes to his mind, and then simply to float in imagery from one scene to another. After a few minutes he recounts the sequence of images as vividly as possible. In other respects Reyher's psychotherapy continues along much the same lines as a classical Freudian psychoanalysis. It seems clear that emergent uncovering may be a fruitful way to circumvent much of the talkiness and redundancy that so often characterize psychoanalytic sessions. The method seems to have possibilities for reaching the crux of many of the patients' problems more rapidly, and helping them face these problems without the defensiveness that is characteristic if they are simply verbalizing freely in the therapy session.

Even in its more traditional format, psychoanalysis of course makes extensive use of various forms of daydreams and imagery. Patients are always encouraged to remember their dreams to present to the analyst during a session. If one attempts to recall a dream during the therapeutic hour, one is in effect generating a series of images and fantasies to which one then associates other sequences of thought. In the course of dream interpretation, therefore, psychoanalysis is establishing conditions for the patient to become increasingly sensitive to the nighttime imagery that we call dreams, and to his ongoing imagery as well as he narrates the dream to the psychoanalyst.

Patients are also encouraged to remember any daydreams or fantasies they have had during the week or within the session itself. Special importance is attached to the daydreams that occur during a given psychotherapeutic session because they often turn out to have some implication for the relationship between therapist and patient, which becomes the heart of analytic interpretation. Typically a patient lying on the couch, the analyst out of his sight, might say something like this:

"I suddenly had this fantasy that you were sitting there in terrible pain. Then I realized in the fantasy that perhaps you were suffering from an incurable disease. I pictured you in the hospital and then saw myself visiting you, with you lying on the bed while I stood beside you holding your hand and trying to console you as death approached."

Needless to say, this kind of daydream will lead to an exploration of the patient's mixture of positive and negative feeling about the therapist, and might also revive memories of comparable ambivalence toward a father or older brother.

The daydreams patients have in psychoanalysis are often clues to their transference experiences. The notion of transference is a central one to psychoanalytical treatment. It is the phenomenon that has led to some of the rather wild assumptions that "all patients fall in love with their therapists." Transference is critical in the theory of analysis because it brings into the session itself the basic orientations that have been leading the patient to many of his distortions and mistaken anticipations in the course of his social experience. By transferring them to the therapist by virtue of the therapist's relative ambiguity of role, the patient achieves the opportunity to see very clearly the extent to which he has developed in his family experiences a set of images and fantasies that are impeding his development and leading to gross confusions in the pattern of his interpersonal relationships.

The important thing to notice for our purposes here is that most people in the course of the many daydreams they generate are piecing together complex clusters of fantasy that become in effect their view of what "real" and "ideal" human relationships are and ought to be. These long-standing fantasies become the basis for our hopes and expectations. To the extent that they are grossly distorted because our own childhood experience was necessarily limited in scope to a particular family in a particular cultural milieu, we experience painful disappointments and social confusion.

In addition to helping patients clarify their own transference distortions and to analyze their fantasies and dreams, psychoanalysis provides a form of training for heightened self-awareness. A patient who has done well in psychoanalysis is likely to have greater respect for his dreams and daydreams and also for the many associations that flit along on his stream of consciousness. He will have learned to use his daydreams and occasional odd or peculiar thoughts to help him identify his moods or aroused emotions, and also to alert him to distortions about relationships that may have arisen as a result of his transference tendencies in a given social situation.

A young man may enter a room in which several people are gathered and suddenly find that he is feeling extreme anger at one of the people nearby. He finds himself beginning to enter into an argument and then suddenly realizes, "Uh-oh. Here I go again. I don't even know this man and here I am picking a fight."

This self-awareness alerts him to replay mentally his train of associations upon entering the room, until in the course of the replay he realizes that in general age and physical appearance the man resembles an uncle who had been the source of great conflict and difficulty in his childhood. He then can tease out the distinction between what the man he has just met is saying and what he expects of a person like this man because of the numerous difficulties he had with his uncle. All this occurs with great rapidity, and he is able to avert an unnecessary and self-defeating quarrel with an otherwise perfectly innocent person puzzled as to why this young man should take such a dislike to him.

European Mental Imagery Techniques

Even greater attention to the imagery and fantasy capacity of adults is evident in the uses made of mental imagery by a number of European schools. Many of these stem from the work of J. Shultz, a German physician at the turn of the century, who may be viewed as a pioneer in the method of biofeedback. The European schools also reflect the influence of the great Swiss psychiatrist Carl Jung.

Jung's description of the ways in which various symbols in Oriental and Western religions and art recur through the ages as representative of basic human experiences is widely accepted. European mental imagery therapists have accepted the great importance attached to the inner world of the human being and to the complex underlying pattern of symbolic representation that is continuously manifested in this world, particularly in dreams; and they have made it a critical part of the interpretation of the contents of their patients' fantasies. In addition, the fact that daily experience does get translated by the individual into some form of symbolic imagery is taken as a basic assumption in most of these techniques. The mental imagery therapists do not actually attempt to retranslate the images produced by patients into more common language; they are content to let the images speak for themselves.

Let us take a closer look at how this method works in practice. A patient comes to a psychotherapist with a specific complaint—for example, recent headaches, bursts of anger and difficulties in his relationship with his fiancée. After taking a reasonably full history and ascertaining that the problem is likely to be psychological, the therapist begins training the patient in relaxation, using the well-known Jacobson method of progressive relaxation. This involves reclining on a couch, tensing muscles and then relaxing them, moving up the body from toes through the face in rhythmic sequence. Many people report this to be an extremely relaxing exercise and it is also widely used in the behavior modification therapies of American psychologists. Next the patient is encouraged to envision a particular scene as vividly as possible, and to try to maintain a sequence of imagery generated by this vision. In the case of men the first image encouraged may be that of a sword, while in the case of women, the picture of a vase is suggested. Clearly, this reflects a somewhat sexist orientation to intrinsic imagery, and it has Freudian overtones as well. These imagery exercises help the patient become accustomed to the production of images, and also provide the therapist with some clues as to how easily the patient can generate visual images.

Following various training exercises of this kind, the patient then embarks, at the suggestion of the therapist, on a series of imagery trips. "Trips" is literally the word the therapist uses. It is quite possible that our own use of the term for drug experiences stems from the earlier European use of a travel metaphor in connection with mental imagery therapy. A patient may be encouraged to imagine he is lying in a meadow, and then to picture himself moving along in the meadow, or perhaps flying up into the sky and traveling through the sky, or sometimes traveling down into the earth. The therapist, who is referred to as a "guide" or "operator," takes a relatively passive role. Having assigned a specific imagery task, he merely attempts to facilitate the patient's trip, occasionally asking a question to clarify the description of the sequence of images, or simply encouraging the patient to keep going. If a patient comes up against an obstacle. that arouses anxiety in the course of the imagined voyage, the therapist may suggest that he start over again, or suggest that he can help the patient continue by offering a magical prop that gets one through the difficulty. Often enough, for example, a patient in his imagery suddenly finds himself up against a huge rock that blocks his entire path; he tries to move around it, but at each side finds that it extends beyond his vision. Desperately, he hammers against the gray stone. In distress, he says, "I cannot go on. There is simply no way of going further; the huge gray rock blocks me."

At this point the therapist may intervene by suggesting, "Why don't you look down at your feet. Do you notice a little gold key? Pick it up and see if you can find a little lock into which it will fit."

The patient generally elaborates that image, searches the ground, and does indeed imagine a little key, which he inserts into a lock on the rock, so that the door swings magically open. He can then continue his fantasy journey inside a cave, which may yield other images.

The images that patients produce in the course of one of these trips are generally relevant, of course, to the major problem areas in their lives, but they are frequently cast in symbolic terms. For example, a patient who has many current problems because of early teasing by a vicious and embittered nursemaid may find that during an imagery trip this woman is represented as a witch or demon who torments him or tricks him into playing a child-like role. After confronting this frightening image again and again while undertaking several trips, the patient will often find that the monstrous figure from his past begins to lose its power over him; and the demonic woman turns into a harmless old crone. Sometimes the traveler kills off the frightening image with a weapon, but often enough he mollifies it or simply confronts it bravely and finds that it backs away.

In the course of the imagined trips narrated to the therapist the patient relives important parts of his life and begins to see his experience in a new perspective. It should be stressed that by and large, the therapist does not interpret the patient's experience in the way that a psychoanalyst might. The experience of the trip into this symbolic realm is felt to have its own essentially curative aspects. The therapist mainly keeps the patient on course, helps him face up again and again to frightening figures so that they gradually lose their intensity, and often suggests ways of circumventing anxieties, so that the patient can attain a fuller awareness of conflict areas.

The method I have been describing was developed by a French engineer, Robert Desoille, and was elaborated by psychiatrists and psychologists such as Drs. Roger Frétigny and André Virel. A particularly systematic approach in the use of mental imagery has been developed by Dr. Harscarl Leuner of the University of Göttingen, West Germany. Dr. Leuner, who calls his method "guided affective imagery," proposes that the patient go through the same series of ten images several times in the course of treatment. These images all represent major conflict areas in life, and each is the starting point for an imagery trip that may take up an entire psychotherapy session. These trips include:

1. Following a stream or river to its source, which often represents an attempt to come to the source of one's problems or to find one's way back to intimacy and warmth. The healing powers of water and the imagery associated with cool springs play an important part in this series.

2. Walking through a meadow. Here the patient is presumably close to a basic experience related to the mother and the sources of growth.

3. Climbing a mountain. In this imagery the patient can reflect his aspirations for achievement or his struggles to surpass others.

4. Encountering an ideal figure from one's life. Here the image is likely to be presented in symbolic form. Leuner cites the instance of a young woman who meets an elephant, which frightens her. Encouraged to confront the beast, she finally lies down and feels his foot pressing on her chest. To her surprise, the pressure is not painful and she no longer feels afraid. It turns out that the image she presented leads her to recall an incident from her childhood. When she was thirteen her father came into her bedroom, where she was pretending to be asleep. He put his hand on her breast and said, "Well, she certainly seems to be developing nicely." For years afterward, she had considerable guilt and confusion about what she took to be a sexual overture from her father. The imagery sequence with the elephant helped her to confront these fearful and long-hidden feelings.

5. To explore areas of sexual conflict, Leuner proposes that women begin their imaginary trip by picturing themselves on a lonely road trying to get a ride from a passing vehicle. For men, the sexual imagery begins with the picture of a rosebush. Americans may be somewhat confused about the sexual implications of this particular floral scene, but in Germany there is a very popular poem by Goethe, set to music by Schubert, called *"die Heidenröslein"* ("The Hedge Rose"). In it, a little boy who wants to pluck a lovely rose is warned by the rose that it has thorns, but he plucks it and ends up getting stuck. It has often seemed to me that this particular image would not be especially likely to generate sexual fantasies in American men, but a collaborator of Dr. Leuner's, Dr. Paul Kosbab, formerly at Virginia Commonwealth University Medical School, has been making use of the guided affective imagery approach in the training of medical students there, and says that they do indeed use the

rosebush scene to generate fantasy trips that have clear sexual implications.

One need not detail all of Dr. Leuner's images for the reader to grasp how their careful use can gradually help unfold a vivid diagnostic picture of the patient's problem areas.

It is important to note that many of the European mental imagery approaches have been applied to a wide variety of psychological disturbances, ranging from more classical neurotic conditions through various psychosomatic problems. To my knowledge, however, there has not been extensive use of these methods with psychotic patients. It seems to me especially important to call attention to the following points about the use of the mental imagery techniques as reflected in the various case reports, published largely in French, German and Italian. First of all, the treatment is considerably shorter than traditional psychoanalysis and generally yields very good results in the sense that symptoms disappear and the patient's life situation improves. The therapy trip itself, rather than the therapist's minimal interpretation, is the essentially ameliorative experience. Finally, a reading of the reports of what patients say as they produce a sequence of images, and describe the ongoing trip, suggests very strongly that the human capacity for producing elaborate and complex sequences of visual scenes—in effect, walking daydreams in the presence of the therapist—is truly remarkable.

AMERICAN ADAPTATIONS OF MENTAL IMAGERY TECHNIQUES. While the major thrust of the mental imagery movement has been in Europe, in the last decade there have been increasing usages of varieties of imagery techniques in this country. The technique of psychodrama, in which an individual's personal problems are reenacted on a stage with the help of trained "auxiliary egos" who play parent figures and other key individuals in his life, was introduced into this country in the 1930s by Dr. Jacob Moreno. This emphasis on overt enactment of fantasy has not really developed as a major movement. Instead, many of Moreno's early innovations have been incorporated into a variety of psychotherapy techniques such as group therapy, encounter group therapy, Gestalt therapy and T groups.

A brief example may point out how psychodrama works to take the private fantasies of an individual, make them public through reenactment, and then help to recast the imagery and anticipatory thinking of the individual into a more socially adaptive mold. Moreno describes the case of a boy of about seventeen who was arrested after an attempt to break into the White House either to meet with or perhaps to attack President Truman. The young man was considered severely mentally disturbed and referred to Saint Elizabeths Hospital in Washington, which has had an active psychodrama program for many years. At first very withdrawn, the youth was gradually able to present his problem to the group of patients and staff participating in psychodrama. He was provided with auxiliary egos, staff and patients who role-played members of his family and others whom he had encountered in his travels and efforts to make contact with the White House. In the reenactment of his terrifying attempt to somehow make his life meaningful, the young man began to see his life situation in a different perspective. He realized to what extent much of his behavior represented a conflict between himself and an aunt who was his guardian, and to whom he was emotionally tied in a deeply ambivalent fashion. Given opportunities to reexamine this situation, he began to change his picture of himself and his aunt, and he saw that many of his actions were attempts to overcome his dependency rather than to act in a truly heroic fashion. Once he realized this, and also could look at things from the perspective of his aunt's problems in dealing with a rebellious young man, his point of view was altered. He began to perceive more realistically what was possible for him and to set goals that were more socially appropriate and attainable. The psychotic aspects of his behavior disappeared, and by the termination of treatment he was launched on a training program toward the goal of becoming a commercial airline pilot.

Most cases are not nearly so dramatic as this one. Still, role-playing—including the technique requiring the individual to reverse roles and try to play the part of his parent or of his "enemy," so that he can change his own concept of these individuals and experience to some degree what they are experiencing—has now become a regular part of many forms of individual and group psychotherapy. Gestalt therapy, which has attained great popularity in recent years because of the exciting presentations of the late Dr. Frederick Perls, has incorporated into its format aspects of both psychodrama and the European mental imagery therapies. In Gestalt therapy, the emphasis is much more on the current life situation of the patient and his current perspectives and fantasies, and less on an effort to trace their origins. There is also much more stress on the individual's body posture and physical rigidities. Frequently such rigidities of movement or facial expression reflect inhibitions and blocks in the fantasy perspectives, which the individuals learned in earlier childhood and are still carrying around with them.

A technique that seems particularly influenced by the European mental imagery movement is the "inside the body trip," which is also used extensively in encounter groups and various Gestalt therapy or humanistic therapy approaches. A patient complaining of heart palpitations and problems in her experience of her body may be encouraged to relax and then to imagine herself going on a voyage into her own body, not unlike that in the science fiction movie *Fantastic Voyage*. The patient's own imagery serves as the basis for the trip and she may produce a sequence of images, one after another, as she sees herself within different organs, her throat, her lungs, her chest, her breasts. In the course of a trip like this, the patient may also become aware of particular body attitudes that are carry-overs of early experiences or childish fantasies, which have never been modified and have therefore led to distortions of her current self-awareness. Some of the examples given by William Schutz in his work on encounter groups make it clear that such imagery trips can often have very useful effects, not only in helping the patient gain more insight into his problems, but in actually relieving certain psychosomatic symptoms.

Still another popular form of psychotherapy is derived from the work of Eric Berne, whose transactional method of psychotherapy emphasizes (in a perhaps oversimplified version of neo-Freudian psychoanalysis) the various "games" or "scripts" that all of us play out in relation to other people. For example, the individual whose private script leads to the game of "schlemiel" may be the kind of person who, early in life, felt that the only way he could gain the attention and interest of others was to play a kind of clownish oaf. By enacting publicly his private fantasy of how to get by in life, this individual repeatedly engages in routines that call attention to him as a clown or mild incompetent, and win him sympathy at the same time that they provide him with excuses to be vulgar or inadequate. Such behavior relieves him of having to make a serious effort at effective social or emotional interaction. This kind of long-standing life script is sometimes referred to as an unconscious fantasy. Within a family setting, and sometimes even in a broader social arena, such fantasies often work well enough for the individual to become somewhat fixated in the role. Only later does he find that in the greater complexities of adult life, the situation leads increasingly to difficulties and problems which can only be cleared up through some form of direct psychotherapeutic intervention.

There are a host of other methods in use in America that involve forms of more or less direct imagery and fantasy or daydream approaches, as part of a humanistic or psychodynamic therapy orientation. Indeed, many of the quasi-religious movements, such as transcendental meditation or Zen Buddhism, in their emphasis on meditation and perceptual directness also call for certain kinds of focused imagery. Frequently a patient will be encouraged to imagine an object like a vase or a flower as vividly as possible and to limit all attention to a very thorough examination of the details of this very specific visual image. In effect, it is an attempt at highly focused attention, the exclusion of external competing stimuli and the training of one's capacities for private concentration. This may also lead to some control over certain biological rhythms and possibly even the alpha rhythms of the brain.

It is certainly true from research indications that people who have a rich imaginative life that they enjoy and feel some control over can enter more effectively into certain types of trance states or transcendental meditation. I would argue that even the kind of imagery that I have reported in my own daydreams, and the football fantasies I use to put myself to sleep, represent much the same kind of processes as hypnosis, on the one hand, and various forms of transcendental meditation, on the other. It is my impression that many of these phenomena about which there seems so much mystery are really relatively straightforward aspects of our human capacities for concentration and focused imagery. Man has evolved a complex faculty for rich and varied imagery and for anticipatory daydreaming, which is an important asset that can be used in a variety of situations. The crucial element is careful awareness and training. Without consciously intending it, the skilled daydreamer has apparently trained himself to greater control over these capacities than the average person. This may also be true of the skilled meditator or the yogi or Buddhist monk. For most people, "The world is too much with us; late and soon,/Getting and spending, we lay waste our powers . . ."

Under the pressures of daily demands many people find that exercises like meditation are a revelation of how much they can learn about their own thoughts and fantasies, and how much relaxation is to be attained by systematically shutting out either their worries or the constant exploration of the external environment. The practiced daydreamer or aesthetically oriented person may find such meditation experiences less necessary or dramatic in their implications.

The various uses of imagery in psychotherapy that we see in the mental imagery movement in Europe, and in its somewhat wilder variations in the many American psychotherapies, do require that we constantly evaluate the actual process itself. Unless we can tie the therapeutic efforts back to a scientific foundation, we run the risk of merely offering a great variety of techniques. Some of these may work some of the time with some people; but they may not have the consistency that is a touchstone of a truly scientific method. I believe it is possible that most of the imagery uses that one sees in the various humanistic games, or in the psychotherapeutic approaches described in this last section, produce their results for the following reasons:

1. For many people the very fact of looking more closely at their own fantasy and daydream processes is exciting and intriguing because they have, in effect, practiced avoiding these experiences from early childhood. They are greatly relieved and intrigued by the fact that in psychotherapy or in encounter groups they are encouraged to revive some of these long-suppressed patterns.

2. In addition to the novelty of the experience, there is important insight to be gained from explicating one's private daydreams and scripts. One begins to see the extent to which many of one's actions have indeed been governed by childhood fantasies that may no longer be appropriate to adult life, and one may also see the connection between these fantasies and the family situation in which one developed. This can lead to a broader perspective on one's role in the world.

3. In addition to these gains, it also becomes evident that one

can use imagery and fantasy to control and redirect one's own thoughts and images. This is an exciting and new experience for many people, who have somehow believed that their thoughts and daydreams come out of the blue and are frightening intrusions into their normal, "logical" thought processes. Once one perceives that one can indeed control one's thought, and yet *play* with thought in an active and interesting fashion, one has a greater sense of one's general powers as a human being.

The notion of control may be a key feature of the effectiveness of imagery and fantasy methods in psychotherapy. The methods I have just described focus more on the "total personality" and less on specific relief of symptoms. In this respect, these methods represent a marked contrast to the powerful movement known as behavior modification, which has developed in the last decade primarily in the United States and England, but is becoming increasingly influential on the international scene.

Imagery in Behavior Modification Therapies

SYSTEMATIC DESENSITIZATION. Behavior modification approaches to the amelioration of emotional disturbance and psychological symptoms derive from a somewhat different tradition than do the dynamic orientations. These methods look not to Sigmund Freud but to Ivan Pavlov, the great Russian physiologist who was the discoverer of the conditioned reflex. The most widely used of all behavior modification techniques for the amelioration of emotional problems is known as systematic desensitization, and sometimes as the method of treatment by reciprocal inhibition. It owes its present development to the work of Dr. Joseph Wolpe. The method has been applied especially in the treatment of irrational fears or phobias, but it has been expanded increasingly to deal with a great variety of other specific and fairly circumscribed symptomatic patterns that are part of most neurotic disturbances.

Basically, systematic desensitization involves a careful analysis of the nature of an irrational fear. Some people are afraid to ride in elevators, others to climb up to high places, others to mingle with large crowds in marketplaces or on subway platforms; and others are terribly distressed if they have to make a telephone call in a confining booth or must sit in a small waiting room with one or two other persons. While the psychodynamic therapies have emphasized the profounder meaning of these phobias in terms of early childhood conflicts about homosexuality or sexual capacities, etc., the behavior modification therapists are not interested in the history of the disturbance; they view it as an autonomous problem that needs to be eradicated for its own sake. They conduct a very careful inquiry to determine the range of situations in which the individual reports that he experiences anxiety. A hierarchy, or sequence of different images relating to the frightening event, ranging from the least to the most frightening scenes, is constructed as a first step in the treatment. The patient is then encouraged to engage in a profound relaxation exercise following the Jacobson method. While the patient is relaxed, he is confronted with the items in the hierarchy progressively. In theory, as each image is presented to a patient in this deeply relaxed state it loses a certain increment of its associated anxiety. Use of the hierarchy ensures that the individual is never faced with a situation in which his anxiety is greater than the degree of relaxation he is experiencing. If he should experience too much anxiety, he is encouraged to start back at earlier scenes in the hierarchy.

In a sense, these scenes are daydreams and vivid images based on the careful description by the patient of the kinds of situations that have been differentially frightening. A man who is afraid to ride on buses, for example, might begin using the fact that the least frightening level is just to think at home of the possibility that he may have to ride on a bus. This arouses a moderate amount of anxiety. The next most frightening image is going out of the house and walking toward the bus stop. Next in order might be the thought of waiting at the bus stop and watching the bus approach. Then would come actually having to step aboard the bus and pay the fare. By constructing such a hierarchy of increasingly frightening scenes, the individual pinpoints the exact sequence of fearfulness and then systematically eliminates the anxieties associated with each element in the total picture.

The critical thing to notice here is that the whole method, despite its behavioristic emphasis, essentially depends on the private imagery of the individual. In effect, the therapist merely establishes conditions of relaxation for the patient, and a systematic way for the patient to engage in the imagery. Basically, the images or the responses that will be desensitized to anxiety are developed by the patient himself, and are completely under his control.

There seems little question that this method of treatment has been remarkably effective in relieving phobias, particularly where they are not part of a massive and complicated neurotic pattern. What does this tell us with respect to daydreaming? Since the key feature of the treatment is the patient's ability to produce imagery and to carry out, in the presence of the therapist, the daydream about various events in his life, the effect of the treatment is in part a testimonial to the great human capacity for producing fantasy material with the power to modify behavior. So in a curious way, we come full circle. The behaviorists, who have been most critical of the emphasis by psychoanalysts and humanists on private experience and internal events in the personality, have ended up developing a treatment method that is particularly effective because it relies extensively on the imaging capacities of the patient!

In a variation on the systematic desensitization method, the relaxed patient is encouraged not only to produce the frightening scene but to balance it with an image of a very pleasant one. This use of positive imagery to weaken the effects of fearful situations or stresses can be traced back to an experiment carried out in a New York City hospital in the 1930s. Peptic ulcer patients trained to anticipate the occurrence of a stress situation, and then produce a state of relaxation by the use of positive fantasies, showed a remarkable recovery and remained symptom-free for several years, despite a long history of ulcers. A control group of patients who were not trained in the use of the positive imagery technique but received the same medical care did not exhibit a comparable resistance to the recurrence of symptoms. Almost all of them relapsed shortly after their discharge from the hospital.

The power of positive imagery, as one might call this technique, ought not to be taken lightly. It is not the same thing as simply saying nice things to oneself or pepping oneself up, as encouraged in a number of popular self-help books on mental health. Positive imagery seems to have a much broader effect. It involves, first of all, relaxing the patient and encouraging him to generate very vivid scenes that are associated in his mind with specific positive emotions such as joy or peacefulness. Quite often, people come up with scenes from vacations they spent at the seashore or on lakes or in wooded areas or on skiing trips. The extensive relaxation plus fixation on these positive images can create a state of private peacefulness that often will help to counteract the anxiety aroused by the thought of various phobic events. For example, in the case of a young male patient with whom I used this method, his phobia about loneliness and possible intrusion by the neighbors, and his excessive annoyance at any noise in the hallways of his apartment house or the corridors of his office building, were relieved relatively quickly although they had persisted for years in the face of more extended dynamic psychotherapy. A student of mine had a female patient with a dread of flying who was quickly able to confront the various stages of flying by the use of this procedure; she eventually made a number of successful flights after practicing this method on her own as well as in the treatment hour.

Extensions of the positive imagery method also provide opportunities for patients to learn how to distract themselves from the kind of recurring attention to a painful or frightening situation that reinforces its negative content. Part of treatment may include training people to develop a repertory of positive images to draw upon during periods of excessive stress.

AVERSIVE IMAGERY METHODS. Many people come to therapists because they find themselves engaging in behavior they are ashamed of, or that is illegal or likely to cause them great social difficulties. The most extreme examples of such behaviors are of course alcohol and drug addictions, various sexual deviations and acts of an antisocial nature such as compulsive stealing. One approach utilized in the behavior modification treatment of such conditions has been to provide the patient with an extremely negative experience at the same time that he imagines or actively participates in the unwanted behavior. The unwanted behavior will increasingly be associated with pain and distress and therefore will be less likely to be carried out in the future. Examples that have been widely publicized include electrically shocking men who are homosexually inclined as they watch pictures of nude males, to the point that even the initial flashing of a picture of a man generates distress on the part of the patient, who then gratefully flicks on the picture of an attractive female.

Since many of the techniques—mechanical or chemically induced shocks or the creation of nausea through drugs—are hazardous and complicated to perform, a number of behavior modification therapists have now moved more actively toward using the patient's own imagery capacities, rather than an external agent, to provide a repellent experience for someone who is trying to control an unwanted behavior. For example, in the covert sensitization method developed by Dr. Joseph Cautela of Boston College, a young man who is attempting to control a drinking habit may be encouraged to imagine himself going into a bar and asking for a drink. As he leans his elbow on the bar, he realizes he is immersing it in a pool of green vomit. In disgust, he withdraws his arm, only to realize that there is vomit all over the floor at his feet, and the stench is rising slowly around him. The bartender hands him the glass of liquor, but almost immediately he himself becomes sick and vomits over it, enveloped in the smell and seeing particles of half-digested food spraying all over his drink and hands as he stands there at the bar.

I don't believe it is necessary to continue with this image, if I still have any readers. Needless to say, cast in the setting of a psychotherapy session where he is being systematically trained in the use of such nauseating imagery, the patient becomes able to picture his unwanted behavior repeatedly in this noxious manner.

A young man I treated had a long history of homosexual activity, about which he was deeply distressed. He basically perceived himself as wanting a heterosexual life and family. The covert sensitization method was instituted after a fairly intensive course of psychoanalysis, and proved to be extremely effective. By joining offensive imagery to a careful presentation of imagery of the desired but unacceptable homosexual events, and following this with rewarding positive imagery associated with encounters with women, we were able to eliminate the patient's homosexual activity within a few months, and he moved rather naturally in the direction of a full and meaningful relationship with a woman.

OTHER IMAGERY TECHNIQUES IN BEHAVIOR MODIFICATION. It does not seem necessary to detail the many other variations of imagery used in behavior modification. Some methods, by systematically conjuring up reinforcing images, reward behaviors that the patient is trying to increase as part of his overall lifestyle. Other techniques involve the use of imaginary models, whom one sees going through desirable acts of various kinds; these models are intended to encourage the patient to try out new kinds of responses not attempted before. Many patients in traditional psychotherapies have tended to imagine that the analyst was accompanying them in a new situation and to model themselves on him. Symbolic modeling techniques derived from the work of Dr. Albert Bandura of Stanford University are used to help children and adults try out new kinds of attitudes and orientations in social behavior.

A method that has achieved some fame but is the subject of considerable controversy because of its possible harmfulness is the technique known as implosive therapy. This approach encourages the patient during a given session to imagine all the horrible consequences of a behavior about which he is frightened. The assumption is that since he imagines the worst and nothing happens, he will reduce his tendency to associate fear with this image in subsequent confrontations. While the method has had some successes, there are technical reasons for feeling that it may actually increase fear under some circumstances, and therapists are cautious about its wider use.

SOME BEHAVIOR MODIFICATION IMAGERY APPROACHES WITH CHILDREN. As the reader may recall from our chapter on child development, the use of make-believe and imagery methods in child training has certain positive advantages. It should also be clear from our discussion of adolescence that many adolescents who have not developed an active capacity for imaginativeness often are likely to find themselves engaging in overt acts of an antisocial nature that cause them to end up in difficulties. Recently a number of psychotherapists and specialists in behavior modification have experimented with a variety of methods for helping children enhance their imagery capacities and use them to control their behavior.

In the more traditional psychotherapeutic orientation, we have work such as that of Dr. Richard Gardner or Dr. Nathan Kritzberg, both child psychiatrists. Dr. Gardner encourages children to tell stories in the course of psychotherapy sessions, and then responds to the child's story with one of his own—based on what he has just been told—that helps the child resolve the conflict that may have emerged in the course of the child's fantasy. The therapist listens to the child's story carefully and then, rather than trying to give advice or resolve the conflict by a direct interpretation, which might be in too intellectual a form for the child to grasp, he reformulates the original story, but offers alternative possibilities or solutions to the problem, which the child can then try out.

Dr. Kritzberg's approach is somewhat similar but more elaborate, because it is built around a number of special board games that are played with children. By the use of these games and by systematic reinforcement of the child's production of story materials, Dr. Kritzberg greatly increases the likelihood that the child will be motivated and excited by the situation and will produce a variety of interesting stories. He deals with these stories by providing counter stories, which are perhaps somewhat less pointedly moralistic than those used by Gardner but convey in symbolic fashion reasonable dynamic solutions to the problems posed in the children's stories. I find Dr. Kritzberg's use of board games a particularly intriguing way of reaching the child between six and twelve who is familiar with this type of game and generally enjoys playing it, and who may not be as readily verbal or is possibly too old to engage in the more traditional forms of play therapy.

Both Dr. Gardner and Dr. Kritzberg, as I indicated, have been oriented toward a psychodynamic approach in their concept of the symbolic mode of communication and in their emphasis on the underlying conflicts in the child's behavior. The work of Dr. Donald Meichenbaum of the University of Waterloo in Canada offers a contrasting emphasis. Dr. Meichenbaum has been working particularly with hyperactive and semidelinquent boys who are given to a great deal of physical attack or antisocial behavior. He believes that many of these boys do not engage in sufficient private thought to lead them to recognize the consequences of their actions. He has therefore developed techniques to help them slow down their behavior, and to interpolate, in the gap between their awareness of desire and the overt action to accomplish that desire, a sequence of self-communication that spells out each of the steps involved. By slowing down the process thus, the children become aware more precisely of what they are doing, and also of some of the harmful consequences to others and to themselves that may accrue from this behavior. Evidence gathered by Dr. Meichenbaum and his various collaborators shows that this type of training can be accomplished quite rapidly with fairly tough kids and does lead to very effective modification of antisocial behavior.

The use of television programs such as "Mister Rogers' Neighborhood" or specialized materials that are prepared and shown on video tape, either to provide children with techniques for increasing the level of their make-believe play or to train teachers to serve as live models for make-believe play, is also being explored by a number of investigators. Dr. Dorothy Singer and I have been attempting to help nursery school children to enjoy their play more and also to find ways of enacting active and adventurous scenes without necessarily engaging in direct aggression toward the other children in the game.

The reader will realize there are many wide-ranging possibilities of utilizing our capacity for daydreaming and imagery to ameliorate emotional disturbance, control distressing behaviors and aid in the more effective development of the individual.

While we still have a great deal to learn about implementing many of these therapeutic techniques, improving their effectiveness and increasing our ability to train teachers or other clinical workers to use them, it should be obvious that there is, in our own imagery capacities, a vast untapped resource for psychotherapeutic good. While one cannot question the fact that certain drugs have been effective in easing fears and in quieting some of the more flamboyant psychotic behaviors that patients used to show in the past, the fact remains that we are pouring into the bloodstreams of such individuals a vast quantity of chemicals whose many side effects and long-term implications for the brain are not yet well understood. Surely it is more reasonable for us to put at least a comparable amount of thought, research money and effort into devising purely psychological approaches to developing our imagery and fantasy capacities as means of effective self-control. So far, the investment by the mental health establishment in such methods is extremely slight, yet there are good reasons to believe that they are potentially far more effective and socially meaningful than the drug therapies. We need to pay a good deal more respect to ourselves and to the fantastic properties of our own consciousness as a resource for effective human experience and social behavior.

CHAPTER 10

Daydreaming for Child Training, Education and Self-Development

Enhancing Make-Believe and Fantasy in Children

In this concluding chapter I should like to move somewhat away from the comforting scientific basis of the material I have presented on daydreaming, and provide a series of suggestions of a practical nature that may be of use to the reader. I have tried to maintain as many links as possible to actual research evidence, but accumulating the information that would forge *all* the links in the chain of evidence is beyond the capacities of most researchers at this time.

In proposing some ways in which what we have learned about daydreaming can be applied, I am hopeful that the reader will recognize the difference between a perceptive understanding of material of this kind and gimmickry or game-playing. For the person who is primarily oriented toward solving immediate day-to-day problems, I suggest that some of the skills and fun that can come from fantasy activity be applied with tempered judgment. As with any human capacity, making the most of one's daydreaming skills requires training, sensitivity to realities of one's immediate social situation and a cutting down of false aspirations. Daydreaming is only one of many important human functions and there are numerous other skills and capacities that have psychological significance.

THE PARENTS' ROLE. One way to begin to understand the fantasy capacities of children is by careful observation. Many parents do not really take the trouble to watch their children closely, as if through the eye of the psychological observer. This is important because of the general tendency to view psychologists as prone to excessive interpretation. When I talk of observing children, I mean recording carefully the actual sequences of behavior and the patterns of verbalization they show. The tendency too often is to move too quickly into a psychoanalytically oriented interpretation of spontaneous patterns.

A child who gnashes his teeth or growls and says, "I'm going to bite," is quickly assumed to be expressing oral-sadistic tendencies. Hasty labeling of behavior patterns as manifestations of extremely dubious hypothetical concepts must be avoided. It is bad enough that psychologists, psychiatrists and social workers fall into this error as much as they do. I would hate to see parents caught in the same tendency toward overanalysis.

In observing children's play one can make judgments that are tied closely to the actual behaviors and on which it is possible to get independent viewers to agree reasonably well. For example, if we limit ourselves to the fairly gross indications, such as laughter, crying or vigorous motor activity, the mood of the child can be described reasonably well.

Based on extensive observations and some formal research with children, one of our hypotheses is that fantasy or make-believe games are intrinsically enjoyable to most children. A first task for the parent, then, is to observe *systematically but unobtrusively* the spontaneous play of the child in the playpen, or bedroom, or in some similar situation. The things to look for are indications of make-believe play, the kinds of themes that are introduced, and the characters—whether imaginary, from stories that have been read to the children, from television or from their family experiences. Often, oddly named figures will come into the stories and it may be fun for the adult to try to speculate on their origins. But one need not feel anxious or concerned if there are imaginary playmates or references to strange events. A number of science fiction writers have demonstrated, in their occasional use of a child's play situation to introduce invasions of Martians or of child characters with sinister inclinations, that parents may frequently feel a certain creepy quality about the ongoing play of children. Perhaps this is because children in their accommodation processes often mimic adult experiences and in a sense hold up a mirror to the adult world.

Careful observation of the spontaneous play of children can therefore be useful in giving the adult some clues to major preoccupations in the child's experience, possibly indications of areas that are very troubling (such as overheard conversations between parents that frightened them or other adult concerns that probably ought not to be expressed before the children). Angry words between parents or threats that are made but not really meant are often taken literally by children. It is these situations that can come up in play and alert the parent to the possibility that the child may have been more deeply troubled by some event than had been realized.

It would probably be a mistake to interfere with the child at that point in the course of play. Spontaneous make-believe play is both precious and delicate in the preschool years, and has to be nurtured sensitively. The parent who feels that some of the overheard content needs to be addressed with the child ought to wait for some other moment, when the two are engaged more directly with each other, to mention the disturbing issue.

Another useful observation the parent may make on make-believe play is whether their children are finding sufficient content and themes for such games. Sometimes children seem at a loss as to how to carry further certain types of play or to vary the range of the content. They will show this by skipping rapidly from one game to the next, by evidences of anger or frustration, or by running constantly to the adult for support. Here is a point where rather than intervening immediately, a thoughtful person might plan to introduce more interaction between parent and child built around make-believe and fantasy or storytelling. The practice of reading to children at bedtime is probably one of the moments of greatest intimacy and enjoyment for the child. Most children have difficulty contemplating sleep. It is a strange land. The turning off of the lights and the play of shadows on the wall hold many fears and ambiguities. This is why many families develop rituals to make the bedtime sequence more routine and reassuring. One of these rituals can be the reading of a story or two—with very definite time limits set and a clear definition of the child's obligations to comply with the conditions.

Reading to a child has both the quality of giving that only an adult can provide and a sharing of enjoyment in the story and in the make-believe play as well. After all, the adult was once a child, and the revival of the fantasy material provides a pleasant recollection; there is a mutual positive emotion experienced.

In addition to bedtime rituals there are other occasions, on weekends or in the evening after meals, when the father or mother may take a child off alone and initiate some kind of make-believe game, or show him how to develop some type of fantasy activity with the toys that are available. This has to be done in such a way that the parent can quickly phase out his or her extensive involvement in the process. By introducing a variety of such games, a parent is increasing the child's repertory of make-believe activities that can either be played alone or used as a bridge with other children in nursery school or a day care center.

What types of content ought parents to present to their children in the form of fantasy and make-believe games? In general, it is important for the child to experience some of the same kinds of things that make up the adult's subculture. Make-believe stories based on common ethnic themes, on figures from American history or the cultural history of the parents are obviously desirable. In the use of such material, there seems no harm in emphasizing qualities of adventure, excitement, bravery, kindness, loving tendencies. The parent should be careful not to introduce material that is either cognitively too complex for the child or that carries with it any strong threat. Thus many fairy tales, such as those from Grimm, need to be read carefully before being presented to children, because they do involve a good deal of violence that can be very frightening if heard at too young an age. Here the parent has to use sensible judgment in defining the line between exciting adventure and potentially terrifying violence.

An important aspect of make-believe play has to do with the way in which it helps children develop a sense of the various roles that they will gradually have to undertake at later ages and in adult life. It can be shown that by two and a half years of age, boys and girls manifest striking differences in the content of their pretend play which suggest that there has already been inculcation in boys of more adventurous themes and in girls of more nurturant, caretaking motifs. A parent who is concerned about avoiding the extreme forms of sex typing that have been characteristic of our society in the past, and about which women have been complaining with good reason in the past decade, might give serious thought to changing the pattern of orientation in girls and boys. It should be acceptable for girls to launch into adventurous make-believe play without being teased as "tomboyish." By the same token, boys could benefit greatly by having the opportunity to engage in make-believe play around more socialized activities such as playing school, house and doctor.

Dr. Dorothy Singer and I noticed one of the boys at a nursery school marching around wearing a man's hat. Asked who he was pretending to be, he replied, "I'm Daddy. My daddy irons the clothes, does the laundry and cooks the macaroni." Clearly this boy was already being exposed to a father who was taking a much more active role in domestic affairs than most men do.

I do not believe that increasing the scope of make-believe play for boys around responsible household activities or the more socialized forms of play that generally characterize girls' fantasies will impede the normal development of the masculine role. Indeed, we need the greater acceptance by adults, both men and women, that the warrior role needs no encouragement in our society, and that by fostering it we push boys into excessive hyperactivity and aggression; and create as well the differences in cognitive skills that we find regularly between boys and girls at early ages.

If ultimately we are going to raise boys who will be prepared to marry the new breed of women, these boys will have to antici-pate that the women they encounter will not be combinations of sexy mother figures and domestic servants. The marriages of the future are going to demand more genuine sharing of all the details of child care and the running of a household, and mutual respect for each other's work skills.

This important point about increased commonality of roles for the sexes is not meant to suggest that one give up history and mythology or culture, which are so valuable a part of our fantasy experience. There is no reason why girls cannot continue to role-play at being princesses or mothers, nor boys enact knights, pirates or other adventurers. What is necessary is that parents become more open to allowing both sexes to move more freely into each other's role-playing within imaginative play situations, and also from time to time to encourage this cross-sex exploration of traditional roles.

Most important, parents should use their own imagination and allow themselves the luxury—indeed, view it as an essential—of helping their children develop fully their fullest capacities for cognitive enrichment. Make-believe and sociodramatic games represent important ways for the child to practice the various elements of the cultural roles that we all must eventually undertake. The alert parent should be sensitive to the value of this early play practice. Children seem happy when they are engaging in make-believe. Parents can make this a smoother passage to adult life by increasing the child's capacities for practicing a great variety of roles, so that when the time comes to make commitments to adult situations, children will have had a repertory of images on which they can later draw, and will not be intimidated about trying out new experiences.

MONITORING THE CHILD'S USES OF TELEVISION. A very important area in which the parent needs to play some role is the child's television viewing. Television is now an inevitable and permanent part of our lives. Most children begin watching before the age of two, and between two and four this form of stimulation undoubtedly becomes a critical part of their entire cognitive repertory. The parent who tries to limit drastically children's viewing of television is running the risk of establishing conditions of tyranny over the child and of separateness from other children; and this must be weighed against the potential benefits the parent assumes will accrue from the reduction in television viewing time.

Although we have very little formal research data on this subject, it does appear that to some extent television viewing *at moderate levels* acts as a significant stimulant to the imaginative capacities of children. It provides them with a much greater amount of material, novel creatures, interesting combinations of music and words, and exposure to far-off countries and different customs, all of which undoubtedly lead to an enrichment of the assimilated cognitive schema of the child. At the same time this greater enrichment *must* take place within some kind of organized setting. Here again, the role of the parent in providing information to the child about the meaning of different material on television, or telling stories or reading books to the child that provide a framework into which he can fit this material, is crucial. Otherwise much of the material from television may be assimilated in disorganized or faulty fashion and in ways that may not be as useful in later life.

There is also the likelihood that some of the features that are presented on the television screen may be lost on children whose attention span is limited, unless there is some feedback from the parent. In our research, described earlier, on the "Mister Rogers' Neighborhood" program, viewed by our nursery school children, we found that this sensitive but low-key program was particularly effective if an adult sat in the room with the children and interacted with the program from time to time, thus encouraging the children to respond to some of Mister Rogers' suggestions.

Parents have a real responsibility to pay attention to the kinds of television materials their children are confronting daily. Indeed, many parents find themselves caught up in some of the children's shows themselves and enjoying the material. This mutual enjoyment of well-chosen shows has a strongly positive effect on the children. It makes it possible for the parents to talk to them subsequently about some of the episodes or adventures they both saw, thus enriching the material for use in private make-believe play.

In contrast, the child who watches alone and is relatively unsupervised may find himself exposed to many kinds of complex adult material, some of which may be frightening and confusing or tend to provoke aggressive imitation. The very popular "Batman" and more recently "Kung Fu," among boys in particular, are examples of violent programs that are supported either by adult encouragement or by the failure of adults to supervise what their children watch. Many aggressively predisposed children imitate violent acts they witness on these shows, acts which outside of a make-believe context can actually lead to dangerous battles between children.

In addition, unsupervised viewing will expose children to particularly frightening scenes. As mentioned earlier, adolescents enjoy monster movies because they have enough differentiated cognitive structure to recognize them as unreal, yet retain just enough uncertainty to share in the fearfulness before finally laughing it off. But younger children are likely to believe what they are watching. Even if adults dissuade them later from accepting the reality of these frightening events, they will already have begun to assimilate the material into their limited cognitive schema. Night terrors and bizarre and weird fantasies and dreams can haunt them for years to come.

One must be especially careful in connection with animal stories. While children love them and identify easily with the animals, there is research evidence that programs in which an animal is harmed or in real danger are very frightening to children. Very young children should not watch them until they seem ready to deal adequately with the threats to Lassie or the other animals pictured. Adventure movies that take place in earlier periods and involve some stylized violence, such as knights jousting, or films of exploration and adventure, seem reasonably comprehensible to children between four and six but are out of their ken much earlier. A program in which an adult figure talks directly with the child may be a good early start. "Mister Rogers' Neighborhood," for example, deals with many of the frightening situations children confront—going to the dentist or doctor, the anger of adults, fears of losing teeth or being flushed down the drain—in an eminently sensible and apparently quite meaningful way.

Parents should also pay attention to commercials and help the child distinguish between reality and fantasy. Commercials are very artful at persuading children that the toys and games being merchandised are much larger and more lifelike than they turn out to be in reality. A panel of psychologists and child care specialists has been working recently to develop standards for children's commercials that take into account young children's limited ability to separate fantasy and reality. But careful monitoring by parents is most critical.

I have gone into detail on the question of television viewing because it is my experience that this profoundly influential area is being grossly neglected in our educational system. Parents have had very little help in understanding what to look for and how to enhance children's experience in television and movies. Indeed, parents lacking funds for baby-sitters often take their children to movies that are probably extremely frightening and beyond their capacities, only to realize the mistake later when they are awakened in the middle of the night by the screams of a child in the midst of a nightmare.

Parents, after all, have usually had no special training for their role. For many adults, spontaneous play with their own children is often not a natural thing. Some of our work on the uses of television in day care centers, and also in studies of make-believe play, have led us to consider various approaches not only to guiding teachers but to training parents themselves to engage in a variety of playlike interactions with their children.

A final word about the relationship of the parent to the play of the child. We are increasingly concerned about the fact that the educational process itself somehow detaches young people from contact with children and from preparation for the role of effective parent. It seems to us that there ought to be built into the high school and college curricula many more opportunities for young people to assume caretaking roles with children and in fact with other dependent persons in the society, under supervision that will present some technical methods of interaction, which will stand them in good stead later on. This is all especially necessary for those young people who may be interested in fields in which human relationships are not a primary part of their work, for they are still likely to end up being parents as well as engineers, technicians or bookkeepers.

An important feature of the relationship between the parent and the child, which derives not only from imaginative play but from many other kinds of mutual play situations, such as board games with rules and sporting activities, has to do with the opportunity of the child to identify effectively with adults of both sexes. There are many ways in which the identification of child and parent is enhanced, including the sharing of a variety of communications and pleasant interactions. To the extent that there is any merit in psychoanalytic concepts that stress the importance of identification in the development of a healthy and adaptive ego, then the availability of at least one parent who is benign, loving and close to the child is critical.

THE EDUCATOR'S ROLE IN DEVELOPING IMAGINATION. If I have placed a large burden on the parent in the socialization of the child, it is because I believe the parent is indeed the critical individual in the child's development, and it would be folly to think that surrogates such as day care centers can ever provide a true substitute. Nevertheless, it is also true that more and more families are made up of working parents and that children are put into group situations at earlier ages than ever before, supervised for four to eight hours at day care centers. Our interviews and observations of a variety of day care center teachers and workers suggest that however eager they are to be useful and pleasant to the children, many lack spontaneity and the ability to move easily with the child into a variety of fantasy games. All too often, what happens to the child placed in a center at ages two to four is that he or she becomes part of a moving and shifting multitude in which there are constant changes in the sequence and direction of play. It is hard for the child to establish phases of the relatively sustained concentrated activity that eventually develops into the more general style of concentration, organized play and cognitive focus that will soon be demanded of him in the first grade.

The day care center and nursery school present early opportunities to begin socializing children into play and game situations that they can enjoy and involve themselves in quite fully;
and that will have, in addition, a preparatory quality for the
kind of "as if" behaviors that will later be expected of them in
the school setting. Again the question is one of training staff to
bring out their own latent imaginative capacities, and to provide
them with the specific approaches and skills they can use to establish an enjoyable setting for make-believe play. With Dr.
Dorothy Singer I have been working recently on sets of play
materials, exercises and games for make-believe play in children.
Some of the exercises begin simply with having the children
imagine little sounds and sights, such as the wind blowing
through trees or a flower growing. Then the children are encouraged to imitate different animals or voices. They can be given
simple props and shown how these can be used for more elaborate series of movements, such as the imitation of the flight of an
airplane.

Depending on one's direction, one can set up for the children
exercises in the area of imagery that may be, on the one hand,
specifically cognitively oriented and prepare the child for reading
experiences, or that may be more dynamically oriented. A useful
and enjoyable set of such exercises is found in a book entitled
Put Your Mother on the Ceiling by Richard de Mille. Dr. de
Mille, who is a California psychologist specializing in imaginative play, comes naturally to the area of fantasy since he is the
son of the famous director of film spectacles Cecil B. de Mille,
certainly a man who translated his fantasies into a popular
medium. One exercise in the book is a game called "Boo!" Here
Dr. de Mille focuses his attention on helping the children develop their imagination as a means of coping with the many
frightening experiences they have in the dark or during the
night. They are encouraged to pretend they are awake or asleep
and to alternate these roles. Then they are given opportunities to

practice being afraid and not being afraid. From there they move to exercises of specific fears they may have, such as being locked in a closet or having something large run toward them out of the closet door. Then they are given an opportunity to practice being something scary themselves. This game continues over a period of time so that they test both sides of the experience and eventually realize that they have some control over the process.

One can move from exercises like these to establishing broader contexts for make-believe play. A game can involve a pirate burying a treasure and then having others look for it, engaging in various adventures along the way. Or a game can consist of an imaginary boat trip, perhaps using a prop of blue crepe paper spread out, as Dr. Freyberg did in her research, with pipe cleaners to represent sailors and Playskool blocks for boats. The children can be encouraged to practice different voices and to imitate the sounds of the wind blowing or the thunder crackling.

The teacher should begin the game, set up conditions for its play and then back out of the situation after fifteen minutes or half an hour of such involvement. It is extremely important that the children see opportunities for themselves to engage in these games privately.

Our experience at nursery schools has indicated pretty clearly that within two weeks of such daily half-hour training periods, children show a considerable increase in their spontaneous make-believe play. The group atmosphere changes in the direction of much more varied, interesting and enjoyable interaction among the children, and in their solitary play as well. Parents who were unaware of the specific conditions of our experiment were struck by the greater enjoyment and imaginative qualities the children were showing within a few weeks.

A word must also be said about the role of the nursery in continuing to foster certain sex role differences that continue the stereotypes of the role of boy and girl, rather than encouraging a more genuine independent development. Many nursery school and day care centers have their separate "doll corner" and "block corner," which tend to support a firm division of the sexes. Boys are allowed to be more rambunctious and girls are called to task for lively activities. Some of our interviews with nursery school teachers suggest that though in their personal lives they want very much not to be "type cast" for the traditional female role, they are still not prepared to allow their young charges leeway in developing overlapping roles in their spontaneous play. All too often one observes a teacher approach a young boy who has isolated himself for an elaborate private make-believe game, and try to get him to join a larger boys' group. The child may go along, with some reluctance, but the teacher may be doing him a disservice despite the best of intentions.

I should stress that I am not urging that teachers be trained to be play therapists. Indeed, I think such an effort dangerous, because it can involve them in overinterpreting behavior psychodynamically. The games and exercises in imaginative play that I have been describing, and flexibility in role modeling, seem to me a much more natural part of the curriculum.

At this time nursery school teachers tend to be women. This is unfortunate indeed, because it could well be that we need many more men in early childhood education as well as in the early elementary school grades. With male teachers, boys would find more positive identifications and better accept the cognitive and emotional or imaginative characteristics of school. The greater availability of young men as teachers would also help greatly in dispelling some of the queasiness our society experiences about homosexuality and the sharply delimited male-female role functions. Further, it would provide the children with male models whose activities are clearly quite different from athletics and aggression. Female teachers often either scold boys for their activities, causing them to feel resentful of female authority and somewhat inferior in the academic setting, or else (accepting the traditional female view of the aggressive male) subtly encourage boys to be aggressive and tough, thus impeding their development of a capacity for attentiveness and self-control, necessary for early acquisition of cognitive skills. As day care centers increase in the next decades and we begin to pay more serious attention to early education (a field that Americans have neglected much more than many of the Western European or Socialist-bloc countries), it is incumbent on parents to insist that schools seek to employ more men and introduce training programs that will genuinely prepare boys for the new kind of relationship they will need if they are to get along with more liberated females of the species.

In the later preschool and kindergarten years, make-believe play and games tied to the exploration of novel experiences and settings can generate increased vocabulary and be linked to learning materials that encourage reading and arithmetic. Games like "store" or "auto mechanic," or adventure situations that also require some use and recognition of letters and numbers, may be extremely important techniques for moving children into the more formal school situation.

In response to the recent research on learning in children that supports the significance of imagery as an aid to acquiring new information, teachers might well emphasize a variety of imagery exercises as part of the curriculum. Some teachers already use this technique to teach vocabulary. It could be elaborated even further and made a more regular part of the curriculum by using some of the methods of imagery practice that have been developed by people like Dr. de Mille. Practice in imagery and make-believe will also help the child deal with some of the materials in his textbooks. After all, even the simplest arithmetic examples presented to children take the form of an "as if" situation. If the problem says that "Mr. Brown is selling ten yards of ribbon at three cents a yard and Betty needs only eight and a half yards," the child is already required to suspend reality to enter into the situation; indeed, the form has been devised because many children find it enjoyable. One could take this a step further by encouraging children to act out many of these situations directly, and to experience the rewards of getting the problems right through some variety of systematic reinforcement program.

Even at the older grade levels children retain a strong interest in make-believe, despite the fact that they may have been humiliated into suppressing its overt manifestations. Again, good teachers instinctively recognize the value of little plays in class. Children from poor socioeconomic backgrounds often are reached especially well if they can become involved in a dramatic production in which even the less articulate children play useful roles. There is a great deal of material in the classroom that lends itself to playlet expression. In addition, the sociodramatic format can become a basic training in a variety of early citizenship roles.

Role reversal, for example, is an especially useful method of training people to recognize the feelings of others in a given social situation. The child may be asked to enact the role of himself asking a parent for money to go to the movies or for permission to stay out later at night. Another child is assigned the role of the parent. After experiencing what it is like to be in another's shoes, the children can be asked to reverse positions. The child who has thought his demands incontrovertible begins to realize what the parent may be going through. He may not only gain a better perspective on how to approach the parent and obtain what he wants, but will also perceive the parent as something other than an ogre. And there is a further benefit that may accrue from such training in empathy through sociodramatic means. The research of Drs. Norma and Seymour Feshbach of the University of California at Los Angeles indicates that children who are capable of empathy—that is, who are able to experience more of the feelings of other people—are also less likely to show overt aggressive behavior or initiate physical attacks on others. Again, all these methods seem to tie together as means of increasing the complexity of a child, so that he can make a more appropriate response in a greater number of situations rather than relying primarily or excessively on avoidance or aggression.

There are two major characteristics of the cognitive development of a child that need to be viewed as a part of normal growth. One of these consists of skills in convergent thinking and behavior. This is the sort of thinking that is evaluated primarily by intelligence or achievement tests. It involves producing the single right answer or producing a set of responses to questions for which the society expects a relatively uniform reaction. Clearly spelling or arithmetic involves such processes. On the other hand, there are many aspects of human experience and adaptive behavior that call for diversity and the ability to shift away from a limited set. These processes, which Professor J. P. Guilford has labeled "divergent production," are also an important part of what education ought to enhance. The capacity for daydreaming is a special instance of this basic divergent functioning. There has perhaps been overemphasis in some books on the fostering of creativity in children, as if creativity were a panacea for many difficulties of adult life. I prefer to take a more limited view, and argue that divergent processes like daydreaming are important parts of the overall armamentarium of the growing person, along with the convergent skills.

It is certainly true that many people whom society evaluates as highly creative adults showed strong early indications of divergent processes. College students who have already demonstrated creativity by production of artistic or literary works (which were so regarded by their teachers or were published or shown publicly) have proved on inquiry to have had a considerable tendency to daydreaming or imaginary companions in early childhood. Biographical accounts of famous individuals in the creative arts suggest similar early expressions. Goethe was given a puppet theater to play with as a child and he spent long hours entertaining himself.

The private value of fantasy experiences is movingly attested to by Goethe in one of his last and most moving poems, the preface to the complete version of *Faust*. In it he describes how the images of his characters from the past returned to haunt him and to create for him a reality more immediate than his present life. Dickens, too, revealed how caught up he became in the characters of his novels and how exciting he found the process. When he finished a book, he said that he felt as if he were "dismissing some portion of himself into the shadowy world where a crowd of the creatures of his brain are going from him forever. . . ."

Very few children in school are likely ever to come close to being creative geniuses in their adult lives, but they can experience some of the same excitement and pleasure as they grow if encouraged in the use of the divergent processes of their brain. The popularity of stories on television makes it clear how much the hunger exists in human beings for such divergent experiences. If we allow children to practice and play with their own divergent capacities at an earlier age, it is very likely that they will tolerate a much wider range of thoughts and story lines than the somewhat limited fare currently available to them.

Personal Development Through Control of Daydreaming

So far I have been emphasizing the development of the capacity for daydreaming in the growing person. What about the adult? Daydreaming skills can be fostered and employed adaptively by the average individual, even if he or she lacks the benefit of the training opportunities I proposed earlier in this chapter. For most people, unless they are caught in an unremitting grind of poverty and near-subsistence existence, the world today has opened unusual avenues for leisure, travel, individual hobbies and aesthetic appreciation. Television and the movies, opportunities for travel, do-it-yourself skills and a greater diversity of types of work, all offer a basis for a richer and more varied storage of material in our brain, which can become the basis for more complex fantasies.

Recently there has been increasing attention to enhancing our capacities for inner awareness. Long ago John Dewey endorsed activities such as those exemplified in the work of Dr. F. M. Alexander, who developed special training exercises in self-awareness. Aldous Huxley, in many of his articles and novels, urged that man take advantage of his potentialities and look to himself both for creativity and modes of relaxation. In his novel *Island,* Huxley describes a society that attempts to build self-awareness into the fabric of its play, work and education. On his imaginary tropical island the myna birds are trained to say "Attention!" and thus alert the people to becoming more aware of their own thought, so as to engage in fuller contemplation both of the detail and beauty of the environment and of their own fantasies and images.

We need to build into ourselves a series of alerting myna birds, so that we pay closer attention *each day* to the fleeting fantasies and other divergent processes of our brain. Almost every individual could benefit simply by keeping a log of his dreams for several weeks. One doesn't have to be a psychoanalyst to notice that certain themes or contents or characters crop up again and again. Apart from the recognition of important motives and interests that will become apparent, one will suddenly become aware of the great diversity and richness that goes on inside each of us. This is fascinating in itself. One night we may be in our old homestead in another state or country, another night we may find ourselves engaged in an adventurous flight to the moon, another night we may be involved in an odd sexual encounter with a stranger, still another night may reflect some peculiar interchangeability of various relatives or friends. Examination of our ongoing dreams or fantasies may stimulate us to use these capacities more effectively for trying out new situations in the future, or for contemplating new possibilities in our work or in our life planning. William Gordon developed the concept of *synectics,* which has encouraged engineers and industrial planners to rely on their own symbolism and fantasy capacities in helping them solve specific problems in their work.

It is important to recognize limitations, of course. I do not believe dreams necessarily foretell the future or that one's unconscious processes inevitably predict where one has to go. But I do believe that dreams or fantasies can signal a strong need or desire, and lead one to assess chances of fulfillment. Unconscious processes represent a playful combination of possibilities which most of the time we tend to reject too quickly in the course of our busy workaday life.

An important thing our dreams and daydreams can make us aware of is the value of the concreteness in our experience, which we ordinarily pass over by relying on clichés or stereotyped phrases. As children we were truly alert to the smell of another person or to the roughness of texture of our grandfather's skin when he picked us up to kiss us. Many of the current humanistic, Oriental or encounter-derived exercises and meditation methods, such as Zen or Yoga, reflect an effort to recapture this concreteness. As the research by Dr. Caroline Spurgeon has demonstrated, one of the bases of Shakespeare's greatness as poet and playwright is his use of imagery involving the greatest range of taste, touch and smell as well as vision and hearing modalities. We delight in Falstaff or Caliban because their language or the language of others describing them makes us feel their reality through the sense of smell or taste or touch. Falstaff is referred to as a "tub of guts" and Prince Hal talks of his "unbuttoning himself" after meals; immediately we have a vivid picture of this fat knight belching loudly and loosening his clothing after gorging himself on a table groaning with viands. Caliban in *The Tempest* describes the strange music of his island, and for a moment we ourselves seem to hear the lovely sounds and surrender to the same sense of peace and illusion, as he concludes:

. . . in dreaming
The clouds methought would open, and show riches
Ready to drop upon me, that, when I waked, I cried to dream again.

In general, everyone's dreams and daydreams evoke the magic of earlier experiences transformed in imagery that only artistically oriented persons are customarily believed to project. In this sense, we all are poets and artists in our fantasies. While I am certain that the daydreams or night dreams of a Shakespeare or a James Joyce are far more complex and rich in illusion than those of most people, I would still be willing to argue that many of us come much closer to artistic creativity—at least in the diversity of association and the concreteness and variability in modalities we experience in these fantasy realms—than we realize. All it takes is a certain amount of attention for us to become aware of how much is really going on inside ourselves. Research evidence in psychology suggests that we store a tremendous amount of material in some mysterious form through the operation of our brain, and that much of this material is stored in an *active* form which has constantly to be "stirred around." Our memory is not simply an inert storage box, like a computer's, but a system in constant motion. We have available to us many, many unusual combinations of images and associations, only a small percentage of which we notice or use.

Again a note of caution. Paying attention to our dreams or fantasies is not going to lead inevitably to our becoming good writers or creative artists. I remember that shortly after the attack on Pearl Harbor in December 1941, I had a dream during which I wrote a poem. I got up in the middle of the night with great excitement and wrote down the words, feeling that I might have composed the great song-anthem of Americans embarked on this new, perilous adventure. When in the morning I read what I had written, there certainly was a poem there and it was based on the image of the dream, in which I seemed to see marching across a map of the Philippines the three characters in the painting *The Spirit of '76*—the fife player and the two drummers. The recurrent line at the end of each quatrain was "And they are marching yet!"

In sum, the poem was dreadful, although it was technically a real poem. This merely demonstrated that I was not a Coleridge, who presumably wrote about the pleasure dome of Kubla Khan upon awakening from a dream. But it was still an exciting thing to do, to write a poem during one's sleep, and I was the better for it even if I had enough sense in daylight to recognize its ineptitude.

Our lives can be tremendously enriched if we attend to our private processes and allow ourselves the leisure of playing them out for only a few minutes every day. Often, the emphasis of various schools of meditation and exercises derived from Yoga or Zen Buddhism is on helping an individual to obtain a more creative perception of the outside world, to abolish desire and intense longing for the unattainable or for greedy acquisition at the cost of self-respect. Without minimizing the intrinsic value of these ancient philosophical orientations, I want to call attention to the fact that sensitivity to our own ongoing thought processes may accomplish much of this task relatively easily, if we allow ourselves the leisure to remember our dreams or notice our play of fantasy in a relaxed state. This means that we have to sit quietly for a few minutes, or look off into space with eyes shut or focused on a blank wall. On awakening in the morning we will find it worthwhile to lie quietly for a minute or two so that we can fix more precisely in our mind the fleeting dream with which we all awaken. As the chapter on psychotherapeutic uses of imagery has suggested, if one can use a relaxation exercise or recline in an easy chair or couch for a few minutes, the likelihood of vivid imagery and more elaborate daydreaming is greatly increased. Under such circumstances one can indulge in a brief fantasy trip.

Much of our pleasure and excitement in life comes from the recollection or anticipation of exciting experiences and events. Unfortunately busyness and enforced extroversion allow us too little time to get the full pleasure from our own contemplative capacities. We are so bombarded by a tremendous range of stimuli every day that we have scarcely time to elaborate on a particular line of thought or implication before new disasters or desires are presented to us. At a football game last week I observed what was a thrilling and beautifully executed pass play by the University of Pennsylvania quarterback and one of his halfbacks. As the play ended I suddenly realized that since I was actually at the game, I could not see the televised "instant replay" of this exciting moment. But really it was not gone and still is not gone; I can reconstruct it more or less at will and take some pleasure in how well it was done.

Recognizing that our daydreams are in a sense an extension of our childhood capacities for enjoyable play, we can continue this spirit of play and use it for many purposes in our daily life. We have of course to build into it a self-checking system that keeps us from driving off the road or bumping into objects along our walking route. But if we can fit a certain amount of playful daydreaming into our sequence of activities it will serve as pleasant pastime and additional resource.

The art of successful daydreaming lies in the smooth shifting from external awareness to inner concentration. Such timing makes for an enriched and varied stimulus pattern that keeps the emotion of surprise high for longer periods, and also increases the likelihood that we will experience joy by reducing the discomfort of both monotony and anger. To the exploratory approach to day-to-day activities or scenes, one can add exploration *of* and *through* thought and, as well, a touch of gaiety to one's work that will make for much more zestful living. Philosophers, such as Gaston Bachélard, have proposed that the dimension of the unreal in our experience is a critical aspect of our ultimate reality. What is most truly human about man, what is perhaps his greatest gift derived from evolution and perhaps his greatest resource in his mastery of the environment and of himself, is his capacity for fantasy. By dreaming man can examine the alternatives that inhere in every moment. The capacity for make-believe provides us with a power over our environment and an opportunity to create for ourselves novelty and joy.

In his deeply moving drama *The Iceman Cometh,* Eugene O'Neill portrayed powerfully how stripping men of their illusions leads them only deeper into despair and anguish amid their miserable surroundings. But our capacity for inner contemplation and fantasy is certainly not limited to illusion. Attention to our own experiences and dreams brings us into contact with the pettiness and evil within us, with our doubts and failures of the past, and the wishful deceptions or vengeances of the future that flit across our consciousness. Our lives are certainly fraught with impending dangers, with horrors and with the inevitability of death. The daydreamer is therefore not immune to an awareness of suffering and to the tragedy inherent in life itself. But greater enrichment is also part of our human potential and daydreaming is a fundamental means of such enrichment. The practiced daydreamer has in a sense the best and worst of two worlds. What his increased inner capacity offers him is a fuller sense of being intensely alive from moment to moment and this is worth the frequent pain of a deeper self-awareness.

References

GENERAL READINGS

(These include extensive bibliographies for the reader interested in pursuing the issues in relevant technical literature.)

Klinger, E. *The Structure and Function of Fantasy*. New York: John Wiley & Sons, 1971.
Singer, J. L. *Daydreaming*. New York: Random House, 1966.
———. *The Child's World of Make-Believe*. New York: Academic Press, 1973.
———. *Imagery and Daydream Methods in Psychotherapy and Behavior Modification*. New York: Academic Press, 1974.
———. "Daydreaming and the Stream of Thought." *American Scientist*, 1974, 2, 4, 417–425.
———. "Navigating the Stream of Consciousness: Research in Daydreaming and Related Inner Experience." *American Psychologist*, 1975, in press.

CHAPTER REFERENCES

CHAPTER 1

Green, G. H. *The Daydream: a Study in Development*. London: University of London Press, 1923.
Humphrey, R. *The Stream of Consciousness in the Modern Novel*. Berkeley: University of California Press, 1968.
James, W. *The Principles of Psychology*. New York: Holt, 1890.
Lindner, R. "The jet-propelled couch" in *The Fifty-Minute Hour*. New York: Holt, Rinehart, & Winston, 1955.

Rapaport, D. "The Structure of Psychoanalytic Theory." *Psychological Issues*, 2 (2). New York: International Universities Press, 1960.

Spurgeon, C. *Shakespeare's Imagery and What It Tells Us.* Cambridge: Cambridge University Press, 1935.

Steinberg, E. R. *The Stream of Consciousness and Beyond in* Ulysses. Pittsburgh: University of Pittsburgh Press, 1973.

Symonds, P., and Jensen, A. *From Adolescent to Adult.* New York: Columbia University Press, 1961.

Tomkins, S. *Affect, Imagery, Consciousness.* 2 vols. New York: Springer, 1962, 1963.

CHAPTER 2

Foulkes, D. *The Psychology of Sleep.* New York: Charles Scribner's Sons, 1966.

Head, H. *Aphasia and Kindred Disorders of Speech.* 2 vols. Cambridge: Cambridge University Press, 1926.

Kleitman, N., and Dement, W. (1957a) "Cyclic Variations in the EEG During Sleep and Relation to Eye Movements, Body Motion, and Dreaming." *EEG*, a: 673–690. (1957b) "The Relation of Eye Movements During Sleep to Dream Activity: An Objective Method for the Study of Dreaming." *Journal of Experimental Psychology*, 53: 339–346.

Silberer, H. "Report on a Method of Eliciting and Observing Certain Symbolic Hallucination Phenomena." In D. Rapaport (ed.), *Organization and Pathology of Thought.* New York: Columbia University Press, 1951.

Sullivan, H. *Clinical Studies in Psychiatry.* New York: W. W. Norton, 1953.

Ullman, M. "Dreams and Arousal." *American Journal of Psychotherapy*, 1958, *12*, 222–233.

CHAPTER 3

Feger, G., and Segal, B. "Daydreaming and imagery correlates of college marijuana users." *Journal of Alcohol and Drug Education*, 1974, *17*, (3).

Frazier, E. Franklin. *The Black Bourgeoisie.* Glencoe, Ill.: Free Press, 1957.

Fusella, V. "Blocking of an External Signal Through Self-Projected Imagery: the Role of Inner-Acceptant Personality Style and Categories of Imagery." Unpublished doctoral dissertation, City University of New York, 1972.

Guilford, J. P. *The Nature of Intelligence.* New York: McGraw-Hill, 1967.

Jessor, R., Jessor, S., and Finney, J. "A Social Psychology of Marjuana Use: Longitudinal Studies of High School and College Youth." *Journal of Personality and Social Psychology*, 1973, *26*, 1–15.

McCraven, V., and Singer, J. L. "Some Characteristics of Adult Dreaming." *Journal of Consulting Psychology*, 1961, *51*, 151–164.

Meskin, B., and Singer, J. L. "Reflective Thought and Laterality of Eye Movements." *Journal of Personality and Social Psychology*, 1974.

Pytkowicz, A., Wagner, N., and Sarason, I. "An Experimental Study of the Reduction of Hostility through Fantasy." *Journal of Personality and Social Psychology*, 1967, *5*, 295–303.

Sarason, S. "Projective Techniques in Mental Deficiency." *Journal of Personality*, 1944, *13*, 237–245.

Schaefer, C. "Imaginary companions and creative adolescents." *Developmental Psychology*, 1969, *1*, 747–749.

Segal, B., and Singer, J. L. "Daydream Patterns, Personality Traits and Drug Usage in College Freshmen." Manuscript in preparation, 1974.

Shaffer, L. *The Psychology of Adjustment*. Boston: Houghton-Mifflin, 1936.

Snow, C. P. *The Two Cultures and the Scientific Revolution*. New York: Cambridge University Press, 1959.

Starker, S. "Daydreaming Styles and Nocturnal Dreaming." *Journal of Abnormal Psychology*, 1974, *83*, 52–55 (b) .

CHAPTER 4

Antrobus, J. S., Antrobus, Judith S., and Singer, J. L. "Experiments Accompanying Daydreaming, Visual Imagery, and Thought Suppression." *Journal of Abnormal and Social Psychology*, 1964, *69*, 244–252.

Antrobus, J. S., Greenberg, S., and Singer, J. L. "Studies in the Stream of Consciousness: Experimental Enhancement and Suppression of Spontaneous Cognitive Process." *Perceptual and Motor Skills*, 1966, *23*, 399–417.

Bakan, P. "Hypnotizability, Laterality of Eye Movements and Functional Brain Asymmetry." *Perceptual and Motor Skills*, 1969, *28*, 927–932.

Broadbent, D. *Perception and Communication*. New York: Pergamon Press, 1958.

Fiske, D., and Maddi, S. (eds.) *Functions of Varied Experience*. Homewood, Ill.: Dorsey Press, 1961.

Meskin, B., and Singer, J. L. "Reflective Thought and Laterality of Eye Movements." *Journal of Personality and Social Psychology*, 1974, *30* (1) , 64–71.

Segal, S. *Imagery: Current Cognitive Approaches*. New York: Academic Press, 1972.

Singer, J. L., and Antrobus, J. "Visual Signal Detection as a Function of Simultaneous Speech." *Journal of Experimental Psychology*, 1964, *68*, 603–610.

Singer, J. L., and Antrobus, J. S. "Signal Performance by Subjects Differing in Predisposition to Daydreaming." *Journal of Consulting Psychology*, 1967, *31*, 487–491.

CHAPTER 5

Berkowitz, J. *The Roots of Aggression*. New York: Lieber-Atherton, 1969.

Biblow, E. "The Role of Fantasy in the Reduction of Aggression." Unpublished doctoral dissertation, City University of New York, 1970.

Freud, S. *The Interpretation of Dreams*. In *The Standard Edition of the Complete Psychological Works*. Vols. IV and V. London: Hogarth, 1962.

Murray, H. *Explorations in Personality*. New York: Oxford University Press, 1938.

Paton, R. "Fantasy Content, Daydreaming Frequency and the Reduction of Aggression." Unpublished doctoral dissertation, City University of New York, 1972.

Pytkowicz, A., Wagner, N., and Sarason, I. "An Experimental Study of the Reduction of Hostility through Fantasy." *Journal of Personality and Social Psychology*, 1967, *5*, 295–303.

Rapaport, D. *The Structure of Psychoanalytic Theory: a Systematizing Attempt; Psychological Issues. 2*, (2). New York: International Universities Press, 1960.

Singer, J. L., and Rowe, R. "An Experimental Study of Some Relationship between Daydreaming and Anxiety." *Journal of Consulting Psychology*, 1962, *26*, 446–454.

Werner, H. *Comparative Psychology of Mental Development*. New York: Science Editions, 1948.

CHAPTER 6

Erikson, E. H. *Childhood and Society*, 2nd ed. New York: W. W. Norton, 1963.

Fein, G., Branch, A., and Diamond, E. "Cognitive and Social Dimensions of Pretending in 2-Year-Olds." (Monograph, Yale University, 1974).

Freyberg, J. "Increasing the imaginative play of urban disadvantaged kindergarten children through systematic training." In J. L. Singer (ed.), *The Child's World of Make-Believe*. New York: Academic Press, 1973.

Goldberg, L. "Aggression in boys in a clinic population." Unpublished doctoral dissertation, City University of New York, 1973.

Gottlieb, S. "Modeling Effects upon Fantasy." In J. L. Singer (ed.) *The Child's World of Make-Believe*. New York: Academic Press, 1973.

Gould, R. *Child Studies through Fantasy*. New York: Quadrangle Books, 1972.

Groos, K. *The Play of Man*. New York: Appleton-Century Crofts, 1901.

Piaget, J. *Play, Dreams, and Imitation in Childhood*. New York: W. W. Norton, 1972.

Pulaski, M. "The Rich Rewards of Make-Believe." *Psychology Today*, 1974, 8, 68–74.

Singer, D., and Singer, J. L. "Fostering Imaginative Play in Pre-School Children: television and live model effects." Paper presented at American Psychological Association, New Orleans, 1974.

Singer, J. L., and Streiner, B. "Imaginative Content in the Dream and Fantasy Play of Blind and Sighted Children." *Perceptual and Motor Skills*, 1966, 22, 475–482.

Stein, A., Friedrich, L., Dell, K., and Vondrassek, F. "Television Content and Young Children's Behavior in Television and Social Behavior." Vol. II, *Report to Surgeon General's Committee on Television and Social Behavior*, N.I.M.H., 1972.

———. *Report of the Surgeon General's Committee on Television and Social Behavior*, N.I.M.H., 1972.

CHAPTER 7

Campagna, A. "Masturbation Fantasies in Male College Freshmen." Unpublished doctoral dissertation, Yale University, 1975.

Ellis, A. "The New Cop-Out Theory." *Psychology Today*, 1973, 7, 56–60.

Giambra, L. "Daydreaming Across the Lifespan: Late Adolescent to Senior Citizen." *Aging and Human Development*, in press, 1974.

Hariton, E. B., and Singer, J. L. "Women's fantasies during sexual intercourse. Normative and theoretical implications." *Journal of Consulting and Clinical Psychology*. 1974, 42, (3), 313–322.

Kinsey, A. C., Pomeroy, W., and Martin, D. *Sexual Behavior in the Human Male*. Philadelphia: Saunders, 1948.

Piaget, J. *Play, Dreams, and Imitation in Childhood*. New York: W. W. Norton, 1972.

Spivack, G., and Levine, M. "Self-Regulation and Acting-Out in Normal Adolescents." Progress Report for National Institutes of Mental Health, Grant M–4531. Devon, Pa.: Devereaux Foundation, 1964.

Symonds, P., and Jensen, A. *From Adolescent to Adult*. New York: Columbia University Press, 1961.

CHAPTER 8

Berne, E. *Games People Play*. New York: Grove Press, 1964.

Ekstein, R. *Children of Time and Space, Action and Impulse*. New York: Appleton-Century-Crofts, 1966.

Freud, S. *The Interpretation of Dreams*. In *The Standard Edition of the Complete Psychological Works*. Vols. IV and V. London: Hogarth, 1962.

Fromm, E. *The Forgotten Language*. New York: Holt, Rinehart & Winston, 1951.

Krafft-Ebing, R. von. *Psychopathia Sexualis*. New York: Pioneer Publications, 1946.

Lindner, R. "The jet-propelled couch" in *The Fifty-Minute Hour*. New York: Holt, Rinehart, & Winston, 1955.

Schatzman, M. *Soul Murder*. New York: Random House, 1972.

Sullivan, H. S. *Clinical Studies in Psychiatry*. New York: W. W. Norton, 1953.

Wagner and Stegman, "Does the Schizoid Child Develop into an Adult Schizophrenic?" Empirical data. Unpublished report submitted in connection with State of Washington Grant 171 "Imagination and Impulse Control in Children," 1964.

CHAPTER 9

Bandura, A. *Principles of Behavior Modification*. New York: Holt, Rinehart, & Winston, 1969.

Bandura, A., and Walters, R. H. *Social Learning and Personality Development*. New York: Holt, Rinehart, & Winston, 1963.

Barber, T. "Imagery and Hallucinations under LSD and with Hypnotic Suggestions." Paper read at the Third Annual Conference at the Center for Research in Cognition and Affect, City University of New York, June, 1970. In Segal, S. *Imagery*. New York: Academic Press, 1971.

Berne, E. *Games People Play*. New York: Grove Press, 1964.

Cautela, J. "Covert Sensitization." *Psychological Reports,* 1967, *20,* 459–468.

Gardner, R. *Therapeutic Communication with Children: the mutual story-telling technique*. New York: Science House, Inc., 1971.

Hilgard, E. *Hypnotic Susceptibility*. New York: Harcourt Brace Jovanovich, 1965.

Jung, C. *Man and His Symbols*. New York: Dell, 1968.

Kosbab, F. "Symbolism, Self-Experience and the Didactic Use of Affective Imagery in Psychiatric Training." *Zeitschrift für Psychotherapie und Medizinische Psychologie*, 1972, *22*, 210–224.

Kritzberg, N. "Structured therapeutic game method of (child) analytic therapy." Manuscript in preparation. Grune & Stratton, 1975, in press.

Leuner, H. "Guided Affected Imagery (G.A.I.) : A Method of Intensive Psychotherapy," *American Journal of Psychotherapy*, 1969, *23*, 4–22.

Meichenbaum, D. "Training Impulsive Children to Talk to Themselves." *Journal of Abnormal Psychology*, 1971, 77, 115–226.

Moreno, J. *The Theater of Spontaneity*. Beacon, N.Y.: Beacon House, 1947.

Orne, M. "The Nature of Hypnosis: Artifact and Essence." *Journal of Abnormal and Social Psychology*, 1959, *58*, 277–99.

Perls, F. *In and Out of the Garbage Pail*. New York: Bantam Books, 1972.

Schultz, J., and Luthe, W. *Autogenic Training: A psychological approach in psychotherapy*. New York: Grune & Stratton, 1959.

Schutz, W. *Joy: Expanding Human Awareness*. New York: Grove Press, 1967,

Singer, D., and Singer, J. L. "Fostering Imaginative Play in Pre-School Children: television and live model effects." Paper presented at American Psychological Association, New Orleans, 1974.

Singer, J. L. *Imagery and Daydream Methods in Psychotherapy and Behavior Modification*. New York: Academic Press, 1974.

Wolpe, J. *The Practice of Behavior Therapy*. New York: Pergamon Press, 1969.

CHAPTER 10

Alexander, F. *The Use of Self*. New York: E. P. Dutton, 1932.

De Mille, R. *Put Your Mother on the Ceiling: Children's Imagination Games*. New York: Walker & Co., 1967.

Feshbach, S., and Feshbach, N. "The Relationship between Empathy and Aggression in Two Age Groups." *Developmental Psychology*. 1969, *1*, 102–107.

Gordon, W. *Synectics: The Development of Creative Capacity*. New York: Harper & Brothers, 1961.

Guilford, J. *Personality*. New York: McGraw-Hill, 1959.

Singer, D., and Singer, J. L. "Fostering Imaginative Play in Pre-School Children: television and live model effects." Paper presented at American Psychological Association, New Orleans, 1974.

Spurgeon, C. *Shakespeare's Imagery and What It Tells Us*. Cambridge: Cambridge University Press, 1935.

Index

About the Author

Dr. Jerome L. Singer was born in New York City in 1924, and educated at City College. He received his Ph.D. degree in clinical psychology from the University of Pennsylvania and his psychoanalytic training at the William Alanson White Institute of Psychiatry, Psychoanalysis and Psychology in New York.

From 1963 to 1972, Dr. Singer was professor of psychology at City College of the City University of New York. He had a private practice of psychoanalysis in New York for twenty years. He is now professor of psychology and director of the graduate program in clinical psychology at Yale University. An active researcher in the areas of fantasy and daydreaming since 1949, he has carried out or supervised more than fifty different research studies and experiments in these fields.

Dr. Singer and his wife, Dr. Dorothy G. Singer, who is herself a psychologist and university professor, and has collaborated with him on some of his research, have three sons and live in Connecticut.